CORRIDOR

CORRIDOR

Media Architectures in American Fiction

KATE MARSHALL

MINNESOTA

University of Minnesota Press
Minneapolis
London

The publication of this book is made possible in part by support from the Institute for Scholarship in the Liberal Arts, College of Arts and Letters, University of Notre Dame.

Portions of chapter 1 were previously published as "Dreiser's Stamping Room: Becoming Media in *An American Tragedy*," *Novel* 46, no. 2 (Summer 2013). Copyright, 2013, Novel, Inc. All rights reserved. Reprinted by permission of the present publisher, Duke University Press. www.dukeupress.edu

Portions of chapter 2 were previously published as "Sewer, Furnace, Air Shaft, Media: Modernity behind the Walls in *Native Son* and *Manhattan Transfer*," *Studies in American Fiction* 37, no. 1 (Spring 2010): 55–80. Reprinted with permission by The Johns Hopkins University Press. Copyright 2010 The Johns Hopkins University Press.

Published by the University of Minnesota Press
111 Third Avenue South, Suite 290
Minneapolis, MN 55401–2520
http://www.upress.umn.edu

Library of Congress Cataloging-in-Publication Data

Marshall, Kate.
Corridor : media architectures in American fiction / Kate Marshall.
Includes bibliographical references and index.
ISBN 978-0-8166-7927-0 (hc : acid-free paper)
ISBN 978-0-8166-7928-7 (pb : acid-free paper)
1. American fiction—History and criticism. 2. Space (Architecture) in literature.
3. Architecture, Domestic, in literature. I. Title.
PS374.S73M37 2013
813.009′357—dc23
2013010191

Printed in the United States of America on acid-free paper

The University of Minnesota is an equal-opportunity educator and employer.

20 19 18 17 16 15 14 13 10 9 8 7 6 5 4 3 2 1

In memory of Melissa Marshall

But the gold, the mirrors, the miles of Baroque ornament drove von Göll himself a little daft. Especially those *long corridors. . . .* "Corridor metaphysics," is what the French call this condition. Oldtime corridor hepcats will chuckle fondly at descriptions of von Göll, long after running out of film, still dollying with a boobish smile on his face down the golden vistas.

—Thomas Pynchon, *Gravity's Rainbow*

CONTENTS

PREFACE

"All That I Need Is a Hallway"

In July 1919 a song premiered at the *Greenwich Village Follies* that suggested a change of affiliation for moderns in pursuit of intimacy. The song trades in mixed clichés, routinely dismissing Shakespearean lovers and serenading knights as "freakish men," and chastising these icons for an overreliance on "atmosphere" ("they couldn't spoon without the moon above") and spectacle ("sometimes they'd fight a duel to win her hand") as available tools for the desiring subject. Amid these banalities, however, lies what seems to be a modally inappropriate substitution. The singer declares that instead of these models for a quasi-literary kind of person on which to pattern his behavior, he requires a kind of space, declaring in the chorus, "all that I need is a hallway," a declaration that also constitutes the song's title. But what kind of person needs a hallway? The chorus continues:

> All that I need is a hallway,
> And you can have your Lovers' lane,
> I never seem to care about a morris chair,
> But when I'm in the hallway that's the time I'm a bear.[1]

Making the move from emblematic person to more material locations for intimacy—Lovers' Lane and the Morris chair each having the capacity alternately to stand in for and facilitate the proximity of lovers (or perhaps thinly disguised sexual violence)—the singer dismisses them for a location that would seem to do the opposite. For a hallway's representativeness is as a communication space. The American idiom for corridor, the hallway facilitates movement between discrete spaces and discreet spaces, making privacy and intimacy possible by sequestering the interior social space of domestic and institutional architecture from its more private retreats. And yet the singer is adamant. Not only does he insist that the hallway is the place where "there's no one there to see," but

> I never escort them home as a rule,
> Unless her home has a nice vestibule,
> All that I need is a hallway.[2]

Persons who "need" vestibular and communicative spaces to manage and stage relation and desire signal their modernity not, as the logic of "All That I Need Is a Hallway" could be seen to imply, through the straw-man differentiation of new from old. For to say "all that I need is a hallway" invokes at least two sentiments. First, it dismisses the accouterments of communication a lover might require in favor of a space that can stand in simultaneously for the linguistic, literary, and symbolic forms of communicating desire. In doing so, the statement also replaces the communication of desire with the desire for communication. It is my contention, that is, that desire for communication is explicitly encoded in the desire for hallways. In this I am adopting the thick definition of communication as a transit system for moving bodies, things, and messages—a definition that informs, for example, the media theory of Friedrich Kittler and the communication history of John Durham Peters, both of whom underscore the dependence of modern individuals and their modern loves on the network of epistemological forms and technological apparatuses of communication.

The story of these communicative individuals and loves has become a powerful one in American literary study and in accounts of the modernist aesthetics forming the larger cultural matrix in which "All That I Need Is a Hallway" is embedded. A key narrative engine of this story can be found in the technological media, which dominate literary accounts of the "materialities of communication."[3] While the technological media and their specific materialities, as well as the emerging body of work energized by attention to them, informs the approach I take in this book to exploring the dense connections between forms of communication, architecture, and mediation in the modern American novel, they also form a point of departure. Though guided by an awareness of the technological "conditions of possibility" from which, *pace* Kittler, the discursive networks of modernity and its literary forms emerge, I attend to a related but distinct system of language and materiality, especially as it involves the supposed interiors and forms of interiority attached to the persons populating the American novel in the first half of the twentieth century. These fictional persons are *medial:* comprising not only the technologies making their material production in novels possible, but also the reflexive reincorporation and reference to that process itself. This formal reflexivity can be understood in systems-theoretical terms as the parallel process of making persons and novels, retaining the movement-based sense of communication mentioned above, but describing what readers of novels are accustomed to thinking of as psychological interiors as communications systems.

Instead, returning briefly to the *Follies,* the focus of this book moves from the first sense of the song's title (the conflation of communication and communication space) to its echo, which sounds a more melancholy tone. A hallway is something no singer should need, given its ready-to-hand ubiquity in modern architecture. And yet, "all that I need is a hallway" indicates a more basic lack, or a longing for something that has disappeared. Although this nearly transparent architectural form has clearly survived challenges to its use in domestic and institutional architecture, such as interwar housing reform and the rise of the open plan, the security of its epistemological status became a topic of heightened anxiety in the first half of the twentieth century. These are the years when "things, like ourselves, were losing their qualities with astonishing ease."[4] The consolidation of what Mark Jarzombek has called "corridic modernity" gives rise in turn to what Gilles Deleuze refers to as "a generalized crisis in relation to all the environments of enclosure."[5] The consequences of both this consolidation and crisis are registered in the forms of individuality and interiority that such spatial, medial, and institutional structures make possible. They reflexively produce and are produced by, I will argue, the novel, which insistently dramatizes and reenacts what it might look like for a modern person to inhabit a modernity shaped by its corridors. This is a landscape in which the hallway works simultaneously as medium, communicative conduit, and destination for novels and persons alike.

This book is a study of novels and corridors, and what the relationship between the two reveals about the modern media. It situates in the discourses of reflexive modernity the particular dynamics of exchange between physical circulation systems and media forms that constitute the landscape out of which modernist American fiction emerges, and through which it observes its own operations. I show how a range of novels enact and encode their medial processes in the concrete structures of American modernity—its infrastructural systems, contagious institutional spaces, its corridors—to demonstrate that the consequences for this recursive movement between novels, spatial structures, and media extend to modern individuals and the interiors that house them. The aim of this project is thus to challenge subject-centered accounts of modernist interiority and its narrative modes, and the tradition of modernist literary criticism that examines the architectural materialities of the novel from this perspective. By attending to the relays between physical and informational communication, and the cross-identifications of interiors and interiority as they are expressed as medial forms in these texts, I develop a counternarrative of what it means to figure modern persons and their communicative environment in the novels of early twentieth-century America.

ACKNOWLEDGMENTS

This book is a map of many intersecting corridors. One of my favorites was reached via the north entrance of a large brick building in Los Angeles: on either side of this door, two pairs of windows form the eyes of an appropriately strange face. During the time I was regularly entering the building, the windows belonged to the three people to whom I am the most grateful for the guidance, criticism, and inspiration they provided this project in its earliest stages. Mark McGurl modeled the very best kind of Americanist scholarship, demanded historicity, and showed me a better way to think about modernism. Kate Hayles exemplified the clear articulation of complex thought, took my most abstract abstractions seriously, and consistently illuminated and helped me realize the book's greater vision. And there is simply no way to separate the ideas in this book from the many hours I spent discussing them with Mark Seltzer, for whom my gratitude, not only for his belief in the project but also for his uncanny ability to make everything more interesting, is ongoing.

Also in Los Angeles, Ed Soja provided my work with a deeper sense of spatial theory. Sianne Ngai, Ken Reinhard, Chris Mott, Helen Deutsch, Kirstie McClure, Felicity Nussbaum, Jonathan Grossman, Michael North, and Richard Yarborough taught me the value of rigorous thinking combined with formidable generosity. I was a privileged resident of cohortopia with Melanie Ho, John Alba Cutler, Julian Knox, Tom O'Donnell, and Dennis Tyler, to name a few, and the beneficiary of many sunlit afternoons sharing thoughts and work with James Landau, Glenn Brewer, and James Pulizzi.

I have many audiences to thank for thoughtful responses to specific chapters of this book. The Los Angeles Americanist Research

Colloquium run by Chris Looby not only formed my identity as an Americanist, but also provided important commentary on an early chapter. At the Midwestern Americanist colloquium at Indiana University, Jen Fleissner and Scott Herring raised points helpful for the manuscript revision. Vera Bühlmann, Ludger Hovestadt, and Klaus Wasserman, and their architecture students at the Swiss Federal Institute of Technology in Zürich helped me to adopt a different point of view. I completed revisions of the manuscript after inhabiting a version if this book's dream world: an international conference of architecture, literature, and media theorists in Weimar to discuss the corridors, service architectures, and secret passages of modernity, and I thank both the participants and my co-organizers, Markus Krajewski and Stephan Trüby.

Others provided help along the way. Bernhard Siegert spent a winter in southern California and graciously accepted me into a small media theory seminar while I was writing, thus opening up the range of medial objects I found myself able to consider. Aaron Gorelik reminded me of Enoch Robinson's rooms, and Tom March showed them to me in the first place. With Sam See, I developed confidence in corridoricity. The Getty Research Institute provided me with a bright desk looking out over travertine and bougainvillea for two years, and many of these pages were composed against that view.

Maud Ellmann and John Wilkinson welcomed me to South Bend as though we were old friends, and remain my Midwestern home for talking about art and ideas. At Notre Dame I've had the benefit of the wonderful mentorship of Sandra Gustafson, Steve Fredman, and Laura Walls, and the support of two outstanding chairs, John Sitter and Valerie Sayers. My colleagues in the English department, such as Joe Buttigieg, José Limón, Romana Huk, Barbara Green, Susan Harris, Peter Holland, Sara Maurer, David Thomas, Suzannah Monta, Chris Vanden Bossche, Katherine Zieman, Elliott Visconsi, and Steve Tomasula, as well as Yasmin Solomonescu, Matt Wilkens, Jesse Costantino, and Kinohi Nishikawa, have made this university an exciting environment in which to work and think, as have my students. I was fortunate to find on my arrival a few friends with whom I could not only navigate the profession, but who soon ended up sustaining me through the most challenging times—I could not imagine better people to work and live with than Jason Ruiz, Aaron Carico, Joyelle McSweeney, Johannes Göransson, Tobias Boes, and Tracy Bergstrom.

My first in-person meeting with Doug Armato took place, appropriately enough, in a long institutional corridor. Both Doug and Danielle Kasprzak at the University of Minnesota Press have been insightful and supportive. An anonymous reader for the press provided some of the best advice I received about the book's composition and motives. At Notre Dame I was the fortunate recipient of superb and indefatigable research assistance from Melissa Dinsman and Yugon Kim, and research support from the Institute for Scholarship in the Liberal Arts.

In academic life there is often little distance between friendship and writing, and I'm proud to have written this book for the likes of Joe Rezek, Joyce W. Lee, and Nathan Brown, who were its first and most cherished audience, along with Ian Newman, the best companion for any corridor. Finally, this book is dedicated to my mother, Melissa, and to those who share with me her loss and memory: Tom, Kelly, and Debbie Marshall, as well as Cathy, Amy, and Patrick McGinnis, and their families, too.

INTRODUCTION

Corridoricity

THE CORRIDOR FIGURES PROMINENTLY in the most familiar texts of literary modernism. Virginia Woolf famously described her idea of the structure of *To the Lighthouse* as "two blocks separated by a corridor." The corridors traveled by Kafka's Joseph K. are the iconic image of modern bureaucracy. Marcel of Proust's *Swann's Way* frets constantly about transit between his room and its exterior places of passage. And Robbe-Grillet's mazelike interiors, in print as *In the Labyrinth* and in film as *Last Year in Marienbad,* all point to the representativeness of the hallway as an index of modern interiority, and as the particular concern of a modernist aesthetic. These interiors, moreover, figure through architecture the by-now familiar account of a "culture of time and space" in the early twentieth century.[1]

This is a modernist spatial world described by Walter Benjamin as the product of the previous century's interest in the arcade. Observing the passages that traverse the buildings and social centers of Paris, Benjamin notes a "remarkable propensity for structures that convey and connect—as, of course, the arcades do. And this connecting or mediating function has a literal and spatial as well as a figurative and stylistic bearing."[2] Benjamin's connective structures combine the boulevard with the corridor, overlaying the passage between buildings and the passage within buildings as a model for urban social experience.[3] The play between urban street and corridor pressures the distinction between interior and exterior environments, so that public and private spaces share similar functions as technologies of transport, and mediating functions at that.

But to what, then, do we turn for an American *Passagenwerk?*

The answer provided in these pages lies in dominant topoi of modern American fiction, such as the infrastructure, transit networks, and corridors that organize domestic and institutional space. *Corridor* argues that these structures can be best understood as media, for through them novels encode their own communicative processes. Novels that explicitly stage the coevolution of media technologies and the protocols of modernity, like John Dos Passos's *Manhattan Transfer,* Richard Wright's *Native Son,* Katherine Anne Porter's *Pale Horse, Pale Rider,* or Theodore Dreiser's *An American Tragedy,* often do so by way of an attention to physical transit mechanisms that also operate as communications systems: conduits or corridors for both bodies and information. These built structures are precisely where the constitutive dynamism of the modern media most clearly emerges.

By portraying media not only as objects, but processes—as noisy, contagious, dialectical, and insistently self-reflexive—the novels I discuss foreground their formal character, or what I call their *corridoricity.* This concept encompasses the adverbial and adjectival dimensions of media: how they work, and how fiction observes its own operations through them. Thinking about novels in this way enables a simultaneous analysis of space, media, and narrative structure, and engages with an emerging body of work in the field of media studies that expands the material history of the technical media to account for how things like spatial structures, technologies, and systems have the capacity to become media in a local historical constellation. The concreteness and historical specificity of the architectural designs, factory technologies, transit proposals, and contagious networks that form the topics and locations of these texts inform a material history through which I locate American modernism's medial conditions of possibility.

This book presents a series of interlocked readings that examine how the modern novel charts the organization of the American interior via corridors and corridor-like structures in the first half of the twentieth century, in texts dating from 1919 through the immediate postwar period. In addition to the works by Dreiser, Porter, Wright, and Dos Passos cited above, I discuss such novels as Henry Roth's *Call It Sleep,* Willa Cather's *One of Ours,* and Nathaniel West's *Miss Lonelyhearts,* all of which are underrepresented in discussions of American modernism and its mediations. This scope also reflects a necessarily flexible view of the conventional periodization of postwar American fiction in 1945 to account for the relationship of American novels to the more continuous material narrative that accompanies the developments in media and the built world at the same time. Included in this flexibility is the question of genre, a messier question for many of my texts than the conventional narrative allows.

William Faulkner's 1936 *Absalom, Absalom!*, a novel often thought paradigmatic of American literary modernism but from its least celebrated decade, shows some of this genre noisiness at work. The nexus of house and person in this novel so known for its interest in architectural design and interior states fits uneasily in discussions of modern urban connectivity or into the Frankean idea of "spatial form" so often affiliated with Faulkner's contemporaries.[4] For *Absalom, Absalom!* is a novel about a house. In an oft-cited moment in the novel's opening movement, a recapitulation of an encounter between Rosa Coldfield and Quentin Compson crystallizes the stakes of affiliating architecture with interiority: "Quentin had grown up with that; the mere names were interchangeable and almost myriad. His childhood was full of them; his very body was an empty hall echoing with sonorous defeated names; he was not a being, an entity, he was a commonwealth."[5] Quentin here has been described in the critical literature as a "vehicle" for Rosa's story,[6] as possessed by the South, which has "infiltrated and laid hold upon his consciousness";[7] his "undefined and undefinable self" forms a "daring modernist metaphor,"[8] and, along these lines, Marilyn Chandler's more literal reading of Faulkner's "house divided" sees Quentin in this scene as someone "whose psyche and body provide a vacant space in which all of history and myth are reiterated, shrunken to the confines of a single tortured mind."[9] In these accounts it is Quentin, rather than the forms characterizing him (such as "empty hall," or "commonwealth"), in which an overtly metaphoric quality obtains. He becomes the vehicle or conduit of meaning, narrative, and history, and must surrender his coherent and conscious subjectivity, which is replaced rather than redefined.

But what more could be said of the "empty hall"? What is it about the structure that makes it an appropriate figure not for Quentin's "consciousness" but more insistently "his very body"? The text's rhetorical move from body to echoing hall renders consciousness an inadequate description of the interior in question. What the passage recognizes about a "hall" is that it houses exteriority within the interior. Quentin's body, therefore, is turned inside out. An empty hall, he literalizes the idea of a channel into a concrete structure, one that signals sociality rather than contained interiority. No "being" or "entity," no coherent or self-enclosed consciousness can do the noisy narrative channeling and rerouting the novel requires, just as there is no unified geographical and historical reality for which the South's racial violence can serve as a structurally sound unconscious. In fact, at times it is architecture that comes closest to the status of an enclosed, thinking agent in the novel. Sutpen's house does not have a Bachelardian map of consciousness; rather, it attains the structure and status of what might be called a person. Instead of the "*blind, unsentient earth itself*" beneath it,[10] the house begins to act and think by dint of association: "as though his [Sutpen's] presence alone compelled that house to accept and retain human life; as though houses actually possess a sentience, a personality and character acquired not from the people who breathe or have breathed in them so much as rather inherent in the wood and brick or begotten upon the wood and brick by the man or men who conceived and built them—in this one an incontrovertible affirmation for emptiness, desertion."[11] This passage thematizes the contagious movement of figuration as part of the structure itself, which acquires its more-than-personified "character" not from the surface proximity of its inhabitants but rather from a deeper metaphoric behest from its materials and their manipulators. That figurative relationship is doubled by simile: "as though houses actually possess a sentience" attributes to the house a primary quality of sensate consciousness (which retained its history as a fraught concept of abolitionist discourse in the post-Reconstruction South the novel describes), but more specifically a will or desire for emptiness, and also withdraws it—the house's capacity to be like its materials and their manipulators is reflexively embedded in its capacity to be like a sentient being. And to be like itself means that its interior, like Quentin's, contains an empty hall, irreducible to the singularity of "being" or "entity." So when Rosa later recounts her encounter "*in that barren hall with its naked stair . . . rising into the dim upper hallway where an echo spoke,*" it comes as no surprise that when she hears the voice of Sutpen's daughter Clytie, "*it was as though it had not been she who spoke but the house itself that said the words.*"[12]

What this interplay reveals is that the relationship between spatial materiality and interiority in Faulkner's text is more complex than that captured by a representational vocabulary. Houses are neither directly emblematic of persons nor maps of the structure of a psychic being, for the relationship they express forecloses the possibility of that more familiar form of psychic personhood. The emptiness desired by Sutpen's house and the echoes traveling through its and Quentin's halls renders the representational relationship medial, bound up in the novel's reflexivity even as it pressures the reflexive closure of its characters. In Peter Brooks's classic essay on narration in *Absalom, Absalom!* he mentions not only a "hollow structure, concave mirror or black hole at the center of the narrative"[13] but also "the many metaphors of its own status and production presented by the text."[14] The example he cites of such a metaphor, the loom, anticipates the materialist gestures of medial literary history in its evocation not only of fictional texture and textuality but the apparatus of writing itself—for it prefigures the Jacquard Loom, a key object in media archeological accounts of digital textuality.[15] And while this provides a compelling and important view of the novel's reflexive relationship to its material production, the materiality of its mediations exceeds their technological media of production and dissemination. The house that dominates the novel and the empty halls that speak and stand in for interiors together produce a highly reflexive, medial alternative to modernist narrative interiority. These built structures, in their explicit communicativeness, are like looms, letters, and other writing and print technologies appearing in the text because they figure the novel's materiality as a communicative artifact bound up in the transmission networks recalled by halls and passages. But peculiar to *Absalom, Absalom!* and many novels in its orbit is the double encoding of that materiality *as* interiority itself, the channelness of the hall standing in for the narrative person. Knowing full well that their collective project is regarded even at the time as one devoted to persons and interiors as they confront urban, social, and historical forces (and in *Absalom, Absalom!* these "forces" too are "sentient"),[16] these novels stage that project instead as an exploration of interiority that is embedded in concrete rather than psychic structures. And although this illustration is but a brief glimpse into the interior worlds of Faulkner's novel, it gestures at a medial sensibility that organizes the text's systems of reflexive reference, and repositions its larger concerns within recursive moves.

These moments in *Absalom, Absalom!* provide snapshots of the reflexively material mediality that structures the dense connections between fiction and architecture in the novels gathered in this book. Faulkner's novel also reveals a richly unstable generic sensibility, suggesting that underneath not only *Absalom, Absalom!* but the larger canon of American modernism lies a material and medial aesthetic unaccountable to narratives of the period that imagine a representational relationship between interiors and interiority. In order to account for such discrepancies, I trace what happens to the kinds of persons inhabiting the richly material landscapes of American realist and naturalist fiction of the late nineteenth and early twentieth centuries when they find themselves in more modernist interiors. Rather than policing period and genre distinctions, however, I draw attention to a persistent yet transforming attachment of persons to increasingly mediatized domestic and institutional spaces that appears most forcefully as a topic in criticism of this earlier moment in American literary history, which tends to be more skeptical of psychological interiority than studies of the novel after the First World War. This book addresses the resulting omission of novels from discussions of the period whose narrative entities and environments concretize interiority in something other than a modernist subject.[17]

That said, I also point out how these forms, materializations, and spatializations turn in on themselves. The novels I discuss—often reading more like late naturalist works than modernist—explicitly thematize and reincorporate the recursivity and materiality underlying novels and persons in their immediately preceding literary historical moment. By doing so, and through an active engagement with both the expanding organizational and physical infrastructures of the built world and its increasingly complex communication networks after the First World War, these novels transform Georg Simmel's "mental life" into something closer to what Mark Goble calls "the mediated life."[18] That is, when their forms of material and medial self-reference double back and start to indicate each other, these novels become communications systems in the sense outlined in the systems theory of Niklas Luhmann and the media theory of Friedrich Kittler, a sense that extends to "individuals" and one that develops throughout the readings included here.

Corridor Histories

The corridor, as a literary space and architectural form, has several micro-histories that inform this project. These range from the corridor's development in the eighteenth century alongside the novel and medial infrastructures of print dissemination and postal systems to its threat of unchecked proliferation in the circuitry of contemporary fiction.

Focusing on the corridor's concurrent hypervisibility in early twentieth-century literary and architectural discussions, I describe a situation in which projects mapping the organization of domestic and institutional space are obsessed with the particular structure of the corridor, while at the same time literary accounts of domesticity, institutionality, and the movement between them draw explicitly on the corridor's literal and figurative manifestations. The corridor situates the intersection of all these things, for as a form it is precisely where intersection happens. If, as I have been claiming, the corridor is the architectural form that most insistently encodes the mediality of novels and persons in modern American fiction, a brief tour through its history as a communicative form as well as its increasingly theoretical prominence as the space of reflexive modernity will do some of this project's archeological work. The architectural and planning concerns in the environment of these literary accounts point to the historicity of the novel's concern with hallway forms as well as how their attention to corridor spaces is system-specific.

At stake in my discussion of the corridor and the perspective it provides for a discussion of literary form is the issue of likeness, or what I call *corridoricity,* which describes the strange reflection the corridor enacts of other spaces and its boundedness to structures of fictionality and mediation. Also important are the logics of separation, or distinction, and how proliferating corridors maintain an interest in their constitutive operations, such as public and private, or interior and exterior. These operations are the basic stuff of literary language. Instead of dispensing with literary corridors as "mere metaphor," I take seriously the role of spatial metaphors in reconfiguring ideas of literal space, and attend to flashpoints in several novels in which the figurative spaces double back on themselves and stage the forms of communication they describe. These metaphorics also provide access to the logic of access, for they reinscribe the abstractions of power, institutionality, and bureaucracy in the hard walls of the built world.

The corridor is the dominant organizational structure in modern domestic and institutional architecture. Its varied historical functions—the separation of the servant classes from the everyday circulation of English aristocracy in the country house, the regulation of movement and privacy in apartment and tenement buildings, or the turn-of-the-century ideal of the "functional house for frictionless living" that extends to the requirements of standardized American suburban living—

are each taken for granted in contemporary definitions of architectural layout. In part because of this ubiquity, the corridor tends to disappear from view as one of those necessary yet invisible structures, like a bathroom in a domestic residence or an elevator in a high-rise office building. Yet even the privy chamber and moving platform have histories that shape the structures and narratives that house them.

The corridor creates specific conditions for what media theorist Bernhard Siegert calls "passability" between discrete spaces, and within domestic environments, the story goes, discrete spaces themselves were made possible only with the introduction of the corridor. Before the corridor, the inhabited space of the house was navigated through a series of interlocking rooms—thoroughfares that inevitably resulted in interactions between those who moved through them. Architectural historian Robin Evans traces the history of the corridor as a radical break that appeared "out of the blue" from previous domestic building plans.[19] Rather than arising as a product of an evolutionary development in architectural design stemming from basic human need, he says, the corridor was imposed on interiors to regulate the movement of people in and out of rooms and reduce contact among those moving through the spaces of the home. The management of human relationships and the expression of human relationships present themselves in corridors. In addition, the formation of passageways implicates movement—or passability—in the definition of the private self among social relations: "It is hard to tell now which became more private first, the room or the soul. Certainly, their histories are intertwined."[20] In this narrative, providing the material conditions for private thoughts is the object of the corridor's formation and the impetus for its design.

Evans first published his history of the corridor in 1978, and he points out with some astonishment that "the history of the corridor as a device for removing traffic from rooms has yet to be written."[21] After a flourishing interest in the corridor by midcentury theorists of power and institutionality and in the popular fiction of the time, both of which constitute the culmination of my discussion of twentieth-century corridoricity, the form languished as an object of study until Evans, and remained marginal after that. Corridors have reemerged, however, in discussions of architecture, mediality, and modernity. The most prominent account is that provided by Mark Jarzombek in a 2010 essay, "Corridor Spaces," in which he offers a riposte to Evans's "devastating critique" of the space's ideological history and affirms the corridor as the ultimate architectural index of modernity.[22] Jarzombek is interested in the long history of the corridor's acceptance in architectural design, examining the "corridic revolution" in western architecture that results in an established "corridic episteme" by the middle of the nineteenth century; tracing the resistance to corridors in their early implementation and locating a newer "anticorridic movement" in architecture after the Second World War; and claiming that the corridor's influence reaches its apex by the mid-1930s and apotheosis in the 1960s.[23] Jarzombek's architectural history is, interestingly, a literary history as well, for he constructs his narrative through engagements with the likes of Lord Byron, Charlotte Brontë, Charles Dickens, and Henry James.

Although corridors feature as hallmarks of a modernity interested in both circulation systems and their attendant modalities of privacy and interiority, and although they appear relatively uncontested in contemporary accounts of what movement within domestic and institutional structures looks like, corridors were the specific target of interwar housing reform in both the United States and Europe. This particular "anticorridic movement" does not feature in the histories of the corridor I have mentioned, but has direct bearing on the fictional and corridor worlds of American modernity. The reforms proposed by interwar housing experiments called into question the ideals of privacy and domesticity literally being set in stone by the corridor, and insisted upon the removal of the "channel" model of circulation in order to facilitate more flexible class and social movement. Book titles from Europe and America may help elucidate the sensibility driving this reform: in the United States, Carol Aronovici's 1939 text *Housing the Masses* describes a Depression-era concern with public housing, and Eve Blau's more recent retrospective, *The Architecture of Red Vienna,* traces a pre–World War II vision of utopian housing potential. Both point to two sides of a similar question: how to build for social life when the very definition of "living socially" is called into question as ideologically motivated?

The indictment of the corridor as an installation of social hierarchy and bourgeois ideology depended, of course, on the assumption that architectural forms directly influence social relations. This architectural determinism was hardly inconsistent with the materialism behind many of the socialist and communist political philosophies compelling architectural reform. The corridor's specific guilt in this instance lay in its domestic history. Hermann Muthesius had described, in his popular

1904 text *Das englische Haus,* the origins of the corridor's functionality in British class society: "Perhaps the most striking difference is the lack in England of communicating doors between the rooms, which means that the only access to a room is from a passage or hall. Thus the English room is a sort of cage, in which the inmate is entirely cut off from the next room. Englishmen usually shake their heads at the sight of a continental ground-plan with its ubiquitous communicating doors and in a continental house they might feel as though they were perpetually sitting out in the street."[24] Muthesius goes on to trace the inevitable movement toward the corridor model of domesticity in continental architecture, an inevitability that would be confirmed by the moves to purge the corridor from working-class domestic architecture twenty years later. In his account, the differentiation between public and private within the private realm itself is at stake in the development of the corridor. Socialist housing programs in Vienna, a vanguard city for public housing at the time, targeted the corridor's evolution from bourgeois residences concerned with the separate circulation spaces of servants and staff, to the proletarian apartment (Blau refers to this as "a spatialization of bourgeois domestic ideology"),[25] as encoding middle-class aspirations in architecture and forming a barrier to class consciousness. Working-class dwellings built in Socialist Vienna sought to return friction, noise, or what Muthesius describes as "the street," back inside the living space.

The corridor was the target of a dispute about the acceptable models of communication and circulation in twentieth-century housing projects, and bound up in this dispute was the movement of the corridor into the private spaces it was meant to separate. In her discussion of architectural reform in interwar Vienna, Blau notes a concern among Viennese architects about the passagelike nature of the working-class apartment: "the corridor ran not parallel to an interconnected suite of rooms but perpendicular to the one-room proletarian dwellings that were themselves little more than passageways attached to its spine. Thus the interior space of the traditional Viennese working class tenement consisted almost entirely of directional space, of corridor."[26] The corridor here presents a specter of continuously replicating throughway, of uninterrupted flow standing in for communication. As the corridor begins to enfold all other spaces, the "likeness" of discrete and continuous space within the interior reveals a problem as much with the concept of corridor as with the architectural unit itself. And clearly this problem is not limited to Vienna: as physical and informational communications systems proliferate at an accelerated rate in twentieth-century urban and media environments, their resemblance to corridors puts them in uncanny proximity. The *corridoricity,* then, of room, passage, pipe, and channel, challenges models of communication at the same time that it reveals them. Corridoricity points to the infrastructure of the everyday.

The recombination of street and private room found its parallel in the spaces of Vanport City, a town built in Oregon in 1943 as one of what Dolores Hayden describes as two competing models of American housing. The first, Vanport City, flourished through the end of World War II by deemphasizing the corridor in favor of communal space, specifically in the service of working women. The other, Levittown, returned the corridor models of privacy and organization to the home, the street, and the suburb. According to Hayden, "The second new town—Levittown—becomes known all over the world as a model of American know-how just as the first new town—Vanport City—is being dismantled, some of its housing taken apart piece by piece."[27] Thinking of both of these models in terms of their relationship to the specific structure of the corridor not only highlights the way questions of organized movement were foregrounded in the debates and developments in social housing, but also brings into relief the nested corridors of the prevailing architectural and town layouts. In Levittown, the prototype of the twentieth-century American suburb, interior hallways, street planning, and developing highway corridors refer to and redefine one another. In this light, the seemingly disparate logics of apartment blocks and suburban blocks driving early twentieth-century housing reform register similar concerns.

In John Archer's simultaneously literary and architectural history of the ideas of privacy and identity underlying the evolution of contemporary American domestic architecture, *Architecture and Suburbia,* the corridor features as an explicit agent of change in the development of the "selfhood" he sees as encoded in house design. His characterization of the transformation of interior space by the corridor demonstrates how evocative this form can be of information systems: "Thus as the eighteenth century progressed, the increasing use of corridors allowed the chamber suite to be transformed from part of a route through the house to a nodal point opening onto a corridor system."[28] Evans, moreover, refers specifically to communications systems: "In facilitating communication, the corridor reduced contact. What this meant was that purposeful or necessary communication was facilitated while incidental communication was reduced, and contact, according to the lights of reason and the dictates of morality, was at best incidental and distracting, at worst corrupting and malignant."[29] Both contest what Evans calls the "guileless" equation of architecture and literature "so that it becomes an echo of words,"[30] and instead pursue something more complex: in Archer's words, the "necessary connection between the belief system (or ideology) of a culture and the material apparatus in which people conduct their daily lives."[31]

A systems-theoretical account of the corridor might focus on the point of view of the "system of architecture," in which corridors would look distinct from their observation through literature, although architecture can also be seen as a system of distinctions functioning as working parts of a social system composed of communications. If literary distinctions are made in literary terms, so too are architectural distinctions immanent to architecture. Seen from this perspective, the corridor works as a form in the medium of space, and the distinction between space and the architectural form, and how that distinction constitutes the system, becomes crucial. Architecture itself then functions in the environment of the literary system, and vice versa, and the surfacing of the architectural form in twentieth-century literary accounts of architecture forms a flashpoint in the mutual irritation of both systems. This renewed attention to the function of the corridor in interwar architectural theory and the planning of urban dwellings surfaces at roughly the same time as novelists are making the corridor newly visible in fiction. The corridor becomes a coeval topic in both interwar housing reform and literary production, and while the developments in architectural, planning, and literary debates function according to different terms, both register a concern with the corridor. That this particular space becomes concurrently hypervisible in multiple media has everything to do with the fact that it seems to blend in to so many other spaces.

The twentieth-century interest in the corridor to which I refer does not represent the only instance of spatial circulation systems standing in for descriptions of the social. Indeed, technologies that regulate movement and enclosure emerge in larger accounts of social change, ranging from studies of "the railway age" to globalization, from the spatial structures systematizing Foucauldian epistemological breaks to the border walls and fences organizing recent commentaries on nationality. Nor does the extraordinary visibility of the corridor in this period form a comprehensive explanation for the relationship of architecture in general, or this space in particular, to social movement and collective life. Instead, the corridor indicates a surfacing desire for noise, friction, irritation, and traffic as a countermodel to the organized flow and policed divides between privacy and sociality within the interior naturalized by the corridor's widespread presence in architectural forms. What stands out, what both generalizes and particularizes the turn to the corridor and the other spatial forms I have mentioned, is their communicative functionality and their mediality. Put another way: the corridor's relationship to communication accounts for its reappearance on the scene in the first half of the century at the same time that it indicates larger structural connections that posit communication as a way of thinking about social and spatial forms. This "boundedness" between the corridor and communication, expressed as a mutual contingency that is in turn bound up in the way each is defined and operationalized in discourse, forms a picture of the corridor as the medial space par excellence, and helps to account for its strange resurfacing.

In John Durham Peters's conceptual history of communication, *Speaking into the Air,* cultural definitions of communication in the United States shift from ideas of physical communication exemplified by terms such as "steam communication" (railroad travel) and "communicating rooms" (as seen in Hawthorne novels, for example) in the nineteenth century, to twentieth-century ideas of dematerialized information or message transfer governed largely by developments in media technology.[32] Current definitions of communications systems, on the other hand, internalize the logic of this shift and bump up against the question of materiality. Friedrich Kittler's "History of Communication Media," following McLuhan, describes communications systems as controlling the movement of people, goods, and messages, but emphasizes control to argue for their analysis as information systems: "Ultimately, communication too depends on control signals, the more so the more complex its working; even the triad of 'things communicated'—information, persons, goods—can be reformulated in terms of information theory."[33] Both histories turn on what counts as communications media—what for Kittler can be anything from language to a highway is in Peters's account dependent on cultural definitions—but when each debate is situated in the language of architecture, the corridor emerges as the site in which the functions of communication are at stake both historically and methodologically. And according to a significant body of American fiction, negotiations over what communication is and does happen in and along the corridor.

If the language of "communicating" spaces seems to pass from view at the same time that the materialities of communication render information transport invisible, and if the connection between communication technologies and their attendant social forms cannot be reduced from one to the other, then the surprising proximity between spaces through which information travels and bodily transportation space at issue in the corridor's reimagination insists on a problem of connectivity itself. The corridor appears as both concrete and figurative communications space, and the relays between the two describe a kind of communication with particularly literary ramifications. As a site for the description (one might say communication) and modeling of interiority, the novel constantly reflects back on its multiple materialities of communication. When those material structures surface as interiors themselves, and more particularly as the interior forms that both organize and signify communication, the novel observes, historicizes, and constitutes itself as a medial artifact. And in a social world composed, following Luhmann, of communications, the strange sociality of communicative space made literal by the built world of the corridor and figurative by its descriptions in turn makes visible the distinctions between literal and figurative, or architecture and literature, and demands an account of how these distinctions work.[34] While there seems to be a danger in taking corridors as metaphors for literary communication, the status of metaphor within language as a device of transport between signifiers implies that the figure and the space fulfill the same function, and have similarly attendant problems. Michel de Certeau, for example, points out that the public transportation system in Athens is called the "metaphorai"—quite literally transport—to show that text moves from one place to another in an organizational system that also forms the condition of the railway car: "Stories could also take this noble name: every day, they traverse and organize places; they select and link them together; they make sentences and itineraries out of them. They are spatial trajectories. . . . Stories, whether everyday or literary, serve us as means of mass transportation, as *metaphorai*."[35] Passageways make metaphors in the sense that they transport bodies and communicate between interiors.

In literary study, discussions of architectural form often "read," in the lingering influence of Bachelard, rooms, floor plans, and other elements of architectural design metaphorically.[36] Interiors can, in these accounts, represent psychological states or productively reveal encoded political and cultural distinctions. Rarely, however, do interiors in these studies return reflexively to complex constructions of interiority, something that necessarily happens when literary interiors are read as taking part in a social system composed of communications rather than psyches, or interested in interiority as an unstable attribution of modern novelistic personhood rather than a psychic state. As a literary space, the corridor thematizes both mediality and interiority at the same time that it produces them. The corridor may not only be regulated, representative, and allusive when it appears within a novel, but also self-referential and medial. It becomes its own destination.

The everyday banalities of corridors and their enfolded spaces start to look different in light of this self-reference. While nothing sounds particularly new in figurations of "corridors of the mind," "tunnel-vision," or the "haunted hallway" motif, the self-signification of spatial form, in this case the enclosure of corridors within corridors, once again brings structures of signification and communication into view. The proliferating hallways and their spatial and communicative echoes in modern novels offer examples of what this might look like. This study of corridors and novels is therefore an analysis of the traffic conditions of communication in twentieth-century American fiction. It takes up the dynamic intersections between the physical circulation systems of the built world and the informational networks of the media as they are staged through the immediate postwar period. This requires a perspectival shift away from the modes of spatial interpretation that characterize the scattered history of accounts of literary space, and a resituation of these spaces and persons in the terms of communication and its attendant models of sociality.

Corridoricity: Form, System, Network

The critical idiom of *Corridor,* developed out of systems and media theory, responds to a kind of reflexivity that has emerged in discussions of the objects surrounding these modes of inquiry. It responds also to the possibility raised by Jonathan Elmer that one result of such (systems-theoretical) thinking could be that "our metaphors of communication may be giving way to communication's metaphors of us."[37] Elmer's provocation highlights the most disorienting aspect of thinking about literature from a point of view guided by the assumptions of either Luhmannian systems theory or Kittlerian media studies: their questioning of the status, agency, relevance, or even possibility of a human subject. This question has taken on new life in reflections on the self-observation of systems-theoretical approaches to the humanities found in Bruce Clarke and Mark B. N. Hansen's recent descriptions of "second-order" systems theory, for example, or in post-Kittlerian discussions of "media archeology."[38] I thus work within an approach that combines two strands of contemporary posthermeneutic theory: the work in media studies coming largely out of Germany, and the systems theory of Luhmann. Despite some critical reservations about the compatibility of these two approaches, which arise primarily out of their definitions of what media are,[39] I maintain that it is in fact for the study of media and literature that the merger is most necessary. By documenting how architectures, technologies, and communication systems alike operate as media in novels, I point to the functional and systemic properties of media as a category and generalized condition of modern sociality. Observation machines otherwise known as novels have an affinity for testing and staging their own mediality; the works I treat enact this testing and observation, with an unsettling frequency, by literalizing communication as physical spaces or systems. By thus putting pressure on their own status as media, these often overlooked novels of the era of American modernism turn observation inward by exteriorizing it.

A number of widely spaced but influential collections track the varied fates of systems thinking in the literary disciplines. William Rasch and Cary Wolfe's 2000 *Observing Complexity,* which contains the Elmer essay cited above, gathers articles from an early heyday of systems theory in the American academy (1994–95), and makes a strong claim for systems theory's potential to transform how knowledge is conceived by the humanities:

> It is our belief that scholars in the humanities [10] and sciences alike who are concerned with the general epistemological problems of description, observation, and interpretation have much to teach each other as the search for a truly transdisciplinary research program becomes an ever more pressing agenda at the beginning of the twenty-first century. Now more than ever, scholars in all fields need to be able to theorize the connections

> between different kinds of knowledge in different fields, to be able to situate their work in a world of tightly interlaced and "hybrid" networks (to use Bruno Latour's term) of human, technological, organic, and informational systems.[40]

Alternately, the transformations called for in this earlier collection become the subject for reflection in Clarke and Hansen's 2009 volume, *Emergence and Embodiment*. No longer charting the need for a "transdisciplinary research program" such as that provided by systems theory, they instead reflect on its effects across several fields: "Some of the most important theoretical and critical conversations going on today in the cognitive sciences, chaos and complexity studies, and social systems theory stem from neocybernetic notions of self-organization, emergence, and autopoesis. A growing body of scholarly work is rethinking the shape and evolution of the relations among science, technology, sociology, psychology, philosophy, history, literature, and the arts through neocybernetic terms."[41] They find the predominance of this "second-order" systems theory, or "neocybernetics," in recent work by the likes of Michel Serres, Isabelle Stengers, and Deleuze and Guattari, but also show how the influence of such thinking can be registered in the topics of growing importance to field-specific analyses when they claim that "neocybernetic discourse is central to current historical, interpretive, and theoretical investigations using concepts such as narrative, medium, assemblage, information, noise, network, and communication to remap the terrain of knowledge with reference to the operational boundaries of systems and their environments."[42] A second-order systems theory works in these accounts as the second-order observation of a theory of second-order observation through its manifestation in recent theoretical discourse that often goes by another name. In these terms, too, the concepts driving my analysis of the novels gathered in this book (and in my view driving the novels themselves), "narrative, medium, assemblage, information, noise, network, and communication," are thoroughly embedded in systems-theoretical discourse.

Also at stake in systems theory's reflexive turn is what happens to those challenged "human" and "humanist" subjects when systems replace them as the target of analysis, for "the noumenal unity of the humanist subject gives way to a differential observation of the relations of living and nonliving systems and their environments, such as human and nonhuman bodies and societies."[43] This change of topic appears, although with different effects, in the method of media analysis termed "media archaeology" by what might be thought of as second-order media studies. Wolfgang Ernst, in an essay included in a 2011 volume on the topic of media archaeology edited by Erkki Huhtamo and Jussi Parikka, tracks this shift through a transferal of agency. "Equally close to disciplines that analyze material (hardware) culture and to the Foucauldean notion of the 'archive,'" Ernst writes, "media archaeology is both a method and an aesthetics of practicing media criticism, a kind of epistemological reverse engineering, and an awareness of moments when media themselves, not exclusively humans anymore, become active "archaeologists" of knowledge. This means that when media archaeology deals with prehistories of mass media, this "pre-" is less about temporal antecedence than about the techno-epistemological configurations underlying the discursive surface (literally, the monitors and interfaces) of mass media."[44] Ernst's "epistemological reverse engineering," which he also redefines as "media archaeography," is not interested in the media apparatus as such but rather in the conceptual underpinnings of historically specific forms of mediation, staged as the simultaneity of "method and machine," an assemblage irreducible to the actions of unified subjects. Thus we have the "New German Media Theory," in which "there are no media," only their discontinuous becoming.[45]

The media world that emerges as a result of the move from technology to something more like a system is one that pressures the limits of metaphor in its most direct encounters with the topic of mediation. In this world, the metaphoric conjunction of object and concept, already presumed, becomes a larger theme. Take, for example, Parikka's description of "insect media," which moves from a discussion of critical and cultural "obsession with insectlike modes of media" to the formulation of "'insects as media,' a cultural historical theme that can be catalyzed into media theoretical implications as well."[46] Parikka's move from theme to theory operates similarly to that modeled by Cornelia Vismann's *Files: Law and Media Technology,* in which the titular object operates simultaneously as act and medium in her analysis of the historical mediality of the legal system. For Vismann, moreover, the networked connections of mediality appear in the construction of persons by the medial systems with which they interact. A courier who delivers messages and reads them aloud, in her account, embodies the coincidence of thing and action: "The courier is left with virtually no leeway. In other words, messenger and message coincide. Subsequently, the former is named after the materiality of the medium, *tabula;* and *tabula* in turn give rise to the *tabularius*—he who conveys files and letters."[47]

The courier, the emblematically medial message and messenger for Vismann, is also a corridor. In Jarzombek's history of the form, the story of the corridor's development in architecture cannot be told without attending to etymology. "In the fourteenth century," Jarzombek says, "in both Spanish and Italian contexts, a *corridor* referred not to a space but to a courier, someone who as the word's Latin root suggests could run fast. A *corridor* might have been a scout sent behind enemy lines, a governmental messenger, a carrier of money, or even a negotiator arranging mercantile deals and marriages."[48] The corridor's etymological movement travels from person to more generalized architectural communication channel before it arrives at the most modern form. Taking seriously the historically and linguistically embedded relationship between person, communication, and concrete structure requires maintaining contact with the corridor's immanent mediality and makes its additional recursive mediality in the novel an especially apropos assemblage for media theory.

I am suggesting that corridors and their ambient formations in modern American fiction provide a precise location for the novel's mediality and that their hypervisibility in novels that otherwise relate uneasily to the genre narratives characterizing American modernism reveals a body of work of more importance to contemporary media theory than its critical fortunes would imply. And this is not a one-way relationship, for the double encoding of medial form enacted in these texts through their corridoricity not only highlights the underlying conceptual complexity and systematicity attached to media in its specific historical and material formulation but also theorizes that encoding within the recursive gesture itself.

This is, after all, a self-consciously literary study of media. Recent media studies work across a variety of humanities fields has sought to remove the analysis of media "away from the monopolies of literary studies"[49] and avoid "paying homage to a form of language processing long since deceased,"[50] and as a result has made available for examination a broad range of media-technological artifacts and their attendant cultural techniques. However, it is my contention that to consign literary analysis to what Kittler calls "those quaint but no longer very functional disciplines that should rather be called cultural studies or, even more preferably, become part of media theory,"[51] creates something of a blind spot for media theory itself. By taking this approach, I am not arguing for a reactionary return to the primacy, or monopoly, of the literary that would uncoil a tightly wound discipline.[52] Instead, the importance of the techniques of literary study and of the specific medium of the novel here operates in two simple and related ways. First, it is that the medial specificity of the novel, as a technology and set of observational techniques, makes a difference for the cultural registration and self-observation of other media—the encoding of media in and as fiction matters. In this, my account of media is also very close to that outlined in Vogl's capacious understanding of what falls within the purview of the media studies field. He argues that "media theory might thus axiomatically claim that no such thing as a medium exists, at least not in the stable generic, disciplinary, substantial, or historical sense. Media cannot be reduced to means of representation, like film and theater; or to technologies, like printing or telecommunications; or to machines, like the telegraph or the computer; or to symbolic systems, like writing, images, or numbers. Nonetheless, all these things are emphatically 'medial.'"[53] The objects that exhibit this "medial" character here are also self-producing and self-regulating. Luhmann expresses this in another way when he says, "Processes that can be applied to themselves are reflexive. With communication, this means that one can communicate about communication. One can thematize the communicative process in communication, can inquire about and explain how something was meant, can request communication, can reject communication, can establish communicative connections, and so forth."[54] I turn to novels because they take this mediality, and this communicativeness, and double it—the texts I examine make it their overt project to observe their own mediality by thematizing the mediality in turn of the kinds of objects that form Vogl's wider field.

My second point is that "mediality" itself is another way of talking about form, and the transfer of media from thing to process is of interest both to the novels and to the wide range of media theorists I have been discussing so far. The sustained interest in figures of thought and cultural practice as figures—the metaphors, homonyms, and other forms of wordplay—that dominate so many cultural histories of media and make them so compelling, have also been surfacing in literary study as part of a renewed attention to form and its materialities. It is in this capacity, too, that media studies provides a pertinent contribution to the culturally informed new formalisms that have been developing across a broad range of literary fields over the past decade.

The "centrality of form to contextualist and materialist critique" appears in Marjorie Levinson's survey of the "new formalism" in literary scholarship.[55] She points to a desire across multiple formalist approaches to reclaim a lost attention "to the processes and structures of mediation" that constitute the relationship of literary discourses to that which they represent.[56] In doing so, these approaches recall what Louis Marin sets out in *On Representation* as "the inseparable duality of method and object" that makes language a formal and formalizable object and "double relation."[57] And in his 2008 piece, "The Idea of Observation at Key West, or, Systems Theory, Poetry, and Form beyond Formalism," Cary Wolfe parses these form debates in systems-theoretical terms, identifying in the work of Luhmann two separate claims that redefine form in the context of modernity—"one having to do with the abstract, recursive dynamics of self-reference in relation to the form of the artwork as such, and one having specifically to do with the perceptual, material aspects of words used as an artistic medium, typically associated with traditional prosodic devices."[58] What my readings of the medial forms of American modernism show is that the making-visible of mediality in these texts is always, along these lines, an explicitly formal process (but not, as Wolfe would suggest, that this is a process specifically guided by the "art system" as such). These readings are also geared to expose the particular affinities that modern American novels have for spatial communications systems to do this work.

While Americanist literary scholarship and its historical narratives have accounted for modernity and also, to some extent, the emergence of modern communications systems, my account of the period places infrastructural forms at the intersection between the two. These readings bring together several strands of an emerging conversation extending from transhistorical Americanist literary criticism to modernist literary studies more specifically that uses the figure of the network to account for the confrontations of medial and concrete systems in literary artifacts. These new studies of networked mediality illustrate the consequences for modern fictional personhood that arise from embeddedness in such physical and communicational systems. The psychic persons described in recent scholarship find themselves constantly attacked, infiltrated, or distributed by the pressures of network forms. Most interesting for this study is the way that such discussions open up the possibility for considering in narrative what Eugene Thacker and Alexander Galloway have conceptualized as "the nonhuman quality of networks," equating nonhumanity with materiality. In *The Exploit,* Thacker and Galloway point out a contradiction in the logic of the network, which as a medium is both constructed and constituted by humans, "yet the moments when the network logic takes over—in the mob or the swarm, in contagion or infection—are the moments that are the most disorienting, the most threatening to the integrity of the human ego."[59] Maud Ellmann also takes up this threat in her study of networks and psyches from James to Freud, *The Nets of Modernism.* Looking at the networked physical environment of urban modernity in the early twentieth century, Ellmann notes the invasion of the private home by utilities and telephones, saying that "such networks insinuate the public in the private sphere, creating mysterious and uncontrollable relations of dependency. This networked world threatens to reduce the human subject to a knot or intersection, rather than an independent agent, in the webs of communication, commodities, and capital."[60] This threat extends to the "transferential world" of James, in which a bounded personal identity loses out to "interpsychic networks of exchange."[61]

In Americanist literary study, books such as Matt Cohen's *The Networked Wilderness* employ a capacious idea of communication as encompassing both physical and discursive networks to account for how books, ideas, and bodies travel in their local historical context. Cohen's analysis of communication systems in early New England tracks "Native American and English encounters in American space" and precisely locates them "within a continuous informational topography that forced all interlocutors to contemplate communications systems *as* systems."[62] His focus on the parasitic noisiness of such networks makes visible the strangeness and violence that "permeability of different signifying systems" produces in material, social, and communicative connectivity.[63] The interest in the systematicity of American literary production extends from pre–printing press material mediality to the institutionalization of American literary production throughout the twentieth century described most prominently in Mark McGurl's

The Program Era, and through to texts such as David Ciccorico's *Reading Network Fiction,* which examine the connective forms of digital textuality.[64]

The studies of early twentieth-century and modernist American literature in most direct contact with the approach outlined here, including Mark Goble's *Beautiful Circuits* and recent and forthcoming work by Katherine Biers, draw from the medial matrix of form and materiality the magnetic pulls of "American *autopoesis,*"[65] the kind of self-reference and self-naming that nontrivially connects novels, people, and physical networks in the reflexive movements of what Mark Seltzer calls "the media-modernity complex."[66] In Biers's discussion of "black phonographism" in James Weldon Johnson's 1912 *The Autobiography of an Ex-Colored Man,* the "material logic of the phonograph" has explicit formal consequences for the narrative subject himself embedded in the "mass-cultural and mass-mediated circuits of early twentieth-century America."[67] For Goble, too, a medial apparatus can become a "racial apparatus" with the power to "make material an aesthetic of racial experience," recursively identifying technologized persons with the technical media.[68] Goble positions this movement, moreover, within the ambitions of modernist formalism: "Race was already so inscribed in the language surrounding new technologies that communicated the immediacy of music like never before, that it was difficult for the musical aesthetic of modernism to register its appeal without recourse to a whole network of racial meanings and iconographies that projected fantasies of blackness onto the medium of recorded sound—making U.S. modernism itself into a kind of feedback loop between race and technology."[69] Goble's modernism registers the bodily and subjective pressures imposed by mediations that move phantasmatically between apparatus and form, becoming "medium specificity with a vengeance."[70] *Corridor* tracks the concretization of the movement between technical media and literary form narrated so powerfully by the growing body of media-theoretical readings of American literature. This can also be described as a focus on the second-order observation of communications media in and as novels. I am in turn suggesting that medium-specific analysis of early twentieth-century fiction can include objects and networks not traditionally understood as technical media, and that the double encoding of mediation is unique to the history of the novel and its interaction with multiple layers of materiality.

Novels and Corridors

The novel constantly refers back to its own form. By reflecting on its place within systems of observation, it incorporates the levels of second-order observation that it facilitates for its readers.[71] What this means for literature as a system of self-observed, self-referential communication is that it produces a theory of communication at the same time it enacts it. In the sense that bodies and information are communicated, they are also implicated in the autopoetic construction of fiction. The networks of relation that constitute the situation of novels find their complement in the space of corridors, which form what Michel Foucault refers to as heterotopias, sites that "have the curious property of being in relation with all other sites, but in such a way as to suspect, neutralize, or invert the set of relations that they happen to designate, mirror, or reflect."[72] Corridors, like novels, invert and contest social relations at the same time that they shape them, combining the real technologies of circulation with their idealized images. Corridors in novels provide the space for self-reference—a physical location for the novel to map its own medial processes. Within a fictional form saturated with self-conscious, self-reflexive self-descriptions, the corridor stands out as an image of the transport mechanisms of communicative sociality.

The question then turns to how novels—as medial systems of communication and transport—use the corridor to observe themselves as such systems. More specifically, why do the wayward novels of American modernism so often describe strange, often dangerous corridor spaces where bodies and information flow too freely or not at all? The ubiquity of corridors makes them almost transparent to contemporary eyes, yet they are made disturbingly visible within these narrative environments. The history of the corridor, as a system of communicative noncommunication for bodies within domestic structures, is intimately bound up with the developing structures of interiority and the medial subjectivity of a reading "public." In the novels I discuss, corridors and corridic spaces are defamiliarized by writers who negotiate the possibilities for message and body transport by radicalizing the process of communication *as* transport and exposing the violence that attends obstructed or dangerously open communicative sociality. These novels, self-conscious forms that both communicate and reflexively produce interiority and sociality, indicate their own narrative structures when they query the relays of the hallway.

The corridor, a space in domestic structures that separates rooms and simultaneously facilitates communication between them, is thus a uniquely modern phenomenon—modern in the sense that it became a sudden and forced requirement for the removal of traffic from rooms in the late eighteenth century, and modern also in the sense that the notions of individuality and interiority that developed with the communication channels of the novel, and media infrastructures of print and post, corresponded with the corridor's application to domestic architecture. The private rooms produced by corridors allowed, among other things, the private reading of letters and novels, two key media of interiority. Within the architecture of the domestic, built world, the technology that regulates the communication of and between bodies emerges as a system intimately tied to the forms that communicate interiority, and these forms have intertwined and dynamic histories. The novel formally enacts the corridor by providing the circulatory space for private thoughts within a reading public; it separates in order to reconnect. When a hallway appears within the content of a novel, it thus opens up a possibility for self-reference within the fictional form, for the novel's status as a method of proxy transport for individuals and information is implicated in the corridor's function as a transportation medium. While not every fictionalized corridor produces an explicit discussion of the novel's form, their entwined histories imply that the structures of communication for both bodies and information are constantly indicating each other, and can be historicized.

If the corridor connects and facilitates the interaction styles of privacy and sociality within the home, one counterpart in the territorial geography of the state that has received renewed attention in the wake of material medial analysis, the postal service, realizes the architectural project of the corridor in the transmission of private letters. That the two become institutionalized systems of communication at around the same time demonstrates their functional differentiation as subsystems within a larger framework of communication. Rewriting the connection between the private soul and the privy chamber, Bernhard Siegert, in *Relays: Literature as an Epoch of the Postal System,* implicates the private letter in the same processes: "The private did not precede the private letter in the process of this transformation—in either a chronological or a casual sense. On the contrary: the private medium was defined as the medium for the definition of the private."[73] The postal system in this account not only creates the bureaucratic apparatus for information delivery, but also the subjective apparatus for the individuals entangled in its transmissions. Siegert also claims that the combination of delivery methods for both people and letters within the transportation networks of the post brought together bodies and information in a form of symbolic exchange, inscribed on a geographical grid.[74] The space of circulation has a direct relation to the state of circulation. The physical transit of the letter oscillates with the reading of the letter as the reading of the transported body encoded in writing. In the space between, communication exists as transportation. Because "passability—forming a way and keeping it ready—is just another word for a historical state of the postal system,"[75] the status of the passage within the home represents a form of postal subjectivity and locates the individual historically within a network of allowed communications between spaces and subjects. Implicit in the question of whether communication exists within a continued flow of undeliverable messages, moreover, is the opposite paradigm of undeliverability: the dead-letter office. Siegfried Kracauer, for example, sees the passage and the terminus as imbricated spaces of congestion. He describes the employment office as a "passageway," but in a liminal space of movement—for it seems more like a dead end, or a passage to nowhere.[76] Transport between rooms—and in this case out of them—breaks down when the corridor fails to live up to its ideal mediating function, and the rooms and inhabitants themselves get in the way. Evans also locates the coherence between private space and passage in movement: "Universal accessibility was as necessary an adjunct to privacy as was the one-door room. A compartmentalized building had to be organized by the movement through it, because movement was the one remaining thing that could give it any coherence. If it were not for the paths making the hyphen between departure and arrival, things would have fallen apart in complete irrelation."[77] Obstructed movement, whether blocked by walls or deliberate inertia, signals a problem with the structures of communication.

The structures of conveyance produced in the developing postal relays of house and state share their relationship to the individual with the novel, which incorporates the mechanisms of corridor and letter in its form. This relationship emerges in the history of the novel's relationship to modern interiority, for in order to gain access to the shared experience of fictionalized interiors, the readers of novels must migrate inward, reducing contact with the social traffic of the corridor. The novel works as a communication system that both communicates interiors and communicates the possibility of communication—or passability—within the systems of information transport that organize social life. In addition, the novel becomes a medium for self-observation: the reader of novels can observe his or her individuality by observing the ways in which others evaluate themselves. For Catherine Gallagher, this self-observation works in part via the ontological difference between character and reader, and yet, though "helping us reenvision our embodied immanence through the condition of its possible absence," what she calls the "incompleteness" of fictional characters also "allows us to experience an uncanny desire to be that which we already are."[78] According to Luhmann, the forms of second-order observation enabled by novels constitute the modern definition of individuality: "An individual in the modern sense is someone who can observe his or her own observing. And whoever fails to understand this intuitively or is not made aware of this by his or her therapist can read novels and project them onto the self."[79]

This projection backward in the form of second-order observation places novels in a system of feedback loops: relays between subject and medium in which the medium itself has a determining role for the subject. Self-observation, in Luhmann's terms, attends all social systems as a form of communication addressed to communication.[80] In other words, individual subjects can have individualized, self-observed interiors if they participate in the social systems of communication found in novels, letters, and hallways. The modern individual appears Janus-faced, for occupying public or private space becomes, on the level of social systems, two ways of saying the same thing. And since the private self depends on the modalities of architecture, fiction, and media networks as social systems that communicate bodies and information, that self must be redefined according to the communicative properties of its interlocking material and medial forms. It is precisely in this interlocking interplay—the movement between persons, material environments, and technology—that the novel encodes medial reflexivity, defining media for itself as process rather than product. And it is their insistently concretized implication in that process that attaches the novelistic persons populating the text to its medial self-reference. In Reinhold Martin's account of the "organizational complex" developing throughout the twentieth century, in which architecture forms "one among many media," the consequences for persons are clear: "And so technocratic and aesthetic research accelerated in the direction of ever more efficient mechanisms of *self*-regulation, *self*-organization. These in turn helped invent new kinds of cities, new kinds of architectures, and with them a new 'self,' none of which could be said to possess the traditional spatial properties that divided inside from outside in any meaningful sense."[81] The architectural persons Martin identifies are the modern novel's unlikely but intransigent inhabitants.

The story of the novel's relationship to the corridor and these inhabitants is the longer story of which this account of the intensification of that relationship in early twentieth-century America is a part. Contained within this long narrative are also shorter narratives, such as an institutional interest in corridor spaces in the writings of Henry James beginning in the late nineteenth century and the postmodern corridic abysses dominating recursive fictions in the latter half of the twentieth century, through to contemporary literary engagements with digital media. These narratives operate in the environment of what I present here, but my focus remains on the particular assemblage of materials, novels, and media and their specific interactions in a period that I claim marks a key turn in the reflexive relationship between architecture and literature. Although I acknowledge that there has always been something medial about the corridor in the history of its literary manifestations, here its mediality takes a different form. This difference also makes a difference within the more localized narratives of medial and spatial modernisms and the kinds of informational and physical technologies admitted into those narratives.

Each of the seemingly unremarkable technologies gathered in this book for their corridoricity, such as ducts, pipes, urban infrastructures, factory machines and interiors, and of course the corridors themselves provide an overt rendering of the novel's materiality, a materiality that involves the apparatus of the book as well as its production and dissemination. At one level, these medial objects refer explicitly to the inscription technologies of the book, such as presses, paper, and mass-produced and -circulated writing. The linguistic and figurative layering of sense that attaches to these objects, meanwhile, thematizes the network of relations between the material printed artifact and its fictionality. This foregrounds the novel's status as a printed book, or more specifically as what N. Katherine Hayles calls in her discussion of medium-specific analysis a "material metaphor," a category of physical object that is both constructed by and functions through its metaphoric networks. Her analysis orients toward electronic mediation, but includes a longer history of material metaphoric actions in her understanding of digital textuality and what she calls the "technotext." According to Hayles, "we are not generally accustomed to think of a book as a material metaphor, but in fact it is an artifact whose physical properties and historical usages structure our interactions with it in ways obvious and subtle."[82] The novels included in this book stand out for the degree to which they bring to the surface the implied figurations of its physical medium, that there is already something metaphoric about novels that inheres in their otherwise mundane physical form.

The material metaphor is a key concern because it makes these novels' staged materiality dynamic, so that the materiality itself is part of a movement between object and concept. The novels discussed here take this dynamic sense of figural movement rather than a static object as the index of materiality, and double it, or reencode that dynamism in its multilayered medial objects. These objects operate as *reflexively doubled material metaphors,* constituting themselves through the self-observation of their mediality, and housed with violent consequences in these novels' imagined physical landscapes.

Corridors, furnaces, electric third rails, and other concrete material structures are media in novels because they doubly encode the reflexivity of writing technology and fictional technique: that is, they embed the forms of self-reflection in a material object that also demonstrates a capacity to reflect upon itself. In this way these objects "become" media in the sense outlined by Vogl in his prescription for a media theory that accounts for the confluence of discursive, technological, or symbolic registers in a discontinuous history of emerging media. He claims that "media are specific, systematizable objects of study for the following reason: everything they store and mediate is stored and mediated under conditions that are created by the media themselves and that ultimately comprise those media."[83] Vogl's insistence on a medial "function," moreover, also demonstrates why the medial objects, operating simultaneously as technology and technique in these novels, invite a different kind of formal analysis than that which has previously accompanied them when they do appear in modernist critical discourse.

Like a Hallway

The genre noisiness of the cluster of texts and concerns gathered in this book—novels published in the era of American modernism but uncomfortable fits within its narratives—becomes a way to pinpoint reflexive mediality. This is friction attached to infrastructure: in Henry Roth's *Call It Sleep,* for example, protomodernist narration erupts at the moment the protagonist connects to the electric third rail, and when *An American Tragedy*'s Clyde Griffiths finds his consciousness overtaken by "a sealed and silent hall," that moment corresponds with the incursion of experimental narration into its realist prose. The furnace in which *Native Son*'s Bigger Thomas burns the body of his employer's daughter reappears later in the novel as an excessive restaging of social realism in an autopoetic gesture. These are the kinds of contagions operative throughout this book and overtly thematized in the hospital corridors of Katherine Anne Porter and the bureaucratic architectures of C. P. Snow's corridors of power.

Appearing near the end of this book's timeline, novels like John Steinbeck's late work *The Wayward Bus* (1947) make the entanglement of corridoricity and the self-staging of genre almost too literal. Steinbeck's text follows the mid-1940s journey of Sweetheart, the "common carrier" connecting passengers from the rural valleys of eastern California to the transit hub that will join them to the rapidly expanding highway system, whose presence is felt constantly. Take the novel's opening description of the location of its departure point, the site of the bus station:

> Forty-two miles below San Ysidro, on a great north-south highway in California, there is a crossroad which for eighty-odd years has been called Rebel Corners. From here a country road goes at right angles toward the west until, after forty-nine miles, it connects with another north-south highway that leads from San Francisco to Los Angeles and, of course, Hollywood. Anyone who wishes to go from the inland valley to the coast in this part of the state must take the road that begins at Rebel Corners and winds through the hills and a little desert and through farmland and mountains until, at last, it comes to the coastal highway right in the middle of the town of San Juan de la Cruz.[84]

The bus that travels along these roads becomes a moving analog of the enclosed sociality of the station's café, which must always be a little wayward. Consider, too, the historically layered highway aesthetics that the bus greets on its journey:

> The highway to San Juan de la Cruz was a black-top road. In the twenties hundreds of miles of concrete highway had been laid down in California, and people had sat back and said, "There, that's permanent. That will last

> as long as the Roman roads and longer, because no grass can grow up through the concrete to break it." But it wasn't so. The rubber-shod trucks, the pounding automobiles, beat the concrete, and after a while the life went out of it and it began to crumble. . . .
>
> Then the country maintenance crews poured tar in the cracks to keep the water out, and that didn't work, and finally they capped the roads with an asphalt and gravel mixture. That did survive, because it offered no stern face to the pounding tires. It gave a little and came back a little. It softened in the summer and hardened in the winter. And gradually all the roads were capped with shining black that looked silver in the distance.[85]

This is the environment that driver, passenger, and bus alike enter when they join the highway system—roads "capped with shining black that looked silver in the distance." But, wayward, the bus cannot abide this luminescent modern mirage. Crumbling road infrastructure leads the bus to "the old road that was there before they put in those damn-fool bridges. It goes right around the outside of the bend. The stagecoaches used to use it."[86]

When Steinbeck's emblem of modern connectivity suddenly veers off onto a nineteenth-century stagecoach thoroughfare, it must get stuck. The bus stops, blocking the road, and its passengers enter a scene to accompany the road on which they travel. When the bus stalls, the characters decamp to what can only be described as the primal scene of a version of American naturalist fiction: "Three deep dark caves developed at the bottom of the cliff and a few small ones higher up." We learn that the caves had hosted coyotes raising their young, and even the grizzly bears long departed from the region, but also that they "were not entirely inventions of nature," having housed native hunting parties and traveling settlers.[87] The signs of some cave visitors have been scratched as initials on their walls. These caves, perhaps too predictably, disclose the atavistic drives of their new inhabitants, culminating in a respectable company man (not quite in grey flannel, but close) raping his wife within them. She responds by dragging her fingernails down her face, exteriorizing both her attack and the cave's interior: "She could feel the blood oozing from the scratches. She put out her hand and dirtied it on the cave floor and rubbed the dirt into her bleeding cheek. The blood flowed down through the dirt and down her neck to the collar of her waist."[88] This movement into quasi-natural nature is a familiar one in Steinbeck's oeuvre, but unlike, for example, *The Grapes of Wrath, The Wayward Bus* seems to strip the passage into the cave of any sociohistorical content save the highway itself. Serially equivalent passengers become another kind of character when they fall off the grid, temporarily inhabiting another kind of novel before being reincorporated into modern circuitry. And as my readings of blocked infrastructure will demonstrate, the system's noise, its interruptions, are what paradoxically ensures its ongoingness. In the end the city lights come into view, "lost and lonely in the night, remote and cold and winking, strung on chains."[89]

Steinbeck's novel is no longer a "mirror on the highway,"[90] but the highway itself, and most clearly refers to itself as such in the collisions of bus and genre. Published in the immediate postwar period, *The Wayward Bus* also points to some of the continuities between its scalar infrastructural concerns and the material engagements with the built world developing over several decades prior to its publication.

Theorizations of the postmodern or contemporary physical landscape likewise take for granted the kinds of connectivity between architectural, urban, and national infrastructures and the media staged in earlier decades in the genre frictions and irritations lingering at the borders of American modernist fiction. Thus, when Jarzombek claims at the end of his history of corridic modernity that in its move "from body to building to pipelines" the word "corridor" also leaves the field of architecture, where it "exists only as a residual." In this new corridor world, "what had been locked into the interior of the building—the building serving as an expression of corridic mastery—works now at a megascale and perhaps outside the bounds of representation."[91] But the corridors and the clogged, corridic pipelines and streets of the novels gathered here suggest that the scalar logic of corridoricity cannot be confined to the contemporary spatial scene, particularly when its representability is at stake. They also show a bourgeoning tendency that Bruno Latour identifies with later twentieth-century transportation projects. His *Aramis: The Love of Technology* makes the mediality of the exchange between physical infrastructure and fiction quite clear. Infrastructure engineers are "creating fictions," he says. "They're novelists." What draws Latour to the unbuilt project of Aramis in the latter half of the twentieth century is its failure to be realized in the material world and its persistence in the realm of texts, for "the observer of technologies has to be very careful not to differentiate too hastily between signs and things, between projects and objects, between fiction and reality, between a novel about feelings and what is inscribed in the nature of things."[92]

The novels I discuss as examples of the communicative logic of modern fictionality form part of a cluster of texts that is at times described as "naturalist," "late naturalist," or "neo-naturalist." Corridors and their displaced doubles appear in the foreground of fiction that resituates the apartment blocks and tenement houses so popular in turn-of-the-century novels in the rapidly evolving urban and media ecologies of inter- and postwar America. Formal interest in the hallway and the physical transit networks of modern communicative sociality erupts in these novels. Moreover, the affinities of many late or neo-naturalist writers with movements of proletarian fiction and social realism contextualize their formal and spatial concerns within a longer history of naturalist sensibility.[93] They also have been the cause of several omissions in genre studies. Readings such as those provided in my discussion of the infrastructural modernity of Henry Roth, Richard Wright, and John Dos Passos offer a corrective to the problem Fleissner identifies as a critical inability to include African American texts in larger conceptions of modern and naturalist writing: "It is a curious fact of American literary history," she says, "that, while African American novels like Wright's *Native Son* and Ann Petry's *The Street* have been among the twentieth-century works most often discussed in relation to naturalism, this linkage has had little effect on broader theorizations either of naturalism or of African American literature."[94] The effect of tracing the contours of these intersecting strands through a complex of texts that also problematize their relationship to genre categories informs this book's organizational logic.

My thinking about the displaced genre categories surrounding these texts can also be characterized by its attention to the "lateness" of their engagements with naturalist and realist concerns. This idea of lateness, taken in part from Theodor Adorno, operates at a slight remove from that used by Edward Said in his *On Late Style,* for it takes up the question of form over biography, and is interested less in the aging of the novelists than the reflective aging of the novelistic forms themselves.[95] In his discussion of late style in Beethoven, Adorno writes: "The maturity of the late works of significant artists does not resemble the kind one finds in fruit. They are, for the most part, not round, but furrowed, even ravaged. Devoid of sweetness, bitter and spiny, they do not surrender themselves to mere delectation. They lack all the harmony that the classicist aesthetic is in the habit of demanding from works of art, and they show more traces of history than of growth."[96] Instead of "significant artists," I am attributing an amount of agency and cohesion to generic concerns themselves, but recognizing that they too cannot be contained by a unified identity. And while I am not exactly describing a "minor literature," it seems no accident that Deleuze's reading of Kafka turns again and again to corridic space. "The hallway can be angled," he says of blockages in *Amerika* and *The Castle,* "the little door can be connected to the line of the hallway, in such a way that things become all the more surprising. The line of the hallway, the unlimited straight line, can hold other surprises."[97] The texts of an almost-belated naturalism, of near-minorness, of corridoricity, contain such surprises. They also show how these late-naturalist texts of the era of American modernism produce a media aesthetic just as exciting and experimental as that attributed to more traditionally modernist texts. I will spend the remainder of this overview dwelling on one such text, Sherwood Anderson's *Winesburg, Ohio,* that shows the beginning of this shorter history of corridic engagement circa 1919. Anderson's fictions, like Steinbeck's, make the interplay between literary and material communication too explicit, a move that can only result in breakdown, and a breakdown that figures an uncanny mediality.

Winesburg, Ohio is probably best known for its use of synecdoche. Framed as a found book of "grotesques," the text uses the logic of figuration to present each of the portraits it gathers to tell the story of a place. That each piece is "a story of" becomes very important to its governing tropes: "The story of Wing Biddlebaum is a story of hands," the first chapter following the frame announces, drawing the text immediately into the shifting status of standing in for something else.[98] Following pieces often work metonymically ("Adventure" stands in for Alice Hindman, and "Respectability" for Wash Williams, for example), but in each case, "standing in" marks each character's status as one of the book's grotesques as well as signifying a connection to the writing process. Every individual in the collection is described as being somehow "like" a writer, for the town is not only populated by writers, novelists, journalists, and teachers, but the carpenter is "like the old writer," the telegraph operator has "the abandon of a poet," and the town youth write notes that dangerously "reflect a mind inflamed by novel reading."[99] And while this writerly self-reflection may be a commonplace of fiction, it takes on added significance in the world of likeness that constitutes *Winesburg, Ohio.* To return to Wing Biddlebaum's hands, they are not only synecdochic representations of the character, but "the medium through which he expressed his love of man." Thought of as a medium, Wing Biddlebaum's hands approximate the writer's choice of language for expression, and call attention to an overt concern with how expression takes place.[100] Moreover, the particular deployment of the synecdoche of hands is also the deployment of synecdoche as cliché—what sounds like a Dickensian play on "hands" shifts from a figuration of the workforce to stand in for an individual—and in this way the text's opening figure is also an account of figuration.[101] Put another way, this part–whole relationship, as cliché, is interested less in its referents (hands and Wing Biddlebaum), than in the transfer itself: the focus is not on the fact that "hands" stand in for "person," but that they stand in for standing in.

The multiple modalities of figuration at work in the text—synecdoche, metonymy, simile, for example—all fall under a general rubric of metaphor that is not only a way of operating but also a topic of conversation. Things that refer refer also to writing in a process of continual self-assemblage and self-reflection. An approach to the text that simply decodes its metaphors, then, tells only part of the story, for the story of Winesburg is also a story of metaphors.

But these are also not just any metaphors. Consider the case of "Loneliness," a central story in *Winesburg, Ohio,* and metonymy for Enoch Robinson. The story deals with Enoch's attempt to participate in the face-to-face, mass-mediated, and architecturally marked vicissitudes of sociality, and maps the ways in which he comes into contact with the abstractions of modern institutional life. The story links his childhood proclivities ("He walked in the middle of the road when he came into town and sometimes read a book. Drivers of teams had to shout and swear to make him realize where he was") to adult confusions of the literal and figurative.[102] "The child in him," we are told, "kept bumping against things, against actualities like money and sex and opinions. Once he was hit by a street car and thrown against an iron post."[103] The institutionalized abstractions of "money" and "sex" here are literalized in the hard structure of the street. These abstractions, moreover, resonate with Enoch's earlier problems of reading books while participating literally in the social movement of the thoroughfare. Literary and bodily communication, it seems, do not mix well, even as they indicate each other.

Taking the use of spatial figuration further, the story goes on to literalize Enoch's encounter with sociality in architecture: "The room in which young Robinson lived in New York faced Washington Square and was long and narrow like a hallway. It is important to get that fixed in your mind. The story of Enoch is in fact the story of a room almost more than it is the story of a man."[104] The room in this story is *hallway-like* not only in shape, but because it hosts the character's friends and becomes itself a dynamic, shared social space. Crucially, Enoch lives in a spatial simile, and the entanglement of the categories "room" and "hallway" in the basic language of likeness circles back to the story's original half-comparison of Enoch made metonym by loneliness. The room is "like a hallway" and the story, "almost," is "the story of a room." The near substitution of hallway for room and of room for character recalls the text's original concern with the function of figuration. But it also does more than that: the "standing in" I have been discussing as the novel's operative mode trips up on the form of the hallway. In this case, likeness links more than characters and stories, for spatial forms reference each other as well, and are in turn bound up in the likeness of characters and stories. At issue here is not only the structure of language and what it refers to, but *how* it operates, and where.

Appropriately enough for a text whose title dramatizes the specificity of place, spatial metaphors overwhelm the stories of *Winesburg, Ohio,* as it pictures each of its characters in reference to their residences and trajectories through the town. Transit spaces in particular organize its metaphoric logic, and alleyways, railroads, and hallways appear in nearly every account. The most-referenced structure in the text is the hotel housing George Willard, the protagonist (a term that depends, in part, on reading *Winesburg* not only as a novel, but a bildungsroman), and its supposedly clear divisions between hallway and private room find echoes in the architecture of domestic space as well as in the road and rail systems described throughout *Winesburg.*

The proliferation of hallways throughout the text as sites where observation (usually in the form of eavesdropping), communication between public and private spaces of enclosure, and negotiations over the figurative constitution of personhood happen indicates an urgency attendant to the figurative status of such spaces. Hallways in *Winesburg, Ohio* appear to metaphorize communication—they take the form of metaphor to refer to abstractions of interiority and figurative communication. Additionally, they refer to the logic of distinction that appears to inhere in the structure of the hallway to comment on the process of making distinctions. The corridor, for example, marks the primary distinction of *Winesburg*'s hotel—that between public and private space—and at the same time that the novel constantly refers to the corridor's traffic in order to distinguish the private cells that it communicates between, the presuppositions behind this distinction, and its very possibility, are constantly being challenged.

But what can be said about these distinctions, and why are they rendered in the metaphoric language of the corridor? I would like to argue that the status of these metaphors, their location and how they function, can be best understood from a perspective of communication that, following the work of Luhmann, Dirk Baecker, and Elena Esposito, dispenses with the also metaphoric logic of transmission to focus on the functions of communication rather than the things communicated (or, as Luhmann puts it, "the entire metaphor of possessing, having, giving, and receiving, the entire 'thing metaphoric' is unsuitable for understanding communication").[105] In this case, "things metaphoric" do not provide an account of communication even as they participate in the literary communications system. Tracing the metaphors of communication located in the text's hallways, and stopping there, would be to reduce the complexity in which their likeness has entangled them: hallways as metaphors for communication processes are but one instance of a literary form for talking about communication.[106]

What makes the operation of these corridors so interesting is their transit to the other side of the distinction between form (for representing communications) and medium (through which communication happens). Not only do they signify, as forms, the properties of communication at stake in the text, they *stage* them. Corridors or (to use the text's American idiom) hallways in *Winesburg, Ohio* simultaneously operate as form and medium. Dirk Baecker provides another example of this in his discussion of the genre of film when he points to the human face as the form through which film experiences and expresses its processes. Baecker looks to Alfred Hitchcock's *North by Northwest* to posit the face as an example of the reentry of a form into the medium/form distinction: "Alfred Hitchcock remarks on the human face as the medial form into which the movies transform it when his film . . . shows the unmoving faces of the American Presidents at Mount Rushmore. If these unmoving faces are only form, they are turned into a medium by becoming the stage of a drama of escape, rescue, and recognition."[107] This, of course, is a description of a medial form from the perspective of the medium of film. Film, like literature, marks the distinction between medium and form in its own terms, and this idea of immanence must be applied to any literary system as well. The communicative operations of literature, and in this case fiction (or more specifically, *Winesburg, Ohio*), can thus be parsed in *literary* terms, or how literature observes itself as a communications system. The corridor that is so like both Enoch Robinson and the telling of stories is transformed into a medial form that both comments on communications and stages them. It both conditions and instances the fictional account of interiority and the communicative distinctions under which it operates.

Play between corridor and corridor-like room reveals the boundaries of psychic, social, and spatial interiority in "Loneliness." Furthermore, after Enoch Robinson's failed participation in marriage, the reading of daily newspapers, and engagement with public affairs (all models of communicative sociality he attempts after leaving the hallway-like room), he rerents the narrow room and locks the door, populating the room instead with fictional "shadow-people" who leave him happy, "like a writer busy among the figures of his brain."[108] The "story of a room," or the story of a corridor, here becomes also the story of a writer—or, a corridor-like room stands in for a writer-like character, entangling likeness and fictionality in the hallway both in and as narration.[109]

Narrative movement through the corridor is correspondingly proprioceptive: relationally oriented toward itself and cross-referenced by multiple modalities of communication.[110] The network of correspondences contained by the corridor's self-description also formulates "likeness," or what might be deemed corridoricity, as the networking of space and the social.[111] Corridoricity, here, particularizes the more general likeness I have been describing: it insists upon a boundedness of space and the social for its peculiar form of self-reference. This is not a description of the relationship of "subjects" to "space," but of the spatial forms of communication as the social. The corridors I am describing appear to presume distinctions such as those between private and public, rest and motion, or interior and exterior. However, they also reencode the "street," or public communications space, as an interior form. This further distinguishing of interior space—as private rooms become the interior of the interior, they thematize interiority—is made possible by a kind of negated self-observation of the corridor: it is both the exterior to the private room's interior, and its opposite, the interior to the traffic of the outside world. It observes itself, paradoxically, through these proliferating distinctions.[112]

Corridors organize and systematize space by regulating the communication of bodies and information and reencoding other communication systems with that conjunction. What Kojin Karatani refers to as "intercrossing space" (*Verkehrsraum*) here looks like an overlay of modern sociality's physical transportation networks (e.g., roadway, sewer, or hallway systems) and information networks (e.g., mass media or telephone systems).[113] In the fiction I have been discussing, the corridor seems to theorize itself continuously as it is observed as a vehicle for both literary and architectural self-reference.

Each of the following chapters discusses the spaces, technologies, and techniques that together encode the medial forms of American modernism, and how a cluster of novels treats spaces and objects as materialities and formal processes, inhabiting the paradoxical relation between the two. What I set out is no nightmare or postmodern abyss—instead, I locate in a group of texts that fall within the rough purview of American modernism the more routine relations of novels, corridors, and media. These texts appear at a point in American modernity in which the perceived immateriality of proliferating modes of communication *between* persons (both wired and wireless) confronts the strange and insistent materialities attending the communication *of* persons through increasingly complex urban and national transit networks as well as through institutional interiors. This is the heyday of the corridor, which will begin to give way to a postwar "open-plan" architectural aesthetic even as it theorizes its own recursivity in novels.

Included in the readings gathered here is a catalog of what I describe as reflexively doubled material metaphors—media architectures that reinscribe the novel's self-awareness as a material, medial object. In Henry Roth's *Call It Sleep* this appears in descriptions of corridors that are formed out of the blank pages through which the novel constitutes itself, a move echoed in Katherine Anne Porter's *Pale Horse, Pale Rider,* which stages its narrative in eerily blank sheets, walls, pages, and sterilized masks. In John Dos Passos's *Manhattan Transfer* the communication networks encompassing the circulation of media and persons alike are constituted by blockage, noise, and disruption, signaling an important aspect of the novel's mediality, and in Theodore Dreiser's *An American Tragedy* the stamping of collars in the novel's factory overtakes other writing techniques through which persons might constitute themselves, and the consequences reach an apotheosis when the novel's protagonist finds his interiority usurped by the literal interior space of the hall. Richard Wright's *Native Son* makes its genre specificity material when the blocked furnace signaling the novel's communicative formality is painstakingly reconstructed in the courtroom, materially doubling the project of social realism. And in the reflexive, theoretical transition away from this fraught world of corridoricity, midcentury corridor theorists C. P. Snow and Carl Schmitt dwell on the persistent literariness (and, in the terms of this project, mediality) that attends the most overlooked and powerful institutional and disciplinary space. For Snow, corridors *are* novels, and for Schmitt, they look like metaphors.

My first chapter, "Becoming Media in *An American Tragedy,*" builds on these descriptions of corridors to develop a reading of media and form in Theodore Dreiser's novel. I excavate the medial history of the stamping technology employed by workers in the novel's collar factory and supervised by its ill-fated protagonist. The process of identification central to the novel's narrative movement emerges as one of versioning, a media process encoded in the stamping technology and localized in hallways that behave like characters. The chapter explores how media theorists since Kittler have shifted the focus of materialist critique from the relations of production encoded in technologies such as factory equipment to the study of typewriters: these analyses in turn make possible a return to the previous objects of materialist study, only now, I argue, with a focus on the similarities between both factory machine and writing machine as media. In *An American Tragedy,* a novel otherwise known for its concern with the deterministic force of print and photographic technologies, the collar-stamping apparatus emerges as a more complex formulation of the relationship between identification, interiority, and media. Dreiser's novel positions its stamping device as media, but not only in the sense that it is a writing machine. Stamping the action, and stampers as devices and persons, are embedded in a media process, one with consequences for the possibilities of rendering something like a modern consciousness, its housings, and the spaces it inhabits. The destination toward which this process is oriented, in this account and those that will follow it, is the corridor.

The second chapter, "Infrastructural Modernity," examines blocked infrastructure: the gridlocked roads and fetus-clogged sewers of Dos Passos's *Manhattan Transfer* and the corpse-choked furnaces and airshafts of Wright's *Native Son.* In these novels, and in the third rails and pipe networks of, for example, Roth's *Call It Sleep,* working infrastructure becomes most visible in its breakdown. Moreover, clogged and noisy communication channels become the explicit staging grounds for fraught social dynamics. This chapter considers pipe networks, ventilation systems, and transit infrastructure not as metaphoric but built communication: that is, the novels I discuss explicitly formalize material channels as media processes.

Pipe networks and ventilation systems, however, are not the only physical systems doing this kind of formal work in the fiction of the period. This appears in another historical occasion for infrastructural shutdown, the 1918 influenza epidemic, during which not only public transit, but also telephone and postal services, were suspended under the threat of contagion. In the third chapter, "The Flu and the Media, or Contagion 1918," I analyze the novels published in the wake of the epidemic, including Katherine Anne Porter's *Pale Horse, Pale Rider* and Willa Cather's *One of Ours,* to suggest that the flu takes on the properties of the media, formalizing both as contagious, and challenging the representational burdens of history by doing so. The influenza epidemic, as described in this chapter, is a media event, but more than that as well: it becomes an opportunity for Cather and Porter to theorize mediation, a sense of which I show also operates in Nathaniel West's *Miss Lonelyhearts,* although West's novel does not deal with the contagions of 1918 as an explicit reference. The recursive movement between influenza as a fictional topic and the way that it becomes media provides a case study, moreover, in how medial forms are also the preconditions for the very representability of historical events.

The 1918 influenza epidemic stages its mediality in institutional spaces, or the hospital corridors and bunkers guiding its spread and containment. These spaces point to the forms of communication that underlie modern institutionality, and its formulation in twentieth-century theory. For this, we might consider the descriptions of institutionality that appear in the prominent, if controversial, accounts of two modern theorists whose work explicitly engages the formal character of the spaces of modernity: C. P. Snow and Carl Schmitt. Snow's infamous lecture on the "two cultures" division of the disciplines, which also includes his famously lambasted critique of literary modernism, engages the forms disciplinary distinction takes, and how it works, far more than usually acknowledged in critiques of the cliché. In the fourth chapter, "Corridors of Power," I take up another of his famous coinages, appearing as the title of his 1964 novel *Corridors of Power,* to outline the spatial idiom he develops in fiction to describe what those distinctions look like in modern political institutions. I show how Schmitt, too, demonstrates an interest in corridors and power in his later work, developing a theory of *Korridorbildung* that positions the corridor as the space par excellence of his concrete-order thinking. Schmitt's corridors not only make the acquisition of power possible, but also inscribe its limits. For both writers, the form of institutional communication emerges in its architecture.

The uneasy transfer between points of view formerly understood as persons and points of space, which I have been describing in these fictional texts as bound up in their corridoricity, is central to my discussion of the works of Schmitt and Snow. For both writers, the corridor concretizes the forms of modern power and institutionality, the likes of which exert considerable pressure on *Winesburg*'s Enoch Robinson, *Native Son*'s Bigger Thomas, and *Pale Horse, Pale Rider*'s Miranda. The observational techniques adopted by Snow and Schmitt, however, provide them with an opportunity to give those forms a name.

I conclude with a discussion of the open-plan architectural and informational aesthetic that develops in the latter half of the twentieth century, sketching the contours of a broadcast logic that emerges in postmodern and contemporary novels and media installations. What Derrida calls "these communications or corridors of meaning" stretch out instead into a vertiginous postmodern view of endlessly replicated hallways echoing into infinite and impossible architecture.[114] The open plan recalls and transforms corridoricity in contemporary fiction. It also shows the results of a set of experiments put in place by the overlooked and materially invested novels of American modernism: the persons, "dividuals," and collectivities ensconced in and indivisible from thoroughly mediated space.

1 BECOMING MEDIA IN *AN AMERICAN TRAGEDY*

> She perched on the stool and treadled at her machine all day, turning out collars, the name of whose brand could be noted for its irrelevancy to anything in connection with collars.
>
> —Stephen Crane, *Maggie: A Girl of the Streets*

> Montgomery Clift comes to town, the poor relation of a rich family that finds him a job at the local factory, where he meets and sleeps with Shelley Winters despite stern orders not to fraternize with the other workers. At a party he sees Elizabeth Taylor, the most beautiful of the local rich girls.
>
> —Steve Erikson, *Zeroville*

MAGGIE WORKS IN A COLLAR FACTORY. The eponymous heroine of Stephen Crane's 1893 novel is responsible for "turning out" collars—at her sewing machine, this factory girl participates in the routine transformation from cloth into collar, or from raw material into product. Her role in the transformation and the factory scene she inhabits are familiar enough as the raw material of American naturalist fiction. For Maggie has good company among other characters—especially women—who populate these texts and who perform acts of routinized mechanical labor resulting in the production of objects: for a time, Maggie makes collars, just as Theodore Dreiser's Carrie Meeber is briefly employed in a shoe factory, and even Frank Norris's Trina McTeague creates her own one-woman production line making wooden animals, at least until her lack of fingers prevents it.[1]

Like Trina, Maggie has a slightly more intimate relation to the thing produced than factory work might otherwise imply, because she holds something called a collar in her hand when she finishes her piece of its construction, when she had previously held something other than collar. And like Carrie, she does not abide this work for long, exchanging the hourly wage for the sexual marketplace.

The affinities between these women start to resonate more powerfully when another of Theodore Dreiser's factory characters is included in their company—the doomed Roberta Alden of his 1925 novel *An American Tragedy.* Not only is Roberta's departure from the factory met with consequences as disastrous for her continued existence as Maggie's, but like Maggie she too works in a collar factory. It is precisely in the otherwise remarkable coincidence of collar factories in these two texts that the divergence between them becomes most acute. Located within the shift of interaction with collars that these novels mark is also a shift in the kinds of objects considered the appropriate subject of the modernity being described, as well as the kinds of persons that inhabit it.

In *An American Tragedy,* Roberta Alden may work in a collar factory, but her assignment to the factory's stamping room results not only in her disastrous acquaintance with the novel's equivocal protagonist Clyde Griffiths, but also an interaction with the collars themselves quite different from that experienced by Crane's Maggie at her sewing machine. Roberta, in a process I will discuss in greater detail, stamps her collars with the company information and brand. Although her labor contributes to the production of a packaged and sellable collar, her most direct and profound engagement with what might be considered an object happens as she imprints an ink stamp on the collars (a convergent process involving the stamp, the metal hand-stamper used to place it, and the human stamper employed to execute that action), rather than with the collars themselves. By contrast, consider the brief allusion to this stamp offered by Crane's novel: what begins as a clinical description of the conditions of Maggie's employment becomes slowly infected by a bemused narrative voice that remarks that the brand name of the collars she sews "could be noted for its irrelevancy to anything in connection to collars."[2] While Roberta is identified with the stamp, for Maggie, the collar is the thing that matters. This is made more explicit when she reflects that "the air in the collar and cuff establishment strangled her," thus assigning to the entire factory the properties of the garment it produces, and also in the poignant reminder that when she faces rejection soon after her escape from her factory machine, her rival's "linen collars and cuffs were spotless."[3] As readers of the novel and the large body of American naturalist literary criticism surrounding it will know, any rise or escape from factory life in these novels will likely end in disaster (or at the very least a serious case of ambiguity). Maggie's proudly worn collar makes this abundantly clear.

Roberta's departure from the collar factory means that she is no longer a stamper, and she quickly becomes the kind of character that both the protagonist and novel must purge. It is important to note, however, that a stamp is not worn in quite the same way as a collar. Nor can it be understood as occupying the same figurative and social domains in a text as the collars on which it rests. The shift from collar to stamp is also a shift in the object of analysis, whether that analysis be materialist, medial, or in this case, both. Populating *An American Tragedy* are medial objects, the appearance of which on the 1925 literary scene, and in the particular context of a Dreiserian factory world, is significant. The collars of Dreiser's text, furthermore, can be thought of in much the same way as some of the material media that dominate media-centered accounts of the novel: like typewriters, paper, or telephones, they can stand in too easily for what they describe. By discussing the medial objects of *An American Tragedy,* I will point to the limitations of approaches to media in literary study that either make assumptions about the transparency of language as a medium for representing interiority or about the material force of the technical media making the production and dissemination of literary language possible. Both formally abstract and materially specific, these objects demand inclusion in a conceptualization of media precisely when they encode literary reflexivity in the process of rendering something as bizarre as modern interiority concrete. At stake in seeing beyond the symbolic heft—or, in this case, inside it—of the collar is also the visibility of the subtle variations that identify the media cultures of American modernity, and the role of fiction in constituting that modernity's self-description.

In what follows, I will demonstrate how the play of stamping operates as an overt dynamic of the media in *An American Tragedy.* An excavation of the medial history of the stamping technology employed by workers in the novel's collar factory and supervised by its ill-fated protagonist reveals the process of identification central to the novel's narrative movement to be one of versioning, a media process encoded in the stamping technology and localized in hallways that behave like characters. The factory tools and architectural spaces populating the novel, each rendered as forms of mediation, reveal Dreiser's text to hold a more important place in the story of the novel's relationship to media than it has previously been afforded, especially as that story involves the blurry edges of the modern subject. It will be my contention that it is precisely where the naturalist concern with materiality confronts a modernist preoccupation with interiority, and in the autopoetic impulses the novel assigns to both genre orientations, that *An American Tragedy* provides a crucial glimpse into the kinds of persons developing in the media cultures of the early twentieth century. This double relation of stamping and architectural interiority developed in the novel reveals both objects' status as *reflexively doubled material metaphors,* or medial objects that encode the networked mediality of the print text in recursive figural gestures. In *An American Tragedy,* a novel otherwise known for its concern with the deterministic force of print and photographic technologies, the collar-stamping apparatus emerges as a more complex formulation of the relationship among identification, interiority, and media. Dreiser's novel positions the stamping device as media, but not only in the sense that it is a writing machine. The action of stamping, and stampers as devices and persons, are embedded in a media process, one with consequences for the possibilities of rendering something like a modern consciousness, its housings, or the spaces it inhabits. By examining how the novel's stamping technology operates as an expression of corridoricity, I will unpack its medial legacy in the novel's afterlives in twentieth-century cinema. I will conclude my discussion of *An American Tragedy* in this chapter by drawing an explicit connection between the novel's techniques for representing interiority and its use of the architectural form of the corridor.

Dreiser's Stamping Room

One way to describe the narrative trajectory of *An American Tragedy* is by mapping its corridors and passageways, for it is through these spaces that the novel traces the rise and fall of its protagonist. The story of Clyde Griffiths begins in "the tall walls of the commercial heart of an American city,"[4] where he distributes religious tracts with his impoverished evangelical family. He plots his escape into commercial society by entering the "marbled corridors" of a local hotel as a "hall boy," securing an income and connecting himself with the "moving panorama of the main lobby" and joining the ranks of "individuals who seemed to him curiously filled with the atmosphere of this place."[5] Clyde flees to Chicago after a fatal traffic accident, and takes up residence in a "hall bedroom" as he works to secure employment that will give him the same access to the corridor life of the hotel that he previously enjoyed.[6] A chance meeting with an old colleague grants him that access, and in the corridors of a Chicago hotel he meets his prosperous uncle, Mr. Samuel Griffiths of the Griffiths Collar and Shirt Company of Lycurgus, who offers Clyde employment in his factory. There Clyde navigates its institutional spaces, or "white walls and white columns,"[7] eventually attaining the supervision of the factory's stamping room. This room is strangely separated from the other workspaces of the factory, yet connected through chutes from above, which deliver detachable collars to the women employed to stamp them with the size and brand (see Figures 1 and 2).

Although he is cautioned to observe the stamping and not the women, Clyde begins a relationship with one stamper, Roberta Alden. But while his relationship with Roberta develops, he gains the attention and societal connections of the wealthy daughter of a local manufacturer, Sondra Finchley. As Sondra's attentions to Clyde become more serious, Roberta announces her pregnancy and demands marriage. The hapless Clyde's attempts to escape this predicament, of course, fail, and when he reads of the drowning of a couple at a lonely lake, this newspaper report offers him a murder plot. What results, between the "towering walls of pines" and "long aisle(s) of trees" at Big Bittern,[8] is his unwilling success as protagonist: hesitating while faced with his final task, a startled Clyde semi-accidentally strikes Roberta with a camera, their boat overturns, and he swims away while she drowns. Clyde is quickly apprehended, and after his conviction he traverses the multiple passageways of the prison, taking his final walk down a long corridor to his execution.

The complicity of the mass media and other representational technologies like cameras and film with the deterministic forces propelling Clyde through the passageways I have been describing might make *An American Tragedy* seem a likely candidate for recent accounts of the media ecologies informing American literary modernism. Yet after a spell as the darling of the likes of Penn Warren and others attracted to its repetitive structures and insistent doubling,[9] Dreiser's one-time

Figures 1 and 2. Detachable collars, early twentieth century. Photographs by Ian Newman.

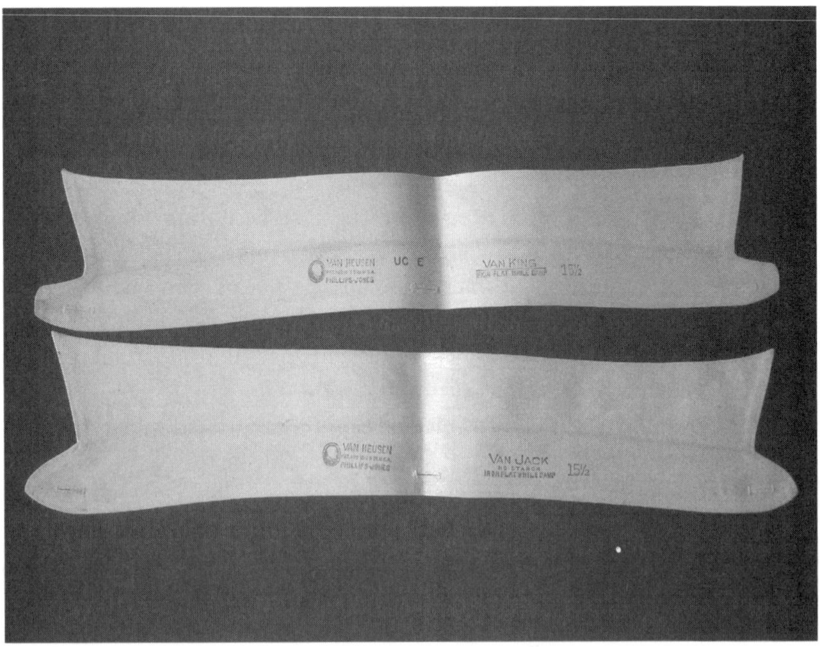

1925 masterpiece has endured something of a critical oblivion.[10] In fact, when, in a recent *New Yorker* article commemorating the novel's reissue in a Library of America edition, David Denby attempts to praise it, he does so by referring to Dreiser's "avuncular stodginess" and asking, "What does it mean to say that a great writer can't write?"[11] *An American Tragedy* is, no doubt, an awkward novel, but its unpopularity may in part derive from the ways it impersonates one kind of novel while doing formal work of an altogether different sort.

In short, *An American Tragedy* looks like a turn-of-the-century factory novel. It shares *Sister Carrie*'s attention to the "machine girls" populating garment manufacturers, or, for example, the spatial organization accompanying industrial life that appears in Rebecca Harding Davis's "Life in the Iron-Mills": "The woman, pail in hand, emerged from the mouth of the alley, and turned down the narrow street, that stretched out, long and black, miles before her."[12] Moreover, the factory occupies the center of *An American Tragedy,* and becomes the object of interest when the novel does enter into critical discourse. Martha Banta, for example, in *Taylored Lives* reads Clyde's downfall as a problem of scientific management exemplified in the factory's operations ("the only way left for him to prove his merit for efficient conduct is through the imagination of murder"),[13] and Walter Benn Michaels looks to the means of production to unpack the novel's delineation of a middle-class consciousness, for, he says, "the rhythm of factory life . . . produces Clydes as well as collars."[14] Their concerns are appropriate, for the labeling and making of collars that goes on in the factory certainly provides a version of the labeling and making of persons that collars do in the society described by the novel. But this is just one version among many, and part of the disconnect that seems to characterize the novel itself as well as its reception resides in just how these versions relate to each other.

The passageways of *An American Tragedy* organize Clyde's movement through its industrial spaces, but in doing so their biggest concern appears to lie in their reference to other, similar corridors, linking otherwise disparate institutions through their organizational protocols. What matters about the hotel, factory, and prison corridors is that they refer to one another, and also that they mark organization as a defining characteristic of the modernity their occupants inhabit. This is a modernity contiguous with that emerging in the novel's ancestor fictions of factory life, but also one that looks at itself somewhat differently. Part of what the concern with factories and collars in *An American Tragedy* registers is the novel's own fixation with things that have the capacity for morphological complexity: collars are clearly things, actions, and symbols simultaneously. However, the fluid transfer between the object and the person who wears it, or between Taylorized factory labor and the making of modern individuals, points to but does not fully capture (or perhaps even masks) the consequences of morphological drift that emerge in Dreiser's novel and how it positions the process of factory production within its portrayal of an insistently reflexive modernity.

The detachable collars the Griffiths Collar and Shirt Company produces are nearing extinction at the time of the novel's publication (they will disappear around 1930, when they begin their transition from material product to the grand symbol of C. Wright Mills).[15] Part of what the factory, and Clyde's position in it, makes visible in *An American Tragedy* is this passing from material object into figure, or doubly so, for the object was doing a lot of figuring work all along (see Figure 3). What the factory also registers is perhaps the strangeness

Figure 3. Collars in Storefront Window, 1899. From Kim Johnson Gross and Jeff Stone, *Men's Wardrobe* (New York: Alfred A. Knopf, 1988), 21.

of thinking about factories at all when the shift is from the work of making white collars to the making of white-collar workers.[16] This strangeness is most palpable when the focus shifts to what happens in the stamping room.

Collars are not made in the stamping room, nor are they cut, pressed, stitched, or packaged—instead they are observed, inscribed, and then observed and inscribed again. By this I mean that the stampers mark the collars according to their size, and Clyde, using a double-entry system, records both the collars and the work of the stampers. This exercise in sorting, marking, and recording reveals much about the apparent disconnect between the factory and other forms of institutional life in the novel, and about their uncomfortable underlying connections. It also reveals that the stakes for the novel in focusing on this set piece of factory life rest not in the production of collars, but in the observation and production of stampers. What happens to stampers in *An American Tragedy* is that they become media. What happens in Dreiser's stamping room is the articulation of a system of stamping that also instances how media work in the novel, and how the novel understands itself as media. This system includes stampers as technology—the devices printing text on collars, stampers as persons—those doing the stamping and their observers, and the action of stamping itself. As a system of interlocking parts, or as it is described in the novel, "piecework," stamping inscribes the communicative forms of identity and identification that begin to stand in for any concern with a recognizable articulation of consciousness or interiority throughout the text. It is precisely in this interlocking interplay—the movement between person, action, and apparatus—that the novel encodes medial reflexivity, defining media for itself as process rather than product. And it is their insistently concretized implication in that process that attaches the novelistic persons populating the text to its medial self-reference.

The narratives of collars and factories demonstrate how collars are aligned with the media in *An American Tragedy*. This is not just a reminder that in Dreiser's novel, Clyde reads about a crime in the newspaper and commits a murder, or, as his detractors would have it, that Dreiser read about a murder in the newspaper and committed a novel. Rather, I'd like to point out that the levels at which media operate in this text partake of the same complexity as its wordplay, and that the parallels and mutual inflections of both have something to say in turn about the media cultures of American modernism and how they are accounted for by the formalisms operative in contemporary media theory.

To return to the stamping room, the stampers and the collars they stamp are shot through with references to writing and media technologies. The collars produced in the Griffiths Collar and Shirt Factory are cloth collars, but as mass-produced commodities they bear strong resemblance to their cheaper paper cousins. These paper collars were stamped, or pressed, from sheets of paper and sold alongside their cloth counterparts (see Figure 4).

The doubling of stamping and pressing becomes part of the stamping technology as well: as inventors rushed to patent machines that would do the stamping (thus combining the stampers as people with the mechanical stampers), they often referred to their designs as "printing presses." In the case of the 1907 design shown here and others (see Figure 5), these printing presses also depend on the standard references to clichés and stereotypes.[17] And, as if to ensure that the many-layered meanings of press would not be forgotten, designs emerged for printing presses that could stamp out the collars and stamp the brand on the collars simultaneously (see Figure 6).

The device used by the stampers in *An American Tragedy* is both more simple and more complex than the devices I have just discussed, but it partakes of their interest in paper, printing, and presses. The stamping technology in Dreiser's novel is more like the device shown below (see Figure 7), which is held in the hand of a stamper, in the case of this novel a woman, who stamps first an ink pad and then a collar.

The text then imprinted on the collars has also been doubly stamped, for the head of the stamping device consists of letters stamped out of metal. This produces a curious dissonance between the stamper and her relation to the prewritten text, for although she is involved in printing on collars, her action is closer to an observation of the printing even as she performs the action. Stamping, figured this way, is a reenaction of a reenaction, made most clear when Clyde introduces Roberta Alden to the piecework she will take up in the stamping room: "He led the way to a near-by table, where the stampers were. After letting her observe how it was done . . . he picked up one of the collars and proceeded to explain all that had been previously explained to him."[18]

The action of stamping and its observation make the intractability of the stamped text seem stranger than the ubiquity of this form of branding might imply: stamping appears to set a fixed text in motion,

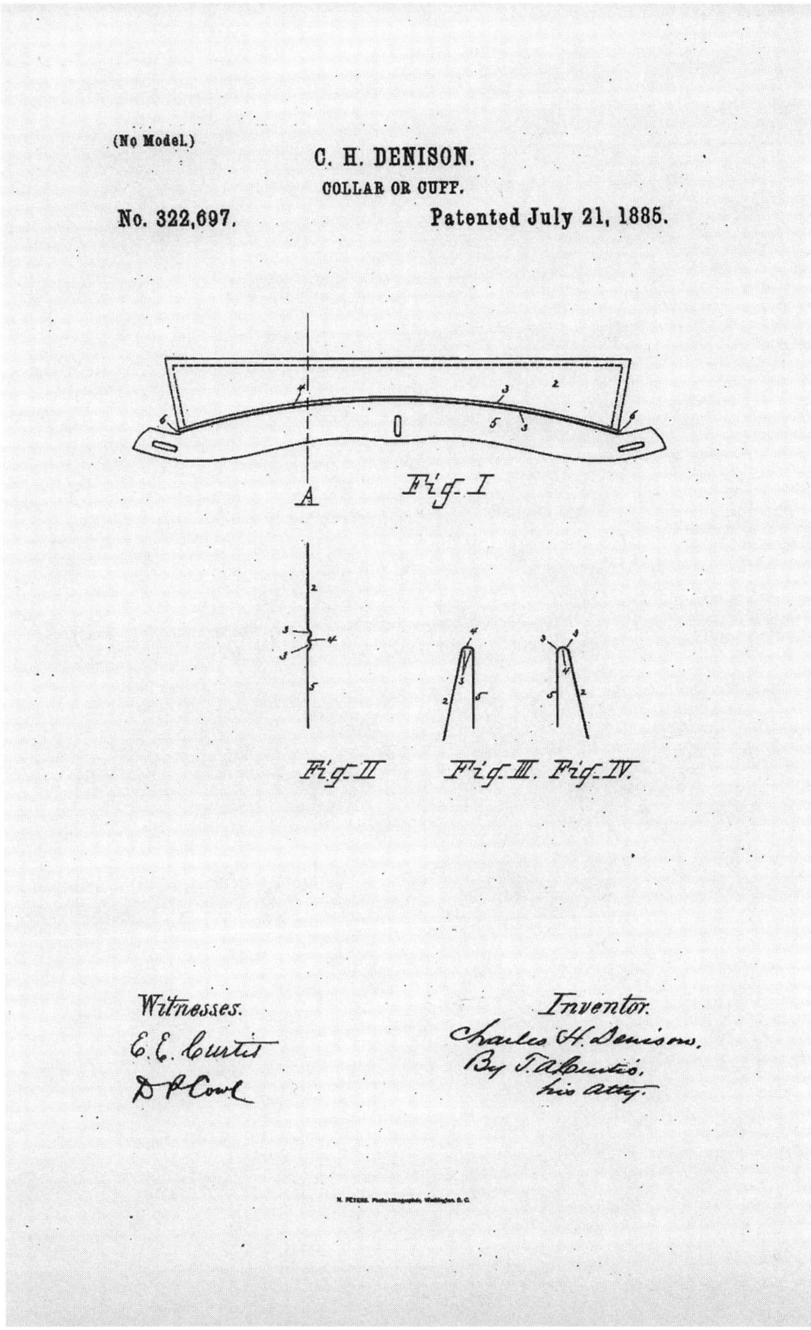

Figure 4. Patent application for paper collar pattern. From C. H. Denison, "Collar or Cuff," U.S. Patent 322, 697 issued July 21, 1885.

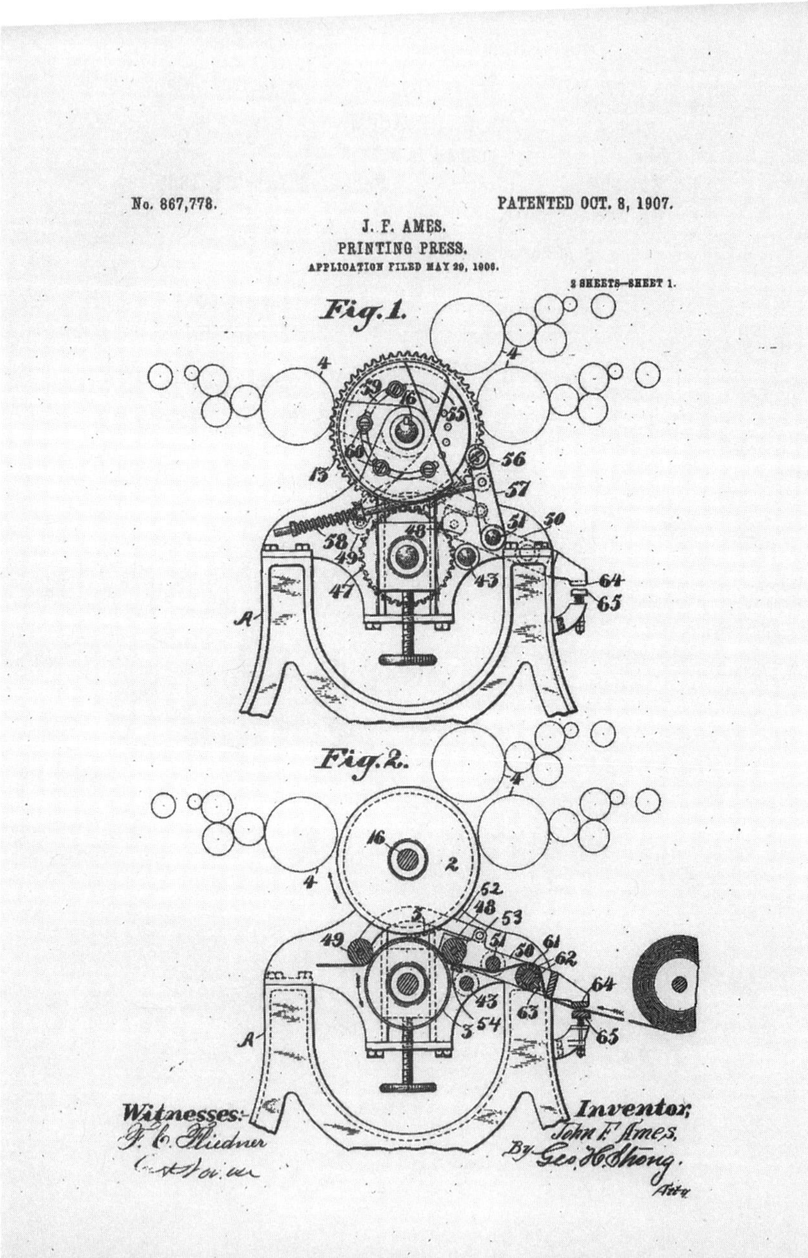

Figure 5. Patented designs for printing presses with fabric applications. From J. F. Ames, "Printing Press," U.S. Patent 867,788 filed May 29, 1906 and issued October 8, 1907.

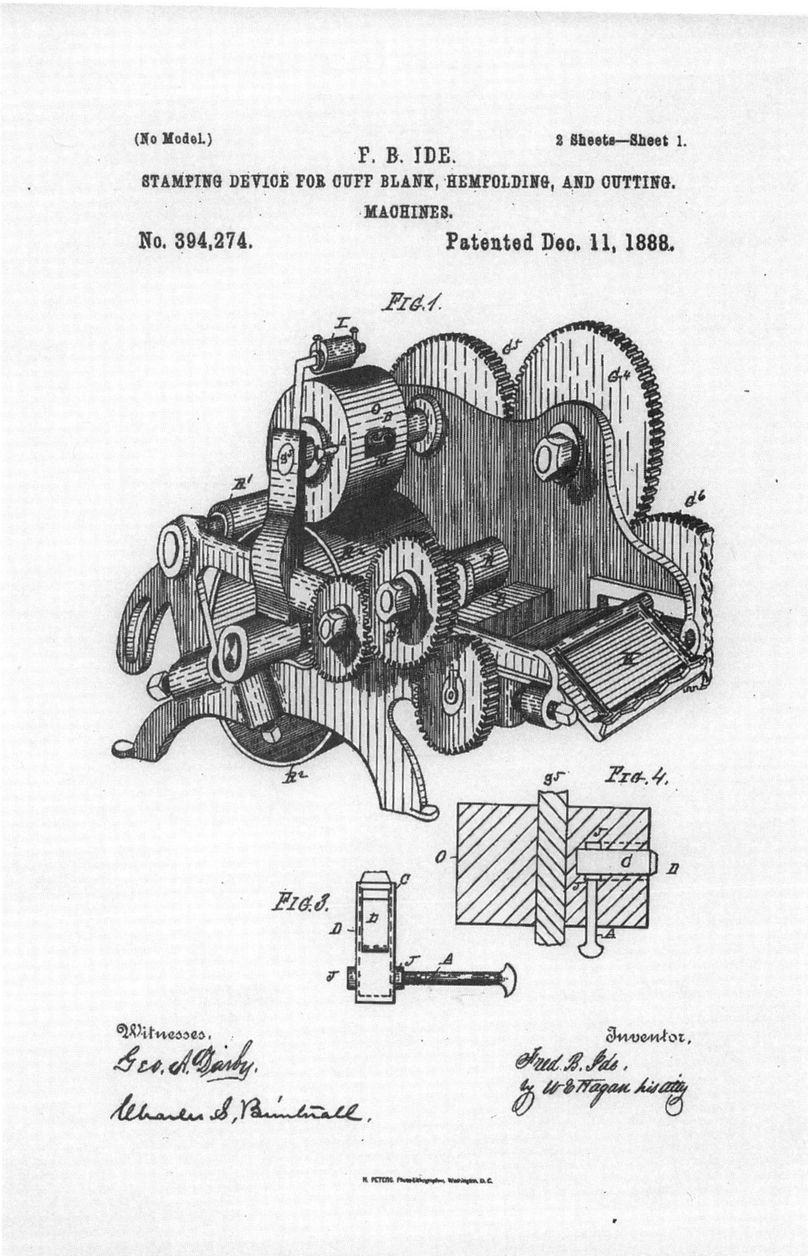

Figure 6. Patented designs for printing presses with fabric applications. From F. B. Ide, "Stamping Device for Cuff Bank, Hemfolding and Cutting Machines," U.S. Patent 394,274 issued December 11, 1888.

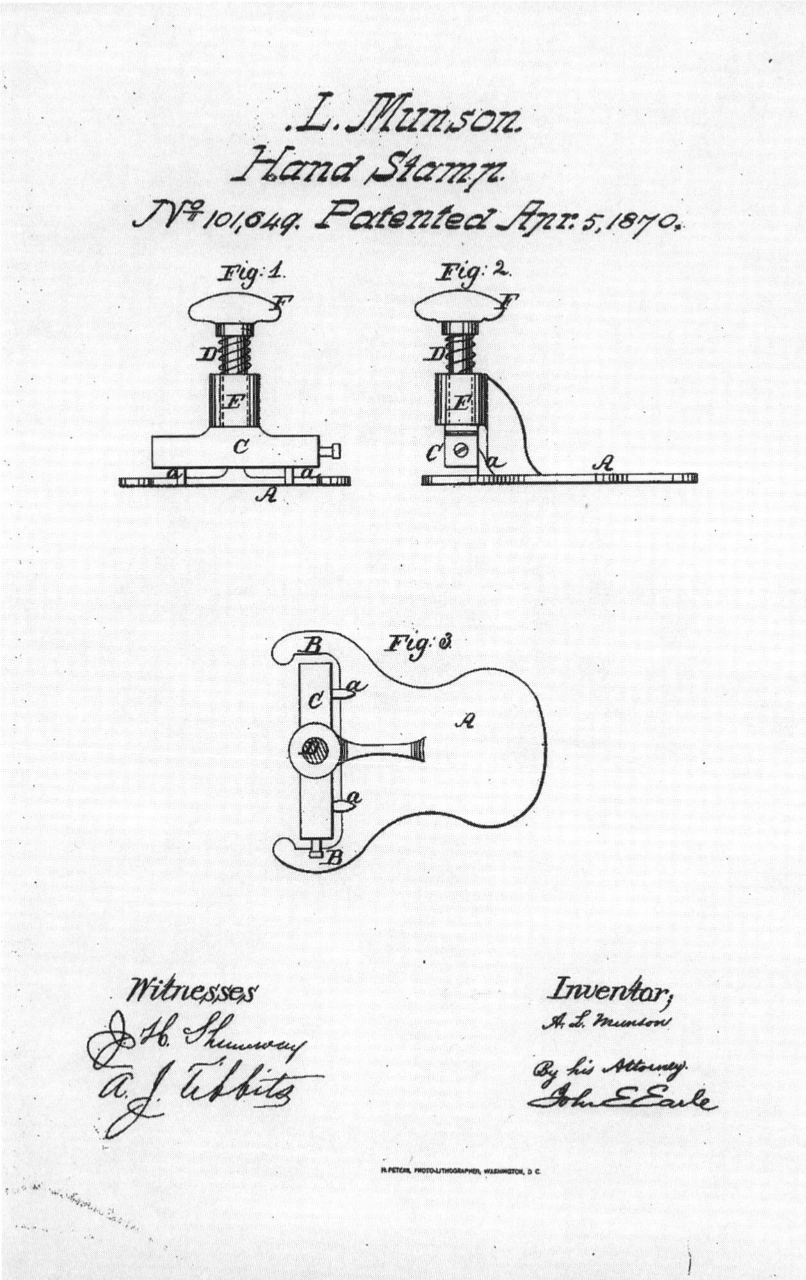

Figure 7. From the patent application for a hand stamper. From L. Munson, “Improvement in Hand Stamps,” U.S. Patent 101,649 issued April 5, 1870.

if only for a moment. It also points to a stubbornness of form associated with the devices, those who operate them, and their institutional regulators: all have been prestamped before they set about making their marks. For media theorist Vilém Flusser, this relationship between form and materials has consequences for how we might understand a concept such as information after the Industrial Revolution: "A steel tool in a press is a form, and it in-forms the flood of glass or plastic flowing past it into bottles or ashtrays."[19] Stamping, in this way, figures the proximities of form and content with some discomfort, as form too can be molded and pressed in steel.

Stampers in *An American Tragedy* provide an overt rendering of the novel's materiality, a materiality that involves the apparatus of the book as well as its production and dissemination. At one level, stampers in the novel refer explicitly to the inscription technologies of the book, such as presses, paper, and mass-produced writing. The layering of stampers and stamping, meanwhile, thematizes the network of relations between the material printed artifact and its fictionality. This foregrounds the novel's status as a printed book, or a "material metaphor," a category of physical object such as a book or interface that is both constructed by and functions through its metaphoric networks.[20] The novel dwells on and makes visible the implied figurations of its physical medium, and shows that a metaphoric nature of novels inheres in their everyday physical form.

The factory's stamping room also highlights what is at stake in housing these kinds of figurations in a factory. Stamping in *An American Tragedy* complements Friedrich Kittler's critique of sociological approaches to literary criticism in his afterword to *Discourse Networks,* in which he notes that when these approaches account for materiality they look to the relations of production rather than information systems: "Steam engines and looms . . . became topics," he says, "but typewriters did not."[21] What becomes interesting here is that the factory technologies themselves are also working as a version of typewriter. Not only does Clyde record the stamping at a desk at the end of the room, but Roberta's table is also pointedly referred to as her "desk."[22] These systems are not contrasted with each other, but juxtaposed. The connections I am describing are more than punned connections, or as I will describe in more detail, they express an attitude toward wordplay very specific to the media forms out of which they emerge. Rather, the cross-identification of stampers with stampers, or stamping desks with writing desks, becomes a problem of identification itself, a process the novel insistently associates with what happens in the stamping room.

The aftermath of Roberta's drowning and Clyde's subsequent trial and conviction demonstrates just how far this association goes. The drowning is immediately recognized as suspicious because the man's hat found at the scene has had its lining removed, a lining that, because of the stamp it would have displayed, would reveal clues as to the identity of its wearer (and Clyde had removed the lining precisely to remove this stamp).[23] A search of Roberta's suitcase, left at the boathouse where the couple had registered under assumed names, uncovers a toilet kit that she had received as a gift from Clyde, which also has a lining, and which also has a "Whitely-Lycurgus" stamp. Once Clyde is apprehended, found in his possession are brochures from the lakes visited with Roberta, and his guilt is partially confirmed when, in the trial, he claims to have acquired them at the lakes themselves, but a closer inspection reveals a Lycurgus House stamp and thus the premeditation of the crime, as the district attorney points out to Clyde's dismay:

> "Well then, explain to me, or to this jury, if you can . . . how it comes that this particular folder chances to be marked, 'Compliments of the Lycurgus House, Lycurgus, N.Y.'" and here he folded the folder and presenting the back, showed Clyde the thin red stamp in between the other red lettering. And Clyde, noting it, gazed as one in a trance. His ultra-pale face now blanched gray again, his long thin fingers opened and shut, the red and swollen and weary lids of his eyes blinked and blinked to break the strain of the damning fact before him.[24]

By folding the folder, about all one can do in a case like this, the prosecutor reveals Clyde's identification through stamping as also a process of self-reflection. Not only does the stamp identify him as one who premeditates, but it also becomes strangely identified with Clyde, whose red eyelids reveal the stamp as a part of his body as well as a mark on a page. In *An American Tragedy,* the identity of bodies and the identity of murderers are determined by the stamps impressed on the goods and clothes they carry.

If stamping had been identifying Clydes and Robertas all along, its more violent recurrence here simply makes their otherwise benign interpolation into the process of their own production more legible. For stampers are not just things or people, but processes that make identification of things and people possible while uncomfortably replicating the identities they represent. Systems theorist Niklas Luhmann puts this another way when he claims that literary techniques for doubling allow texts to "represent the transformation of identity into communication."[25]

The novel binds stamping and identification as indicators of a communications system that is postally instantiated, yet simultaneously repudiates standard associations of post and stamp, or of postal communication with modern identity-formation. Instead, postage stamps and clothing stampers participate in a similar process. It is no accident that the first thing Clyde asks Roberta, when he introduces her to the stamping room, is for her address, which he duly records in the ledger containing the record of the stamping work. The only other clue available to detectives hunting down the identity of Roberta's body is a letter, addressed to her mother and found also in what Clyde had hoped were anonymous belongings left at the boat house. The letter is addressed to a "Mrs. Titus Alden, Biltz, Mimico County,"[26] a town but not a house. The letter here represents not a rival form of the identifications available in the stamps, but another version of them, for the forensic utility of the stamps I have mentioned resides in the information they provide—which is, in fact, a very similar form of address. The Griffiths collars, like most labeled goods produced in factories of this kind, would have carried not just the company name, but its location. Clyde's uncle is Mr. Samuel Griffiths, of the Griffiths Collar and Shirt Company, of Lycurgus, New York. The county investigators fixate on stamps and linings with the same intensity as letters because they too provide an address. Clyde removes the lining of his hat because he has purchased the hat in Utica, en route to his planned murder, and it would not only point to him but also to his planning of the event. Roberta's toilet set directs the police to Lycurgus even as the letter sends them to Mimico County, and the juxtaposition of both places makes the identification of persons and plot possible. It also implicates the strange oscillation between specific location (the towns are specific places) and general address (a place is more general than a house) in the process of identification through stamping. If this was not clear enough, one need look only as far as the method by which Clyde receives his love letters in anticipation of his fateful trip to the lakes: although street delivery became commonplace in American towns and cities after the 1860s, Clyde's letters are addressed to him at Lycurgus, by "general delivery."[27]

Stamping is the process by which the novel signals its own participation in a media culture—a culture that includes newspapers and novels, and collars and stamps, as markers of identity, and as versions of the forms it can take. What matters is that these forms, while related, are versions. Both specific addresses and general delivery, both identity and difference, these medial forms provide a vantage point from which to view the novel's own self-identification as a medium. For *An American Tragedy,* the novel, is as much of a medial object as those it embeds within the narrative. The loops it enacts between its underlying material metaphors, stamping, and something like a modernist narrative interiority are reflexive. The material metaphor shows how the novel's materiality is dynamic, that its sense of materiality itself is part of a movement between object and idea. The novel isolates figural movement rather than static objects as the index of materiality and doubles that dynamism in its multilayered medial objects. These objects operate as *reflexively doubled material metaphors:* they constitute themselves through the self-observation of their mediality.

Stampers become media in *An American Tragedy* because they doubly encode the reflexivity of writing technology and fictional technique: that is, they embed the forms of self-reflection in a material object that also demonstrates a capacity to reflect upon itself. This is a rather abstract way to point out that stampers "become" media in the sense outlined by Joseph Vogl in his prescription for a media theory that would examine a medial function rather than technically specific and historically stable media apparatuses alone. Vogl's description of emerging media outlines a discontinuous history of becoming-media in which those things stored and mediated by medial objects can only be stored and mediated by the conditions produced by the media themselves and even comprising them.[28] Vogl's withdrawn definition of media also demonstrates why stamping, operating simultaneously as technology and technique in *An American Tragedy,* cannot be reduced to either thing or action.

Instead of observing and recognizing, for example, the proliferation of doubles throughout the novel, a media analysis of stamping along these lines operates under the conditions it describes. If stamping indicates that the movement between registers is precisely where the novel points to its own mediality, the observation of that mediality partakes of a similar kind of zeugmatics. A media theory interested in things that do what they are also produces its own conditions. When Cornelia Vismann and Markus Krajewski, for example, read the law and the computer as mutually constitutive media, they abide in the ways in which their approach is subject to the same similes it unpacks: "Law relies on transfer media yet is itself a transfer system; it transfers rights. Like other transfer systems, not the least of which is language, law tends to underestimate media of transfer as mere tools, with the deceptive outcome that media appear as matters that can be regulated. Yet a law that claims to be able to regulate a technological medium merely produces a paradox, because it aims to regulate nothing other than its own grounds of existence."[29] The "mere paradox" of stamping as media in *An American Tragedy,* then, is that it enacts its own grounds as well, and all the more so because it enacts this enacting within the self-producing media system of the novel. Like other familiar media technologies, it operates as a clear writing proxy, it entails the observation of its own process and must be produced by way of an uncanny self-referentiality (stampers are made from stamped parts), and the stamper must also produce what it observes (persons as stampers). Where these loops matter for the medial production and observation of *An American Tragedy* is in the outlining of the forms of interiority and identification that this system makes possible. For stamping is the identification mechanism and technology that brings its own version of identity into being and into view, and is how the novel, in turn, identifies itself.

Literalness Effects

There are many versions of *An American Tragedy.* Versioning, moreover, is a problem with which Dreiser was explicitly familiar: for example, when he introduced a 1928 Doubleday reissue of Norris's *McTeague,* he expressed a hope that the nearly thirty years since the novel's original publication would allow it to be read, finally, "in the spirit in which it was written."[30] His hope, however, was tempered by the observation that *Greed,* the 1924 film that for Dreiser was simply Norris's novel in another medium,[31] had been subject to the same critiques and "ignorance" that had originally greeted *McTeague*'s publication. Since its publication Dreiser's 1925 text has been adapted for theater and film, illustrated, put to music, and reimagined in novels ranging from Richard Wright's 1940 *Native Son* to Steve Erikson's 2007 novel *Zeroville.* In the latter, the mediality I have been describing is instanced and inscribed on the head of the novel's "cineautistic" protagonist, as noted in the opening lines: "On Vikar's shaved head is tattooed the right and left lobes of his brain. One lobe is occupied by an extreme close-up of Elizabeth Taylor and the other by Montgomery Clift, their faces barely apart, lips barely apart, in each other's arms on a terrace, the two most beautiful people in the movies, she the female version of him, and he the male version of her."[32] The scene, from George Stevens's film *A Place in the Sun,* is constantly misrecognized, much to Vikar's often violently expressed dismay. Informing this misrecognition, however, is the novel to which the scene refers. Although *An American Tragedy* never appears directly in the text, the Joseph von Sternberg epigraph, "I believe that cinema was here from the beginning of the world," etches its presence. It refers to the specific counterhistory to *An American Tragedy*'s self-identification as a medium that emerges in its afterlives. That is, through its range of real and imagined film adaptations throughout the twentieth century, which make this problem of media self-reference their own. These include Sergei Eisenstein's adaptation, which was first commissioned by Paramount and then rejected in 1930 and never made; that studio then released a version directed by Josef von Sternberg in 1931; then follows the novel's famous postwar adaptation, George Stevens's 1951 *A Place in the Sun,* which is then revisited and reread in 1988 by Jean-Luc Godard in *Histoire(s) du cinéma;* more recently, the novel resurfaced less directly as Woody Allen's 2005 film *Match Point.* Although the history of these films and their dialogue with one another is fascinating, I bring them up here because of the ways in which they each make dialogue with the novel an overt project of rendering the specificity of the medium in which they work.[33] The novel's persistent recasting in film throughout the twentieth century highlights its insistent techniques for rendering its own mediality: this is, in part, what its adaptations pick up on and reincorporate into the cinematic form.

An American Tragedy, after all, had been imagining itself as its own adaptation all along. Clyde's quest for "connection" with individuals and institutions begins with odd jobs that allow him disposable income to attend the motion pictures and other performed genres to which his parents are opposed. His entry into these forms of commerce gains him employment at a drug store directly connected to a theater lobby ("a most fascinating connection to Clyde"),[34] and which leads him to seek employment at a drugstore connected to what will become his first hotel employer. These adjacent connections become much more direct in book 3 of the novel and its trial scenes, during which the prosecutor famously imagines himself on a movie set ("Were not the eyes of all of the citizens of the United States upon him? He believed so. It was as if some one had suddenly exclaimed: 'Lights! Camera!'").[35] They are also incorporated as technique, for book 3 opens with something like an extended tracking shot, beginning with a bird's-eye view of the county hosting the trial, and magnifying slowly, so that eventually "the central square of the town" emerges, followed by a further revealing of "the office of the County Coroner," which in turn gives way to "one Fred Heit, coroner, a large and broad-shouldered individual" who can be seen "lethargically turning the leaves of a mail-order catalogue" when a telephone call begins the action.[36]

The corrupting influence of film on both novels and Clyde receives another recasting at the end of the novel when Clyde's mother sets her opposition to the industry aside because the only venue open to her public defense of her son is a movie house. Unlike *An American Tragedy*'s novelistic reversioning *Native Son,* the influence does not appear in remediated descriptions of film reels themselves, but rather is restricted to spaces and techniques. The strategy for pointing to mediality and incorporating rival media forms as a process of self-reference is in part what makes *An American Tragedy* such an interesting subject for filmmakers themselves concerned with staging their own medium's reflexive turn. This can be seen in Eisenstein's use of the novel's narrative techniques in order to explore alternative visual sequences, for example, or in von Sternberg's fascination with the liquid medium. As Mandy Merck points out, in *A Place in the Sun* Stevens indicates his interest in the self-reference of film most explicitly through his departure from the novel's manufacturing associations (which include, of course, stamping) by assigning Clyde the last name of Eastman, among other renamings: "Significantly, the director compares his selection of this real-life brand name to the one finally chosen for Angela, Vickers. Unlike the fictional manufacturing firms of Dreiser's novel—whose products are Griffiths shirt collars and Finchley vacuum cleaners—these are actual names from Stevens's wartime experience, with Eastman-Kodak supplying his 16 mm color film and Vickers building British bombers."[37] As an Eastman, Clyde demonstrates that the association of manufacturing firm and movie house works as something more than a basic link between mass production and mass media. Just as stampers disclose their medial character as they go through a process of versioning in the novel, the novel undergoes a similar process at the hands of the cinema.

One charged exception to the novel's omission in recent decades from critical discussion of the modernist novel or a medial modernity can be found bound up in its iterative medial legacy. In Jacques Rancière's 2002 account of Godard's account of the novel, he asks what "the Hollywood version of Dreiser's *American Tragedy* must depend on," and the answer in part lies in what he calls "something other than reproduction,"[38] or the logic of versioning. Putting pressure on how Godard reconciles Stevens's twin roles as the recorder in cinema of both the Nazi death camps and Dreiser's novel, Rancière unpacks a theory of the image, in which the image is prior to, constitutive of, and revealed by the cinema. This, he claims, is what Godard explicitly "opposes to fiction"—it is "not the claimed illusionism of performance," he says, but "the image as the imprint of presence." The particular fiction to which this is opposed, that of *An American Tragedy,* shows this process in reverse through its reference to the medium of photography. Remember that Roberta's drowning begins when Clyde's camera strikes her in the face (in an essay on photography as art, Dreiser refers to camera technology as "a canvas with an eye"),[39] and this emerges in the investigation and trial as yet another literalization of stamping. Marks imprinted on Roberta's face correspond to the physical object of the camera that contains her image within it, but instead of "the image as the imprint," we have something more like the literal imprint as the image.

For Rancière, the movement in and out of the literal register becomes a kind of literalness effect, an experience of the "bizarreness" that accompanies the pasting together (or "redoubling") of, alternately, the visual and semantic, or visual and conceptual.[40] And it is through the turning of Godard's technique of "incisive juxtapositions" back upon itself that the role of *An American Tragedy* in helping to produce this effect becomes clearer. For the Sondra Finchley erased by Stevens to become Angela Vickers is erased again by Elizabeth Taylor, who plays Vickers in Stevens's film, and it is her body that, removed from its prior cinematic surround, becomes Godard's mediation on the a priori of the image. Or, according to Rancière, "a new image comes to bring literariness (*littéraliser*) to Elizabeth Taylor's place in the sun."[41] Although the image is meant to be precisely what precedes the literary, there appears to be a temporal short circuit, in which the simultaneity accompanying the process of juxtaposition makes the desire to uncover that which has come before seem unlikely to receive its reward. Instead, the "new image" is something more like an old character.

What you get when you erase the novel's Sondra twice is, if nothing more, "literariness."

But as either source or destination, *An American Tragedy* is still fiction, whose "artifice" and "perspective" Rancière opposes to the image, even as it provides reading models. For, he says: "It is necessary, while challenging the empire of language and sense, to submit the linkages of images to all of the prestige of homonyms and plays on words. In this way Godard's cinema renews the interminable tension between the two antagonistic and interdependent (*solidaire*) poetics of the aesthetic age: the affirmation of the radical immanence of thought in the materiality of forms and the redoubling to infinity of the games of the poem that takes itself as its object."[42] Cinema, as a linkage of images, becomes literally legible through techniques developed to think about linkages of words. Reading images as one reads homonyms not only points to the "profound paradox" built in to an idea of the visual medium that is simultaneously self-reflexive and material, but the degree to which that paradoxical tension is part of the structure of homonyms themselves and the "empire of language" they participate in and help to constitute.[43]

By calling attention to the "prestige" of homonyms in the context of reading images, Rancière also resituates his longtime attention to form and epistemology in what approaches a medium-specific analysis. When, for example, he discusses the "paradoxes of production" in *The Philosopher and His Poor,* a similar tension emerges: "Thus science and *doxa* trace in a disenchanted world the figure of the new enchantments of *paradox.* These practices that misrecognize what they do, these misrecognitions that take action [*agissent*] themselves . . . they all inscribe in the prose of the world what once had been the weapon of the rhetorician and the sophist."[44] What had been situated in terms of recognitions and caught gazes also attach to forms of rhetoric or are articulated as a grammar. At stake is the structure of the relationship between words, between images and things, and of the words, images, and things to themselves. This structure, and its recognition, then identifies and informs the institutions and abstractions that constitute relations between persons. In *Dis-agreement: Politics and Philosophy,* Rancière explicitly describes these "relationships between ways of doing, ways of being, and ways of saying" as subject to the logic of homonymy: "The overall mechanism of these in-between interpretations has a name. It is called the *social.* If relations between the police and politics are determined by a few key words, a few major homonyms, we could say that, in modernity, the *social* has been the decisive homonym that has caused several logics and intertwinings of logics to connect and to disconnect, to oppose one another and to blur."[45] Although suspicious of what he calls in *The Names of History* the "homonym hunters," who "attribute series of events to subjects" and are themselves "victims of homonymy,"[46] Rancière also acknowledges that underlying the historicization of governing homonyms is the strange homonym of history itself, in which "the confusion of language [is] in fact needed to measure the dilemma in its rigor," and which, as narrative, can only be produced or reflected upon in narrative. What emerges in Rancière's thought is a distrust of the linguistic medium that must always be rendered in language, a relationship itself expressed through a persistent affection for paradox and homonym. The modernity of which Rancière must be simultaneously analyst and symptom becomes, as he puts it, "a question of words."[47]

Rancière's modernity, and its organization by homonym, also has its co-conspirators. This modernity is subject to a formal analysis that is in turn subject to its own gaze. These strange and strangely powerful instances of paradox and homonymy also undergo their own process of versioning in theories of modernity that appear attracted to the same formal drives as the reflexive modernity that forms their object. For someone like Pierre Bourdieu, this looks like a "structural homology," or figure that describes the otherwise counterintuitive relations between groups and persons in different fields (or, put another way, encodes identity in difference). Alternately, for deconstructive media theorist Bernard Stiegler, the "grammaticalization" of relations between media takes on the appearance of a kind of homonymy that he acquires via Gilbert Simondon: "The technological synthesis is not a replica, not a double of life, any more than writing is a replication of speech, but there is a complex of writing in which the two terms always move together, being in transductive relation."[48] Something that Rancière's homonyms, Bourdieu's structural homologies, and Stiegler's transductive relations have in common is their insistent rendering of form and material simultaneously. Their materials move, are in-formed, *relate*. Their forms are reflexive.

The structured relations between form and materiality thus operate as the backdrop out of which Rancière's discussion of the cinema as a medium emerges, a backdrop also very much in line with the observational techniques characteristic of the study of modernity and its media. These techniques, moreover, also fold back on themselves as the idiom for theories of the media cultures of modernity. The media studies I am describing present media objects and technologies as paradoxically self-producing, or technologies that produce their own abstractions. This appears, for example, when Vismann and Krajewski portray a system of law that is "blind to its own dependency on the computer as medium as well as to its structural homologies with it" and that must be analyzed by way of the "isomorphism between legal and digital machines,"[49] or in Vismann's volume on files, in which she describes her object (files as records, effects of records, and recording devices) as "homonym, despite its terminological indifference to matter and function."[50] These studies delight in antanaclasis, but in doing so they also insist that shifts between registers of meaning be taken seriously. The result of such an insistence is that the interpretive goals of a cultural study oriented toward media, or seen from the perspective of the media themselves, are bound to the conceptual and material collision already present in the media of interpretation. Techniques for studying media, like the media they are employed to study, produce their own conditions even as they observe them.[51]

These theoretical housings for homonyms also bring into view the range of accounts that Dreiser's novel taps into with its multiple emphases on stampers. It also provides a possible explanation for why these stampers have remained invisible when the formalisms available to their analysis had room for their hermeneutic implications but not in combination with their materiality as media. And given *An American Tragedy*'s peculiar fixations with the materialities of forms and how they paradoxically signal the ongoingness of self-reflexive observation, its role in this history of media and its incorporation in the cinematic process of versioning seems an appropriate legacy.[52] For before the drama of stamping begins in the novel, something like homonymy, or at least its predilection for a likeness that refuses itself, sets Clyde in motion: "It was that old mass yearning for a likeness in all things that troubled them, and him."[53] On a basic level Clyde wants to be "like" other people, or to find internal correspondences between different exteriors, and the reverse. The novel, too, seems to exhibit this "old mass yearning" as it appears and reappears in alternate media throughout the twentieth century, only it wants to be somehow like itself even as it is rehoused. Whatever self it wants to be like aligns uneasily with the yearning Clyde, who witnesses his own transposition between contexts of interiority that bear a strange resemblance to what happens to stampers. The formal resemblances between stampers and novels that mark them as media, and which appear also in the novel's cinematic legacy, in addition surface in the kinds of persons attached to stampers and novels.

Architectures of Interiority

I bring up the filmic versions of *An American Tragedy,* and the reflections upon them, also to point out the scenes in the novel that seem to present the greatest challenges to and points of differentiation between them. These include the work done in the factory, which for Eisenstein and von Sternberg is stamping, but shifts to the production and packaging of bathing suits in Stevens's postwar film, and, appropriately enough, to finance capital in Woody Allen's. In addition to the stamping room, these films also diverge on the point that drew Eisenstein to the novel in the first place: the experimental rendering of interiority that accompanies Clyde's deliberations about the murder and the event itself. Most revealing about the pairing of these scenes as points of divergence are the ways in which they both work as overt renderings of the novel's medial self-reflection: through stamping, as I have been discussing, the novel examines its medial processes, and through its experimentation with narrating interiority, which I will describe now in more detail, it examines its status as a novel, or more specifically, as a modernist novel. As the story goes, it was Eisenstein's interest in the filmic possibilities of internal monologue and stream-of-consciousness narration in Joyce's *Ulysses* that led him to Dreiser's text.[54] And although *An American Tragedy* is rarely included in discussions of innovation in modernist form, these films' pressuring of its techniques for rendering consciousness may provide an indication of why it should be.

The narrative shift to which I refer occurs just as the novel leaves its stamping room behind, en route to the Adirondack lakes. Clyde has read about the drowning at Pass Lake in the newspaper, gone to mail letters, read the story again, gone out of town, and returned to his room and desk, where he then "rereads" "the disconcerting item" in "the identical paper."[55] Later, he will reread the content of garment stamps in the newspaper reports detailing his crime ("Also in her shoe lining was stamped the name of Jacobs of this same city. But other than that there was no evidence as to her identity"),[56] but the process of imprinting that Clyde initiates with his multiple readings of identical texts has stranger results. Clyde starts to go "over and over his hitherto poorly balanced actions and thoughts but with no smallest door of escape anywhere."[57] But a door does appear, in what starts to look like the infrastructure of his consciousness. What Clyde finds is an instance of what kinds of "identical" figures populate the world of rereading he has entered: "Indeed, it was now though from the depths of some lower or higher world never before guessed or plumbed by him . . . there had now suddenly appeared, as the genie at the accidental rubbing of Aladdin's lamp . . . the very substance of some leering and diabolic wish or wisdom concealed in his own nature, and that now abhorrent and yet compelling, leering and yet intriguing, friendly and yet cruel."[58] This genie, or "the Efrit of his own darker self," speaks, and Clyde enters into a dialogue with himself, somehow half Shaftesbury, half Dr. Jekyll. This dialogue continues as he plans the murder, travels with Roberta to the lakes to commit the murder, and then also while he hesitates in the boat, resulting in a kind of murder. Sometimes this voice is marked with quotations, sometimes with parentheses; sometimes it emerges out of something like the free indirect, and sometimes it allows Clyde to observe himself from outside of himself. All of the time, however, it makes Clyde's crisis one of narrative form as well. The deployment of the genie of the *Arabian Nights* as the housing for this inner speech, moreover, clearly situates this sequence of narrative destabilizations not only as markers of the novel's engagement with similar experiments in the air of the 1925 literary culture, but of its engagement with a longer reach of the history of the novel as a medium. And should this reference to the tales of a thousand and one nights as a marker of novelness seem at all tenuous in this context, consider that as he languishes in prison Clyde is given two books to read: the *Arabian Nights,* and *Robinson Crusoe.*

Although these scenes of novelistic self-reflection sometimes pass into a free indirect rendering of a kind of consciousness, they also pass into passages, or pass back and forth through what Flusser literalizes as the doors of a quasi-Hegelian "unhappy consciousness."[59] When Clyde begins his debates, the figuring of his interior as a more specific form of housing complicates the project of locating his thoughts, for "indeed the center or mentating section of his brain at this time might well have been compared to a sealed and silent hall in which alone and undisturbed, and that in spite of himself, he now sat thinking."[60] At issue is not simply who materializes as another, thinking Clyde, but *where* that happens, or what kind of space emerges. That space is corridor, or corridor-like, oscillating between vestibule and hallway: it is alternately "a sealed and silent hall," "the great hall," "the enormous chamber," and, tellingly, "the silent halls of his brain."[61] Both private retreat and connective space, these halls provide an architecture for interiority even as they act as substitutes for it.

For corridors have a long association with the kinds of interiority made possible by novels and novel reading: an architectural form emergent in the eighteenth century and made dominant in the nineteenth, the corridor dialectically separated communication space from private space in domestic interiors. The private thoughts and private selves associated with those modeled by novels and internalized by novel reading also required private rooms in which that reading might take place, and this is what the corridor simultaneously makes possible and constantly irritates. This irritation is what the uncertainty of Clyde's "halls" makes visible: the paradoxical juxtaposition of corridor, the conduit for bodies and information, and the private retreats produced by corridors, demonstrate that the stakes for this representation of interiority are communicative. If Clyde's halls emerge as "silent" or "sealed," they indicate what might have been otherwise. As is the case for many novels appearing in the orbit of *An American Tragedy,* the structure of modern communication emerges most dramatically in its breakdown.

The replacement of interiority by communication, or interiority as communication, forms the ultimate result of this experiment in rendering interiority in material terms. It presents what John Durham Peters has described as an architecture of modern communication, which "reflect[s] an individualist culture in which the walls surrounding the mind were a problem, whether blissfully thin (telepathy) or terrifyingly impermeable (solipsism)."[62] But it does so by transferring the persistent materiality of that architecture to its narrative technique. Instead of streams of consciousness, Clyde has corridors, and when the novel deploys parentheses as markers of our passage into the inner lives of its characters, they represent not a failure or withdrawal from the free indirect, but its excessive literalization. These thoughts have walls.

But a question remains about what kind of person inhabits himself by accessing this world of genies, sealed halls, and blocked passages. If, as I have been arguing, the stamping room and inner chamber mark moments when the novel examines itself as novel and medium (and here I might mention that neither genie nor chamber survives in any of the films), then the individuals populating them are not exempt from this process. While Dreiser's well-publicized interest in Freudian theories and research into modern psychoanalysis while composing this novel invites a reading of Clyde's inward turn that maps its forms in psychological terms, this tells only part of the story. The vertiginous quality of Clyde's interiority troubles its status as a rendering of consciousness: these halls demonstrate that what you find in the interior is another interior, and there is no sign that there is an outside, or end, to these proliferating insides. Instead of consciousness, what appears is something more like communication: that is, the "self" that is "self-conscious" in these scenes emerges from its media.

What Mark Jarzombek has described as the "making of a modern space," or the formation of the corridor, involves the linguistic move from corridors as people (they were couriers and negotiators) to corridors as architectural constructs.[63] Considering that corridors were people before they were places, and that they were messengers, Clyde's oscillations begin to make a little more sense. Clyde, in fact, begins to enact the reverse movement: the transposition of space back to person. Part of what Clyde himself registers during his internal debates is the degree to which this transformation might take place. Clyde feels "that he himself, cold and numb and fearsome, was being talked through—not actually talking himself."[64] Throughout these scenes, Clyde is simultaneously messenger, thoroughfare, and destination. He is a corridor.

"Once files act like people by staying overnight and spending extended time in corridors," Vismann says, "that is, once files take on the habits of their users, a new time has begun—the time of files."[65] While the presence of the corridor as the staging ground for the bureaucratic rationality of which these files form a media technology could not be more pronounced, I would like to keep in view here the ways in which corridors themselves operate as media technologies, and participate in similar processes of enactment to those Vismann reserves for files. Although the modern-day corridor is removed from its homonymic roots (or twice-removed in its American idiom, hallway), the persons, places, and actions to which it used to refer directly persist quite insistently in the institutional, domestic, and personal vectors of *An American Tragedy*. The Clyde who takes up residence in himself in the manner I have been describing names the corridor as a medium that expresses and encodes the same formal relations as those expressed and encoded by stampers. Not only does this demonstrate modernity's "shift of the corridor from a political space to an epistemological one,"[66] but also that the logic of homonymy that characterizes the novel's presentation of media also relates these otherwise disparate media instances to each other formally. This takes on another guise in the novel when Clyde occupies his "hall bedroom," just before he meets his uncle, for he does so under a different name. This name also appears among the evidence during the murder trial. Clyde's persona as a hall-bedroom tenant of his apartment house had been "Harry Tenet," and when asked whether he feels remorse about appropriating this name Clyde can only reply, "No, sir—I thought there were lots of Tenets."[67] He is, of course, right—there are lots of tenants and Tenets populating his environment, and by naming himself in this way he simply acknowledges (albeit unknowingly) that acting as his own tenant will produce anything but the coherent, motivated subject sought by the prosecution.

In yet another version of *An American Tragedy,* a limited-edition "symbolic illustration" of the text by Hubert Davis that was signed and introduced by Dreiser, the double identification of Clyde with this kind of spatial and communicative interiority is etched, tattoo-like, on the protagonist's head (see Figure 8). What is fascinating about this imagining of Clyde is not only the allusion to architectural interiority running across the surface of his skull as he lingers in prison throughout the trial, but the telephone poles framing the image and organizing its perspectival vectors. The drawing combines the physicality of architectural space and the material infrastructure of the communication network, rendering the overlay clearly on the outside of what would otherwise be Clyde's interface between mind and world.

Clyde adds another layer, then, to the process of versioning that appears in the novel's stamping room, in its self-observation as a medium, and in its legacy involvement with the self-observation of other media. Clyde does not, as has often been argued, formally double himself; rather, he experiences the interiorization of stamping, a media process, as the rendering of his interior as, literally, interior. He produces versions of what he observes. As an alternate housing to the psychological person, and as an observing and self-observing communications system, Clyde's interiority brings out the strangeness of modern

Figure 8. From *The Symbolic Drawings of Hubert Davis for An American Tragedy by Theodore Dreiser* (New York: Horace Liveright, 1930).

communication at the same time that it presents this strangeness not as the exception, but what is simply the case. This is also what Luhmann describes as the reality of the mass media. He says that "when individuals look at media as text or as image, they are outside; when they experience their results within themselves, they are inside. They have to oscillate between outside and inside, as if in a paradoxical situation: quickly, almost without losing any time, and undecidably."[68] I would like to suggest that it is through his engagement with media that Clyde registers the early stages of a twentieth-century shift to the Deleuzean "dividuals"—or, perhaps, the preconditions of why our contemporary fixation with grammars of the multitude so often results in being singular plural.[69]

The Ghost in the Machine

I will conclude this chapter by offering one final version of the experience of the stamping room's medial exteriorities as interiority in the novel: a ghost story. Just before Roberta drowns, and while Clyde wrestles with his inner chambers on the lake, that is, in the brief moments before the so-called murder, he hears the haunting sounds of the "weir-weir" bird, which many see as a direct reference to the lonely lakes of Edgar Allan Poe. Clyde's struggle continues, and he is beset by such sounds. First, he hears the "sharp, metallic cry of a blue jay speeding in the depths of these woods," and then "the lone and ghostly tap-tap-tap of some solitary woodpecker."[70] But Clyde, fatefully enough, is slightly mistaken. When he hears the ghostly "tap-tap-tap," what he is in fact hearing is the same sound that he has already heard, in the novel's terms, a couple of hundred pages before, in the factory. What he hears, more specifically, is "the tap, tap, tap of metal stamps upon scores of collars at once."[71] Ghostly indeed.

When Roberta's parents are informed of her death, they immediately ask whether she has been killed by a machine in the collar factory.[72] What this haunting, or pre-haunting shows is that their insights are partially correct, for the deaths of Clyde and Roberta start to look like side effects of a media culture that has revealed itself by becoming too literal. What this also shows is that the recent tendency in criticism of modernist literary interiors to fixate on architectural preconditions or the rendering of social forms in architectural forms perhaps leads them to lose sight of the formal properties of the architectures they describe, especially as these architectures enact and encode medial processes. These can range from accounts of bourgeois individualism that, like Habermas, make claims that "the privatization of life can be observed in a change in architectural style,"[73] or to more recent studies that, while offering insightful histories of the mutual constitution of social and architectural forms, especially regarding the implications of their constitution for gender, do not turn this analysis back toward the medium studied as well as the role of these forms in its self-constitution. The genre of architecture-in-literature appears, for example, in Elizabeth Klimasmith's discussions of spatial practice, which unpack how urban residences "exemplified permeable architecture," but register only how they affect individual writers as individuals, for whom "architectural vagueness threatens the integrity of the self."[74] To presume that a self occupying these walls will be an "integrated" one in the texts that form the precise objects of these studies, I contend, is to imagine a kind of person inadequate to those proposed by the narratives and their engagements with spatial and medial form. Victoria Rosner, in addition, proposes "a material history of modernist literary interiority," what results is a conception of an architectural home as "a possible antidote or counterbalance to the dangers of the street; it extends a sheltering retreat from the shock and dissonance of urban life."[75] These and other author-centered or phenomenological accounts of architecture and, specifically, modernist literature tend to substitute interiors for interiority, and therefore gloss the highly charged and radically identificatory relationship between the two that, in my view, is inextricable from the media cultures constituting the particular instance of modernity that these modernist texts inhabit.[76] In other words, when architectural forms emerge so resolutely as communicative, they point to a very different way of understanding the forms of social, institutional, and domestic life. These architectures reveal how such cross-identifications as those of stamping, rooms, and stamping rooms extend to the very structure of modern personhood in a media culture.

The final section of Dreiser's novel, titled "*SOUVENIR*," presents the likeness of Clyde in the image of his nephew, who inhabits the "tall walls" of another American city. This "unsoiled and unspoiled and uncomprehending boy" not only sends a postcard greeting from the generic determinism the novel engages and updates,[77] but also offers a reminder that the versioning of what has come before will be its

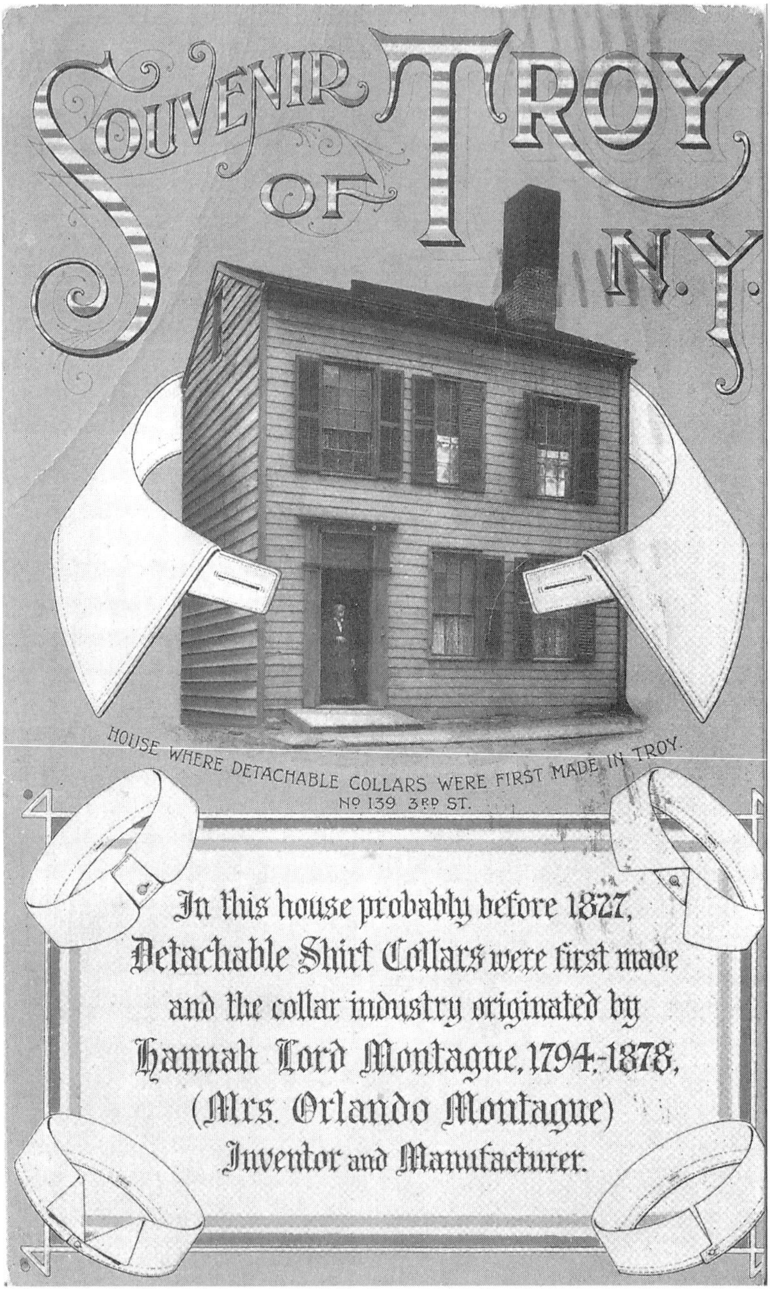

Figure 9. "Souvenir of Troy, N.Y." Collection of Brookside Museum, Saratoga County Historical Society.

ongoing project. Like this postcard from the collar manufacturing capital of New York (see Figure 9), the novel replaces the locus of modern interiority with its bizarre literalization in an architectural form that also happens to wear stamped collars. Souvenirs themselves, the medial forms of *An American Tragedy* prepare us to feel somewhat at home with its otherwise uncanny juxtapositions of collars and houses, and houses and persons.

2 INFRASTRUCTURAL MODERNITY

> Saying that this system includes the telephone, the telegraph, television, the highway system, maritime pathways and shipping lanes, the orbits of satellites, the circulation of messages and of raw materials, of language and foodstuffs, money and philosophical theory, is a way of speaking clearly and calmly.
>
> —Michel Serres, *The Parasite*

> Publicity it seems to me is as necessary as ventilation. . . . It lets in fresh air.
>
> —John Dos Passos, *Manhattan Transfer*

WHEN MELVILLE'S BARTLEBY wants to take in a view of the world outside of his office, he looks out the window at a light shaft. The narrator lingers on this particular technology for circulating light and air: "My chambers were up stairs at No.— Wall-street. At one end they looked upon the white wall of the interior of a spacious sky-light shaft, penetrating the building from top to bottom. This view might have been considered rather tame than otherwise, deficient in what landscape painters call 'life.'" Instead of the airshaft, Jonathan Parker's 2001 film adaptation of "Bartleby" translates the object of the eponymous hero's "dead-wall reveries" into an air-conditioning vent. Parker's Bartleby stares up rather than out, at a dusty, rattling ventilation portal. Lest that vent go unnoticed as the object of and frame for observation (like the "view" it replaces), a repairman painstakingly removes a dead pigeon from the ventilation system to which it provides access. The excessive literalness of associating a dead letter carrier with a former employee of the dead-letter office also includes the blocked conduit fixing both of them, involving and literalizing the ventilation system as a message carrier as well. Bartleby makes the relays between messages, messengers, and infrastructure—already visible in Bartleby the fiction—a guiding concern, but in doing so offers a reminder that what's modern about this instancing of modern communication is not just the communication technology, but the communication process itself.

The air-conditioning system and the earlier ventilation and circulation technologies to which it refers point to a communication process that is at once exhaustively connective and constantly breaking down. This is another way of saying that they point to a communication process that works, for noise, disruption, and breakdown not only reveal that communication was going on in the first place, but also allow it to keep going. Melville's short story and its adaptation draw explicit attention to how things, abstractly informational or aggressively physical, circulate. And the embodied, but dead, letter of the pigeon shows how strangely alike these two poles can be. These two Bartlebys self-consciously operate as story and film, but the tension between their treatments of ventilation instances a problematic particular to printed fiction as it positions itself within a larger field of media forms.

This dynamic operates also in another contemporary interpretation of an infrastructurally invested text, Ralph Ellison's *Invisible Man.* Perhaps the least ambiguous aspect of the collection of 1,369 incandescent bulbs illuminating the narrator of *Invisible Man* is that they are attached, and in turn attach him, to the municipal power grid. Though the significance of the number of bulbs remains as elusive as the narrator's name throughout the novel, it is clear that their function is closely tied to *Invisible Man*'s project as a work of fiction. Not only are these bulbs likened to tiny cinematic observations systems (we are told that the narrator "sat on the chair's edge in a soaking sweat, as though each of my 1,369 bulbs had every one become a klieg light in an individual setting for a third degree"),[1] but their mediality also becomes a question of form. "Without light I am not only invisible, but formless as well," the narrator explains, continuing that "to be unaware of one's form is to live a death."[2]

The narrator's description of a self-reflective, *formal* and formed subject depends on his sometimes gleeful, sometimes rueful theft of energy from Monopolated Light & Power. That theft, while exempting him from one aspect of urban social bureaucracy, also crucially counteracts his enforced isolation from the world above. When he dismissively suggests that "it won't matter if you know that I tapped a power line leading into the building and ran it into my hole in the ground,"[3] he is also assuming that readers (even fictional ones) of modern novels are uninterested in the infrastructural systems that, like the narrator himself, require illumination. When the contemporary visual artist Jeff Wall described the production of his arresting *After "Invisible Man" by Ralph Ellison, the Prologue,* he noted that "working on that picture, I really learned about what Ellison's 1,369 light bulbs means. You can only have a few on at a time."[4] Wall's statement about the paradoxical situation of staging a scene from fiction in material form points out what Ellison's novel registers by other means: you see how the grid works only when it doesn't.

Two aspects of domestic America's favorite cliché during the first decade of the twenty-first century, "crumbling infrastructure," also describe the infrastructural modernity emergent in the American novel of the early twentieth century. The first is that, when invoked, the reference to infrastructure always refers to physical structures and

Figure 10. Jeff Wall, *After "Invisible Man" by Ralph Ellison, the Prologue,* 1999–2000. Transparency in lightbox, 174 × 250.5 cm. Courtesy of the artist.

to the collectivities conjoined by them, that there is always "something metaphoric" about infrastructure. The second is that these structures tend to remain invisible until blocked, broken, or struck by catastrophe. Although these aspects must by necessity be taken for granted in the contemporary narrative (or at the very least obscured by the status of cliché), what becomes more clear in the modern novel are the ways in which infrastructural networks form at once the physical and figurative connective tissue between persons, or operate as material symbols that produce the social and describe it. And in these texts, it is in the insistent and fraught movement between registers of meaning that infrastructure identifies its status as a medial object, one through which the novels identify their own operations as media.

Infrastructure holds a privileged status in the topography of modern American fiction. This is a landscape in which stopped pipes, traffic, congested ventilation, and jammed signals reveal the complex, communicative relays systemically connecting persons and spaces that would otherwise work undetected. It is no accident, I will argue in this chapter, that these blockages are effected by the bodies of infrastructurally connected and constituted persons. My examples, including the corpse-choked furnaces and airshafts of Richard Wright's *Native Son,* the dangerous third rails of Henry Roth's *Call It Sleep,* and the fetus-clogged sewers of John Dos Passos's *Manhattan Transfer,* provide a compact catalog of forms these encounters can take. And it is the explicitly *communicative* status of these forms, I contend, that accounts for the becoming-visible of infrastructure in this particular moment in American literary history.

Familiar materialist accounts of compulsive literary reflexivity focus precisely on the recording and transmission devices broadly understood as the infrastructure of the modern media. Even if the "mediality" of literature (and thus the constitution of literature as such) has specific technological media as its conditions of possibility, referring to these technologies is not necessarily the only method available for novels to think about that fact.[5] There is a way in which dealing with a novel's status as a medium from the material standpoint of its media technologies is both too material and not material enough: to attend to the materialities of literary communication, it also makes sense to attend to the broad range of communication technologies of which the technological media constitute a part. This means understanding communication in its broad sense, as encompassing the transit systems for persons, things, and messages. This also means taking seriously the literal as well as metaphorical implications of a concept such as the "medial landscape" of the literary, in the sense that physical topographies have a constitutive role in describing media relations.[6] This too, as I will show at the end of the chapter, is a form of *corridoricity*. When the physical infrastructure of the built world appears in its most explicit form as the architecture of communication in the novel, it becomes a mode by which the novel thematizes its own participation in the communication systems of modern sociality. Put yet another way, this is where the novel thematizes, and therefore communicates, itself.

This approach to communication and its doubling can be briefly described in systems-theoretical terms by way of the distinction between medium and form.[7] Communication technologies provide the technological conditions of possibility for literary mediality, but the possibility of communication itself forms the medium through which the literary emerges. When the novel names itself as a communication system, it selects among these possibilities of communication and provides them with forms. These forms, which in the novels I am describing include organized communication systems such as pipe networks and transit lines, provide an account of how communication works. The distinction between specific forms of communication and the medium of communicative possibility from which they are selected can then be recognized and reflected upon, and then become another possibility for communication, or another medium. When infrastructure becomes visible in the novel as a communication system through attention to its flow or blockage, the reentry of the distinction between medium and form ensures the continuation of novelistic communication.

Visible infrastructure is itself a paradox, for the catchall term usually refers to the largely unseen underpinnings of physical and organizational systems. And although sight is a powerful sense here, as Bruce Robbins has shown in "The Smell of Infrastructure," it is not the only one available to make the presence of otherwise unnoticed networks felt.[8] Visible infrastructure brings structure to the surface, but not as a superstructure, which would imply that something remains beneath, propping it all up. Infrastructure as a description and concept has come to signify organization in its physical and abstract senses: it can refer to the bureaucratic structures composing the modern state; public works such as mass transit systems, roadways, and power and sewage utilities, technical communication media and their networks; and the organization underlying social formations and modern business. While the inclusiveness of "infrastructure" may seem to rob it of its content, the connectivity between multiple registers that it enacts is also appropriate for the broad scope of its descriptions of communication. Infrastructure makes multiple forms of systematicity possible and maintains them. In what follows, infrastructure will surface in its many valences as "critical infrastructure"—that holdout from the military discourse circulating more loosely in contemporary political commentary—and in doing so reveal the novel's communicative architectonics.

By drawing attention to the medial character of infrastructure in these novels, I am adding to a developing discussion of infrastructure in modernist literature. In recent works by Michael Rubenstein, whose 2010 *Public Works* makes a clear case for the importance of infrastructure for Irish literary modernism, and by Scott Herring, whose *Another Country* (also published in 2010), studies the "self-reflexive ex-urbanites" of American modernism and beyond, the physical networks of urban and national space become definitive for the subjects of fiction.[9] Herring's analysis travels from "modernist metronormativity" to the "queer infrastructure" that underlies it, and he makes an explicit claim for the interpenetration of media and infrastructural materials in the construction of spatialized sexualities: "As much as high modernist books or nationalizing newspapers or Internet chat rooms enable dominant forms of urbanism, so too have the forgotten materials of infrastructure (the gravel, the tar, the asphalt, the buckets of yellow and white paint) enabled imaginary and realized practices of metronormativity to proliferate."[10] For Rubenstein's narrative of the codevelopment of urban infrastructures and Irish modernism, the infrastructural networks invading domestic and public spaces alike have consequences for, and perhaps even produce the modernist narrative subject: "To consider the sewer as the antecedent for the stream of consciousness is, once one thinks of it, almost commonsensical, since to do so is really only to literalize the stream of consciousness for a modern urban setting, where there are few streams other than those in the sewer and where the sewer flows everywhere, underground and unseen. It is to see the extent to which the urban infrastructure impinges on the structures of urban subjectivity."[11] While both of these accounts deal with locationally distinct narrative persons, they point to a powerful sense that infrastructural materiality and the persons who encounter it are deeply intertwined, especially in the media systems of the modern novel. I will examine how that doubly encoded materiality—of infrastructural networks, persons, and media forms—surfaces with violent insistence as mediality in modern American fiction.

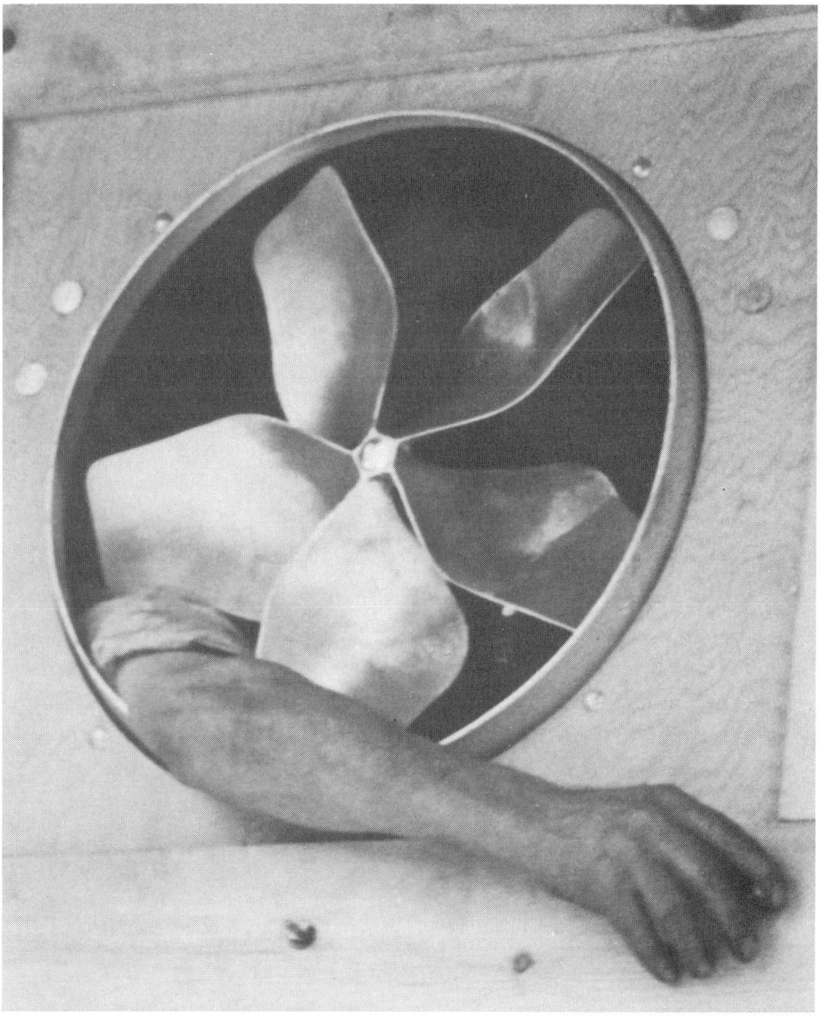

Figure 11. *Arm and Ventilator, New York,* André Kertész, 1937. Gelatin silver print; 5⅜ × 4½ in. The J. Paul Getty Museum, Los Angeles.

Clogged Pipelines, Blocked Airways

In his discussion of the collective topographies of modern socio-technological networks, Bruno Latour identifies a tendency to mistake the expanding scale of media and technological networks for systematized global totality, and suggests that an alternative account of proliferating, expanding networks would "follow the unaccustomed paths that allow this variation in scale, and . . . look at networks of facts and laws rather as one looks at gas lines or sewage pipes."[12] The limitations of large-scale network models, he argues, become visible when compared with localized infrastructural systems. Moreover, these smaller infrastructural networks of "gas lines and sewage pipes" are implicitly involved in the development of wide-reaching, "longer" (a term Latour finds less suspicious than "global") networks. What it means to consider networked abstractions like facts and laws by means of the networked physicality of pipes requires putting some pressure on the distinction between physical and abstract, and taking seriously the similarities (in this case, mutual embeddedness) of both forms of network.

This is not to say that physical infrastructure networks are not commonplace metaphors for describing their abstract—or informational—counterparts, but rather that much is at stake in adopting the same perspective to "look at" laws and sewage pipes, perhaps more so than the commonplace usually registers. The same can be said for the reverse, looking at gas lines and sewage pipes rather as one looks at networks of facts and laws. Both of these perspectival operations dabble in what might be called fiction. This is to a degree unremarkable—when Kojin Karatani, for example, describes architecture working "as" metaphor he refers to the process of fiction-making—but it is also crucial for thinking about overt entanglements of physical and abstract networks within narrative fictional forms.[13] This also reintroduces and reorients Latour's concern with scale, for the gas lines and sewer pipes envisioned as networks present their own ineffable complexities. Pipes and lines, or laws and facts, are both organizational and technological, or social and spatial, depending on the perspective from which they are observed.

What this looks like in the novel is at times an oddly domestic version of the mathematical sublime. In Henry Roth's 1934 novel *Call It Sleep,* the apprehension of pipe networks not only provides a quick index of the relation of "the metropolis" to "mental life," but it introduces the novel itself. After a brief prologue, the novel's young protagonist takes over the narrative focus while contemplating his relationship to urban and apartment infrastructure:

> Standing before the kitchen sink and regarding the bright brass faucets that gleamed so far away, each with a bead of water at its nose, slowly swelling, falling, David again became aware that this world had been created without thought of him. He was thirsty, but the iron hip of the sink rested on legs tall almost as his own body, and by no stretch of arm, no leap, could he ever reach the distant tap. Where did the water come from that lurked so secretly in the curve of the brass? Where did it go, gurgling in the drain? What a strange world must be hidden behind the walls of a house! But he was thirsty.[14]

The novel introduces its project of development, on the one hand, by portraying a literalized imperative to grow into the world described: *Bildung* and building work as related parts of the same project. But David Schearl's realization that "the world had been created without thought of him" involves more than the problem of proportion, for his inability to access the water contained in the apartment's brass tap operates on several registers. "Standing before the kitchen sink" is another way of contemplating, however briefly, the vast infrastructure to which the tap is just one portal. Appropriately, this recognition scene takes the form of an interruption, for considering the water supply ("Where did the water come from?") and its waste system ("Where did it go, gurgling in the drain?") happens between the repeated assertion that "he was thirsty." The moment at which the scale of the water and sewer systems begins to come into view—"What a strange world must be hidden behind the walls of a house!"—is also the point at which the narrative retreats from the connectivity of these infrastructural forms into the solipsism of individual need.

Although *Call It Sleep* lends itself nicely to concerns with psychic systems generally—providing Oedipal dilemmas in family relations and, on the spatial level, Bachelardian basements harboring deep fears—its recognition scenes involving urban infrastructure, including taps, sewers, power lines, and third rails, point to another kind of personhood. The glimpse of proliferating pipe networks, and of the "strange world . . . behind the walls," gestures toward spatial forms not as representative of the relationship between psychic states and the architecture housing them, but rather toward an idea of relationality itself as constitutive of personhood. Or put another way, personhood is a kind of position taking, one interested in articulating a relationship to the connective infrastructure linking other persons in a communicative system that might be called "the social."

In media theory, communicative relationality can be another way of describing interpretation, which in literary form includes recognizing the built-in and assumed interpolation with other texts and media. Novels and other forms assume a distributive quality, and can be thought only in relation to the communicative networks in which they participate. These networks are often discussed in spatial terms. When Elena Esposito, for example, discusses a "medial landscape" expanding from the culture of print, relationality becomes a horizontal project: "It is not only the single text that is decomposed and combined in different forms: the relations among texts, or the general horizon of communication, also become possible objects of decomposition and recombination."[15] Relationality, figured as "horizon," looks a lot like a branching, networked grid, and for good reason. Communication and its attendant positions are inseparable from their infrastructural connectivity.

It may be tempting to refuse a model of relationality that likens pipe systems, media networks, and persons, and look to the literary as a safe haven of particularity that offers an escape from a homogenized medial landscape. Italo Calvino, in his late essay on speed, does this when he discusses communication: "In an age when other fantastically speedy, widespread media are triumphing, and running the risk of flattening all communication onto a single, homogeneous surface, the function of literature is communication between things that are different simply because they are different, not blunting but even sharpening the differences between them, following the true bent of written language."[16] The "surface" becomes the specter here, and Calvino assumes that literature, over other media systems, produces depth through a special relationship to differentiation. In the case of *Call It Sleep,* however, the horizontal expansion of communication as a process of relating things that are to varying degrees *alike* works as an overtly literary project. The novel participates in, rather than offering refuge from, its medial landscape.

It requires only a brief detour through the ur-texts of twentieth-century media theory to discover a fascination with the self-sameness of communication. The most prominent figure in this group would be Walter Benjamin, whose work on language and translation calls attention to the propensity of language to communicate itself, or communicate communicativeness. Similarity as such is emphasized by the

English translator of the essay on the work of art, who doubles Benjamin's reference to reproduction: "Every day the urge grows stronger to get hold of an object at very close range by way of its likeness, its reproduction."[17] The pun on "likeness" here refers to media operating by way of simile, or mimesis as figuration. Adding likeness to reproduction becomes an efficient way of talking about both the media and the mass, for the desire for likenesses as nouns (the physical reproductions themselves) is also the desire for likeness as a state of being. Desire for likenesses becomes a way of articulating likeness, or communicating. This essay might also be revisited briefly by way of another side of likeness, in the Valéry passage that Benjamin uses to discuss the referentiality of media forms: "These convergent endeavors made predictable a situation which Paul Valéry pointed up in this sentence: 'Just as water, gas, and electricity are brought into our houses from far off to satisfy our needs in response to a minimal effort, so we shall be supplied with visual or auditory images, which will appear and disappear at a simple movement of the hand, hardly more than a sign.'"[18] In this loop of referentiality, physical infrastructure and information infrastructure refer to each other with the same "minimal effort." The transit systems of metropolitan life expand via networks of pipes, cables, and airwaves, each working to form a general topography of communication.

Dominique Laporte takes the referentiality of infrastructure to extremes when he says, in *History of Shit,* that "surely, the State is the Sewer," and suggests that the history of humanism is tied to waste generally, and human waste more specifically.[19] The Valéry passage cited by Benjamin, describing the simultaneous situation of infrastructure and media, barely mentions any of its inputs, be they water, electricity, or images, being taken away: although images potentially disappear, there is no visible sewer or waste to complement the things "brought into" houses. The question then becomes where, in the proliferating and overly referential transit modes for moving waste, fuel, or information, does the specificity of the sewer become visible?

Like any good communications system, the sewer becomes most visible when blocked. The novels I am discussing here draw incessant attention to their sewage infrastructure, and they often try to have it both ways: by highlighting the things that travel through and block communications systems, in all of their specificity, these novels bring multiple circulation technologies into relation as part of a broader communication architecture. In the multiply entangled communications systems that form the structure of John Dos Passos's 1925 novel *Manhattan Transfer,* blocked sewers appear alongside traffic jams, missed connections, and clogged circuits as the novel traces the becoming-visible of modern communication. Toward the end of the novel, one of the more developed characters invokes the specific infrastructure of the sewer, but only in reference to her experience of a crowded cross-walk. When Ellen Herf, after pausing to buy flowers, is overwhelmed by the movement of cars and bodies in the crossing, the conflated movements force a kind of synesthesia: "Under all the nickelplated, goldplated streets enameled with May, uneasily she could feel the huddling smell, spreading in dark slow crouching masses like corruption oozing from broken sewers, like a mob. She walked briskly down the cross-street."[20] It is not just that Ellen can "feel" a "smell" or that the smell metaphorically and then synecdochically shifts to a vision of swinish multitude. That Ellen's fear of contact takes the form of a broken sewer demonstrates an odd literalness attending infrastructural forms even as they are invoked as abstractions. If corruption oozes from broken sewers "like a mob," it is because the sewers here form part of what constitutes the mob or the masses—part of what makes Ellen so uneasy is the literalization of the mob, represented by the sewer, and the implication that she does not escape its democratizing function. In the resemblance of sewer, mass, and street (for the figuration of broken sewers begins in reference to street blockage) also obtains an uneasiness, between the specificity of the waste system and its implication in other communications systems.

The encounters with the sewer in *Manhattan Transfer* may begin to read somewhat like a newsreel-sized depiction of the return of the repressed. While there is a certain appeal to lingering gleefully, in the spirit of Žižek, on the portals to the sewer systems eagerly awaiting the return of an obscure object, the systems I am describing here are far more mundane in their operations. Blocked sewers announce that they were there working all along, and call attention to the everydayness of the noise that constitutes them as communications systems. As a result, what they contain also becomes part of the everydayness of communication. A 1916 Futurist work, *Deretani di case,* or *Backsides of Houses,* draws attention to precisely this relation. In it, Vincenzo Volt depicts architectural elevations as poem structures, and the sewage pipe, or "conduit," occupies a prominent position. The left-hand house

Figure 12. Vincenzo Volt, *Deretani di case.* The Getty Research Institute, Los Angeles (90-B23637).

contains "hanging latrines," "condensers of 100 digestions" in which "steep dump entrance = abortions." The casual nearness of multiple waste products in this piece diminishes their capacity to shock. It instead offers up the banality of waste, human and otherwise, as an index of the relationship, literalized in the poem's form, between physical and linguistic architecture. The conduit moves words and waste without dwelling too long on the content of either.

When stuff in pipes becomes suddenly visible through blockage or breakdown, revealing the constitutive noisiness of the communication process, it too participates in this banality. In *Manhattan Transfer,* pipe blockage works as an interruption akin to David Schearl's pause in front of the tap in *Call It Sleep.* Just before the vision of broken sewers and their attendant masses described earlier, the novel provides another detour courtesy of its waste infrastructure. In the final chapter, the narrative turns momentarily to the dilemma of Alice Sheffield, a minor character who has appeared only peripherally in two previous scenes, and who has not yet acted as a focalizer in any of the novel's shifts to omniscience or free indirect discourse. That the novel stops for Alice as it reaches its end is not surprising given its sustained engagement of multiple voices. Moreover, her plight, that "something went click in her head" after she pushed her way through a mass of bodies forming a "stream" from the street into the department store, is not unlike the difficulties experienced by many of the incidental or more developed characters in the novel.[21] She survives her shopping trip, meets her lover, and plans an elopement in just over two pages, and the novel returns to its wrapping-up of several of its more sustained storylines.

The scene may be a throwaway moment, one in which the novel uses a brief encounter between minor characters to reinforce its themes and strategy of polyvocality before getting on with its business. When the conversation turns to the plumbing troubles in Alice's building, however, the "throwaway" reveals itself as the business of the novel: "It seems they've been having the plumbing examined by an inspector," she tells Buck: "There was a woman upstairs who did illegal operations, abortions. . . . That was what stopped up the plumbing."[22] "What stopped up the plumbing," that is, what was thrown away, is an integral component of plumbing as both structure and operation. In this scene, the sewer technologies of modern urban living become visible as an explicitly connective network, linking the supposedly discrete apartments and their supposedly discrete individuals in a system of pipes in constant motion throughout the city. This scene registers a situation of contact between an individualized idea of personhood and the physical architecture of the social—by participating in the process of throwing away and thus entering into the networks of communications between bodies and buildings, Alice Sheffield confronts a double recognition, in which the stream of bodies that triggers her scene is strangely mirrored in her account of the blocked flow of pipes. To return to the stopped plumbing, it is useful to remember that what was thrown away, what was blocking the sewers, was human parts, or to be more precise, human fetuses. The visibility of contact between the body and the pipe, or between the interior and its exteriorized sociality, is also the visibility of the body in the pipeline. In this world, self-enclosure outside of and against social networks is an impossibility, and its reminder makes the recognition of that situation possible. What stopped the pipes stubbornly resists the cooptation of "plumbing" by "women's plumbing"—instead, the illegally aborted fetus is radically dissociated from the organic system.

The clogged pipes so casually referenced in this scene, moreover, dramatize the visibility of the network on the discursive level as well. For Alice's neighbor is likely the same practitioner to which Ellen Herf first takes her former roommate, and then herself, and the byproducts of their procedures could very well be contributing to the building's plumbing troubles. Made visible here is the insistent literalness of association—Alice Sheffield's shock of recognition is doubled by the physical connection of all three characters to one another and to the pipeline. The character networks have their explicit infrastructural analogs. The novel renders the operations and their byproducts casual, even banal, at the same time that it locates a kind of violence in the pipes themselves. Connected also to this scene is Stan Emery, the likely father of Ellen's aborted fetus, who explicitly points to the way that violence and pipelines interact by tapping in to his apartment's gas line as he commits an explosive suicide.[23] Stan, who had earlier informed Ellen that "procreation is the sign of an incomplete organism," is all too complete, or tries to be. When the autotelic self for which he has striven confronts the connective structures of sociality, it explodes.

Although fleeting in the world of *Manhattan Transfer,* these eruptions mark moments when the text draws attention to itself as a simultaneously material and discursive network, and abides in the discomfort that simultaneity produces. Not only is Stan Emery connected by character and bodily association to Alice Sheffield's plumbing, but he operates as a clog as well: shortly after Stan has pronounced his views about procreation, another plumber gets involved. After a show, Ellen prevents Mr. Fallik from entering her dressing room's bathroom by declaring it "out of order," and he promises that he'll arrange "to have a plumber come and look at it" for her.[24] But Ellen has been engaging in some storytelling herself, for the blockage preventing the use of her bathroom is none other than a concealed Stan, whose discovery would be disastrous for Ellen's stage career. If Stan's status as a clog in the sewer system is nothing other than mere fiction, all the better.

When Bernhard Siegert opens his account of the postal infrastructure of the literary field, he is being only kind of metaphorical in his relation of pipes and words: "Language was a pipeline that constantly clogged with the ambiguities of rhetoric. Philosophers were its plumbers."[25] Instead, he claims, the infrastructural metaphor itself has the ability to evade "plumbers" and represent the perceived channelness of language, demonstrating that "figuration and confusion already are present whenever there is communication."[26] In the novel, physical infrastructure works not as "mere metaphor," as if such a thing were possible, but as a figuration of the infrastructural nature of communication. It provides an occasion to comment on the communicative process of fiction and keep that process going. In *Manhattan Transfer,* the sewer system provides another way of thinking about what Zygmunt Bauman has been describing as "liquid modernity": instead of the characteristically modern "melting of solids" standing in for a dissolution of communicative networks and social systematicity, here dissolution and disruption take seriously the figuration implied in liquidity. If on the one hand the appearance of sewer pipes and other conduits reveals an architecture that flows, or even a "permeable architecture,"[27] it also emphasizes that this permeability has always been part of the architecture of communication. Even a liquid modernity needs an infrastructure.

The sewer system is just one of many structures that connect the interior with the grid. Long before Terry Gilliam put bodies in mailbags and sent them to clog a pneumatic bureaucracy in the film *Brazil,* bodies were bringing the novel's multiple circulatory systems to the surface by stopping them up. Communication, both represented and modeled in novelistic turns to infrastructural networks, becomes hyperphysical. This also has consequences for how a novel works out its status as a medium. Increasing interest in media studies and visual culture among scholars of American literature has resulted in the emergence of a growing archive of accounts of media technologies as they appear in texts. These often presuppose a self-reflexive relationship between novels as media and media in novels, but keeping track of media technologies loses something in its reduction of what counts as communication. Moreover, the archeological tendency of media inquiry can at times become too ontological, or perhaps quasi-ontological, focusing despite itself on what media are rather than how they work. Attending to the physical structures of communication as the media's conditions of possibility and occasions for self-reflection helps to shift the focus to how the novel works as a medium.

Choked Furnace

What this means for a novel explicitly concerned with the relationship between media and modernity (and its impasses), such as Richard Wright's *Native Son,* is that overspilling and overlapping circulation systems provide an index of the novel's media relations, and therefore an account of modern relation as such. This is not without its problems, as evidenced by the raised stakes attending the body parts clogging circulatory structures in Wright's novel. While *Native Son*'s interest in cinematic and newspaper media is well documented,[28] these image and message circulation mechanisms can also be read alongside architectural and urban circulation systems.

The early pages of *Native Son* carefully introduce Bigger Thomas to the characters, spaces, and forces that will help determine his role in the rest of the novel. Among these introductions is a set piece staging and thematizing the process of introduction itself, for when he joins the Dalton household as an employee, Bigger must ritualistically meet family members, household staff, and the discrete spaces in which he will live and work. In this introductory reflection on introduction, Bigger is introduced to another household employee, Peggy, who in turn takes him to meet one of his charges, the furnace. Given that the furnace will play an important role in subsequent events, it is perhaps appropriate that it warrants an introduction that parallels others in this scene: shortly after Henry Dalton says, "Peggy, this is Bigger,"

Peggy then tells Bigger, "this is the furnace."[29] Bigger's impressions of the furnace, as well as the furnace itself, are recorded in this scene for future reference: "He rose and followed her out of the kitchen, down a narrow stairway at the end of which was the basement. It was dark; Bigger heard a sharp click and the light came on. . . . He smelt the scent of coal and ashes and heard fire roaring. He saw a bed of red embers glowing in the furnace."[30] The furnace connects Bigger's sensory registers at the same time that it gathers the spaces of the house, and Bigger later notices that his private room has two radiators. Moreover, this furnace draws attention to the household waste economy, for Bigger is instructed to burn the family's garbage as well as its abundant supply of coal. In a scene that introduces introduction, and in a house that (in part) powers itself, the furnace too must participate in the play of self-reference. Peggy says to Bigger, "You never have to use a shovel for coal. It's a self-feeder." Bigger pauses to admire, but she doesn't stop there, telling him "you don't have to worry about water, either. It fills itself."[31]

The "self-feeding" furnace figures one side of the novel's circulatory dynamics, and gives a physical structure to the logic of self-production. That this logic breaks down, or clogs, makes sense given *Native Son*'s generic interest in Dreiserian naturalism and social realism. In Jacqueline Stewart's discussion of the novel's specific engagement with the cinema, both media and space play a part in shaping the novel's generic perspective: "In *Native Son,* set on the South Side of Chicago, Wright's social realism (including his naming of specific streets, films, the Regal Theater) offers a scathing analysis of the oppressive social map that confines young black working-class (male) migrants at the moment the novel was written."[32] In this account, the specificity of spatial and media reference in their combination matters for the conventions we recognize as "realism" and "determinism." Although the furnace's circulatory and self-producing qualities put it in conversation with the circulatory and self-perpetuating logics of the urban and the media as Stewart describes them, the furnace's specificity stops at the description of it as "self-feeding." However, it does follow to think of the furnace in relation to how the novel explicitly deals with the conventions of something like a social realism.

The extensive trial scenes that end *Native Son* test the limits of a social realism that produces its effects via attention to detail. The portions of book 3 most recognizable as staging "production of evidence" take place before the trial itself during the coroner's inquest, and are best remembered for the brutal unveiling of female bodies and body parts. The coroner, whose task to convince a jury to remand Bigger Thomas for a murder trial appears initially straightforward given Bigger's signed confession, theatrically unveils Bessie Mears's "raped and mutilated body" among his other evidence.[33] Bigger recognizes that "they were using his having killed Bessie to kill him for his having killed Mary," drawing attention to the strange circularity of this particular system of association. Not only does the display of a black woman's body as a substitute for that of a white woman pose a problem in this scene, but the associational nature of this kind of evidentiary model does as well: it exposes a short circuit in the ways in which physical proofs stand in for something else. Bigger worries that Bessie's body is "merely 'evidence,'" and both Bessie Mears's and Mary Dalton's remains simultaneously exceed and fall short of what they are supposed to represent. It's not enough that the "bloody and black" body stands in for Bessie and a "pile of white bones" for Mary, but that one body inaccurately stands in for violence done to the other.[34]

That the objects and narratives making up the case against Bigger will be manipulated in favor of the existing power structure is an open secret. This is in fact part of the genre of courtroom drama being described as social reality; what emerges is an oversignification built into the selection and description of the evidence itself. Racial distinctions overwhelm the remains even when, in Mary's case, they are reduced to fragments, and yet the shared gender of the two women allows for a too-easy assumption that both bodies were the subjects of the same male sexual violence, eliminating the specificity of crimes suffered by either. There may be too much evidence, but that evidence also says too much. Moreover, the excessiveness of the evidence does not stop with the bodies, although they are the most visible in this scene. Reenactment and reproduction of what counts as "real" physical objects and spaces becomes an obsession of the inquest and its media presence, and this is nowhere more visible than when, following the coroner's inquest, the police escort Bigger back to the Dalton house, place him in Mary Dalton's bedroom, and order him to reenact the rape that never happened in front of newspaper photographers.

What operates as a version of realism in the courtroom looks a lot like fiction, and in its overtly figurative and associative modes seems to equate "literariness" with "evidence." In the larger context of the narrative of *Native Son,* this demonstrates the reentry of realism into the novel's social realist project (or at least the urban and architectural focus of that strategy), drawing attention to the ways in which truth claims and physical detail interact.[35] The furnace is not only a working model of the novel's communicative process: its reconstruction in the courtroom doubles that reflexivity so that the furnace stands in for novelistic communication and the specifically novelistic project of realism at the same time. The courtroom scenes stage and recontextualize the generic moves with which the novel engages as a novel. And they also stage each other: the inquest, for all of its detail, is merely a rehearsal for the trial it authorizes. The trial also deals in excess—the prosecutor calls sixty witnesses—but the narrative compresses the presentation of physical evidence into a single paragraph, recalling their earlier courtroom appearances with a few key changes:

> Buckley brought forth the knife and purse Bigger had hidden in the garbage pail and informed the Court that the city's dump had been combed for four days to find them. The brick he had used to strike Bessie with was shown; then came the flashlight, the Communist pamphlets, the gun, the blackened earring, the hatchet blade, the signed confession, the kidnap note, Bessie's bloody clothes, the stained pillows and quilts, the trunk, and the empty rum bottle which had been found in the snow near a curb. Mary's bones were brought in and women in the court room began to sob. Then a group of twelve workmen brought in the furnace, piece by piece, from the Dalton basement and mounted it upon a giant wooden platform. People in the room stood to look and the judge ordered them to sit down.[36]

The condensed description of physical evidence included in the trial scene refers both to the excessive displays in the inquest and to the spatial specificity of the novel's urban and architectural landscape. Yet it does so with a difference, for not only is Bessie's body notably missing from the clothes it formerly occupied, but the compression of narrative time spent on the physical evidence is countered by an extreme increase in courtroom space that this evidence occupies. After the successive presentation of witnesses and objects, so that each starts to stand in for the other in a series, everything stops for the furnace.

But what can the gratuitous labor of dismantling, transporting, and rebuilding of a furnace so large it requires a "giant wooden platform" prove, if not that there is something gratuitous, in fact novelistic, about the rhetoric of evidence? The self-feeding furnace takes on an aspect of self-evidence: the prosecutor stages a reenactment of

Mary's disposal and discovery, and after he demonstrates what it would have looked like to clear out the bones clogging the furnace's vent with a shovel, he declares, "The State rests, Your Honor!"[37] It is no accident that it is the too-literalized furnace that dramatically stands in for the prosecution's entire case. The furnace was there, bringing together bodies and spaces in a communication network all along, and if its blockage by a body didn't make it visible enough as such a system, it had to be brought out of the basement and set upon a stage in the public arena. When Jonathan Elmer discusses versions of visibility in his reading of *Native Son* in relation to trauma theory, he invokes the "bottlenecks, knots, foyers, and centers" and "points of fusion, condensation, and boiling" of the Deleuzian event: "Mary's murder answers just this description; we have there a blockage and bottleneck building up pressure."[38] These blockages, moreover, make concrete the communication blockage that afflicts Bigger in the presence of his wealthy white employers, the police investigators, and the reporters covering his arrest and trial, all of whom seem to impede Bigger's capacity to speak by the presence of their bodies, and his. This suggests an interplay that Mark Goble describes as "race figured as medium." In his account, race refigured in medial terms by literary texts can be coded "as a physical, material limit to expression that becomes aestheticized as a vehicle for communication."[39] If Mary's murder metaphorically deals in bottlenecks and blockage, then the inclusion of the furnace as the trial's key witness turns this metaphor inside out. The blocked furnace stands in for the evidence and for the crime, and the evidence was what blocked the furnace in the first place. Although metaphoric blockage in part describes the novel's social reality, literal blockage locates its self-description. The furnace fills itself.

A furnace that fills itself is also a furnace that blocks itself, for in *Native Son* fuel and blockage easily become the same thing. The furnace dramatizes this exact problem when it stops working in a basement full of witnesses, whose attention Bigger must not allow it to attract: "He had gotten some of the ashes down out of the stove, but they choked the lower bin and still no air could get through. He would put some coal in. He shut the doors of the furnace and pulled the lever for coal; there was the same loud rattle of coal against the tin sides of the chute. The interior of the furnace grew black with coal. But the draft did not roar and the coal did not blaze."[40] When Mary's ashes were all that clogged the furnace, it simply did not put out enough heat, but when Bigger sets its fuel cycle going, crisis ensues. The blocked airflow of the furnace repeats that blockage outside of itself by clogging the air of the basement and choking its inhabitants, and the furnace's self-exposure ultimately exposes both Bigger and Mary to public view. In this way, the furnace also literalizes communication theory's greatest paradox: that what keeps the system going ("the same loud rattle of coal") is its noise, or precisely what stops it up.[41]

But the furnace requires something in addition to and slightly less tangible than its coal supply to continue generating heat: ventilation. It is self-contained, but only up to a point, and requires an irritation from the outside both to produce and to forestall its constitutive congestion. This commonsense aspect of the furnace's workings—that all fires must breathe—complicates the ways in which the physical structure of the furnace participates in circulation. Circulation in *Native Son* is always double sided, and so it follows that the circulation system of the furnace relies on another form of circulation to operate. It also makes sense that in a novel so invested in movement, enclosure, and communication, a fiery furnace becomes both a way to locate these things explicitly and the occasion to reflect upon how they work. When the circulation of heat halts in the novel, it draws attention to the fact that the "outside" of the circulation system is another circulation system, albeit engaged with another medium. As the furnace reveals ventilation and combustion to be two aspects of a larger circulatory dynamic, the clogging of that furnace with body parts ensures that the embeddedness of persons within these circulation systems will not go unnoticed.

Native Son is one of many novels that stage the paradoxes of modern communication via the entanglement of ventilation and combustion. In *Manhattan Transfer,* the threat of exploding ventilation shafts periodically reminds the city's inhabitants of its circulation architecture. The alleys, corridors, and airshafts that seem to separate bodies and spaces also constitute the most likely sites for combustible communication between them. In the novel's opening chapters and in several subsequent scenes a "firebug" occupies the background conversation of friends and strangers meeting in the street, and ventilation systems form the arsonists' specific targets. Fire interrupts a meditation on the very meaning of "metropolis" as Ed Thatcher walks home past rows of tenement buildings in the chapter of that same name:

> In the empty space in the middle of the street the fire engine and the red hosewagon shone with bright brass. People watched silent staring at the upper windows where shadows moved and occasional light flickered. A thin pillar of flame began to flare above the house like a romancandle.
>
> "The airshaft," whispered a man in Thatcher's ear. A gust of wind filled the street with smoke and a smell of burning rags. Thatcher felt suddenly sick.[42]

In this scene, street traffic stops for the spectacle of an apartment house on fire, but circulation space takes over the description. Instead of the crowd, attention shifts to "the empty space" left in the street. Play between circulation space and the things that fill it highlights the paradoxical relationship between combustion and ventilation. The fire trucks fill the gap in the street, fire fills the airshaft, and the air and smoke in turn fill the entire avenue. The drama of "airshaft" as a murmured explanation for the fire resides in part in the irony that something designed for protection could turn deadly, but also in the shared knowledge that, like a whisper among strangers, ventilation is a necessarily explosive structure of sociality.

Ventilation systems known as airshafts became a requirement of mass housing after tenement laws enacted in 1879, which required that all rooms have access to air. In large urban dwellings in cities such as the New York of *Manhattan Transfer* and the Chicago of *Native Son,* the scale of building meant that not all rooms touched the outside walls of the building, and provision had to be made to provide ventilation for inner rooms. The answer was to provide some access to the outside from the inside, and tenements incorporated a vertical passage through their center.

The combustible ventilation in *Manhattan Transfer* and the ventilation of combustion in *Native Son* take another turn in the latter, which links the furnace and airshaft as circulation systems by blocking both with bodies. After Mary Dalton's body clogs the furnace draft, Bigger Thomas throws Bessie Mears down an airshaft, and is later told that she literally froze in the passage. A "rattle" of coal "against the sides" of the chute accompanies all three of Bigger's early encounters with the furnace (his introduction to it, the disposal of Mary's body, and the attempt to clear the vent), and when Bigger throws Bessie out of the tenement window, "the body hit and bumped against the narrow sides of the airshaft as it went down into blackness."[43] But the physical similarities between furnace and airshaft in *Native Son* tell just one side of the story. The clogging of both ventilation systems with bodies is simply the most overt way in which the novel makes it clear that communicative circulation is both its location and situation.

The likeness of furnace to airshaft also incorporates scenes of reflection and reconstruction. Bigger encounters the building in which he will rape, kill, and dispose of Bessie also in the idiom of introduction,

Figure 13. "Airshaft of a Dumbbell Tenement, New York City, Taken from the Roof, Ca. 1900." Courtesy of the National Archives and Records Administration.

for "they stopped in front of a tall, snow-covered building whose many windows gaped blackly, like the eye-sockets of empty skulls." After Bigger and Bessie occupy the building with the aspect (or remainder) of personhood about it, the novel carefully stages a meeting of Bigger and the airshaft: "He hoisted the window and looked up the air-shaft; snow flew above the roof of the house. He looked downward and saw nothing but black darkness into which now and then a few flakes of white floated from the sky, falling slowly in the dim glow of the flashlight."[44] This lingering look, and pause in the otherwise frenetic pace of "Flight," makes the airshaft available for another version of the reconstruction that will later take place in the courtroom. Although the prosecution does not rebuild the airshaft into which Bigger throws Bessie (and although there is a sense this would be the case were it possible), Bigger mentally rebuilds the airshaft before he makes use of it. After Bigger rapes Bessie, his thoughts wander before he forces them "back to the room": "He reconstructed in his mind the details of the room as he had seen them by the glow of the flashlight when he had first come in. . . . He remembered hoisting the window; it had not been hard. Yes, that was what he could do with it, throw it out of the window, down the narrow air-shaft where nobody would find it until, perhaps, it had begun to smell."[45] Both furnace and airshaft become blocked, but their multiple reproductions emphasize that this blockage works as communicative noise, and that both architectural and media systems similarly involve persons in their circulation mechanisms.

The mass media circulate alongside the infrastructural systems of *Native Son,* and Bigger proves his credentials as a good modern subject by basing his behavior on the known knowns of crime reporting ("Fingerprints! He had read about them in magazines!") and by following newspaper accounts of his pursuers following him after he has been implicated by the blocked furnace. It should not be surprising, then, that the airshaft has a media sensibility: after all, the same year that marked the publication of *Native Son,* 1940, also saw the release of Duke Ellington's popular song, "Harlem Air Shaft." Describing this song, Ellington juxtaposes the airshaft with communications technology: "'So much goes on in a Harlem air shaft.' Ellington explained. 'You get the full essence of Harlem in an air shaft. You hear fights, you smell dinner, you hear people making love. You hear intimate gossip floating down. You hear the radio. An air shaft is one great big loudspeaker.'"[46] The airshaft works as a topic for Ellington precisely because of the noise it houses, and it thematizes itself as a song by becoming the speaker on which it is played.

The media systems of *Native Son* become three-dimensional not simply as mechanisms through which Bigger learns and monitors his status as modern subject, but rather as oddly physical reflections on modern communication. Bigger doesn't just read newspapers and project them onto himself; he wraps the rat he kills in the novel's opening pages in a newspaper. This overt physicality of newsprint involves urban space as well as bodies. The map Bigger follows of Chicago's South Side printed in the newspapers during his pursuit depicts concentric black and white circles indicating the areas already searched by "police and vigilantes" and those still to be searched. This image looks a little too much like that made on an earlier appearance of newsprint, in which "the blood crept outward in widening circles of pink on the newspapers, spreading quickly now."[47] Newspapers in this second instance catch the blood draining from Mary's head, which Bigger removes in order to fit her body in the furnace. The newspaper's map of Chicago has already been printed in blood on newspaper, and the same newspaper on which the map appears then briefly becomes a makeshift furnace: "He crawled back through the door and into the narrow passage and lowered himself down the shallow wooden steps into the hallway . . . Then he had an idea; he wondered why he had not thought of it before. He struck a match and lit the newspaper; as it blazed he held one hand over it awhile, and then the other."[48] Media circulation happens not simply alongside the circulation systems of urban and architectural infrastructure, but coextensive with them. *Native Son* makes this a problem of perspective, which can change what a newspaper is by altering the position Bigger occupies when looks at it. For Niklas Luhmann, this describes the reality of the mass media: "When individuals look at media as text or as image, they are outside; when they experience their results within themselves, they are inside. They have to oscillate between outside and inside, as if in a paradoxical situation: quickly, almost without losing any time, and undecidably."[49] This also reflexively doubles the material mediality of race in modernism described by Katherine Biers as "the black phonographic voice" and Mark Goble as "race records."[50] Blocked and explosive furnaces, sewers, and airshafts literalize the paradox of the mediated individual. Descriptions of communication systems in these novels function as descriptions of novels as communication systems, and the self-thematization of communication here means rendering the abstract physical. To return to the Latour proposition with which I opened this account, for *Native Son,* it makes sense to look at networks of facts and laws rather as one looks at the radiator.

The Corridor Underground, or Continuous Transit

The clots and blockages I have been describing suggest a nightmarish quality to functioning communication, but their inverse, unblocked flows and unbounded connectivities, often appear threatening as well, as they too reveal the infrastructural workings of communication. The movement of electrical currents and subway trains through an urban infrastructure can be too free as well as halted, and street traffic can jam, crash, or move too quickly. These are what I have been describing as the traffic conditions of modern communication, where "always-on" and sudden shutdown conspire equally to bring its infrastructure into view.

Well-worn narratives of twentieth-century urban development in the United States focus on a double movement: the colonization of vertical space via the skyscraper and horizontal space via the suburb. But as these forms develop, the novel often focuses on another dimension, laying out an urban topography that is subterranean and infrastructural. Transit networks for moving people, refuse, power, and information constantly surface (albeit paradoxically) as places where the novel names itself as a transit network as well. On one level this should be hardly surprising, given the long and intimate affiliation of print and its physical circulation systems—"communication" in novels always harbors the ghosts of its earlier idioms of physical movement and encounter—yet this infrastructure, as it appears in the novel, indicates a kind of irritation or disruption of communicative process.[51] In the communication systems of the built and media worlds of early twentieth-century American fiction, however, irritation is more constitutive than disruptive.[52] The hypervisibility of systems like subways and sewers, figured as media, allows the novels I am describing to add both texture and specificity to accounts of themselves as part of a media ecology.

Take Roth's *Call It Sleep.* The novel tracks David Shearl's encounters with and movements through urban communication networks, including the circulation spaces of the tenement, the ever-expanding grid of roads and power lines, and finally a near-fatal merging with the third rail of the city's transit system. In the infamous scene at the end of the novel, when the narrative moves into David's semi-consciousness, overlapping networks make possible the overtly literary manipulation of form: by literally "tapping in" to the electrical and transit lines, David reveals an excess of interiority and connectivity, which is rendered in overloaded passages of stream-of-consciousness narrative and figurative extremes. The too-muchness of this scene, however, seems precisely the point, especially in light of the novel's infrastructural thematics and urban geography. As the Proletariat gathers around David's 550-volt infused, yet motionless body, the "*doors of a hallway*" slowly open in the parenthetical interludes, and draw attention once again to the architecture of circulation and the corridoricity of media:

> *(As if on hinges, blank, enormous*
> *mirrors arose, swung slowly upward*
> *face to face. Within the facing*
> *glass, vast panels deployed, lifted a*
> *steady wink of opaque pages until*
> *an endless corridor dwindled into*
> *night.)*[53]

Powered by the electrical currents of the city's transit networks, this meditation on the collision of spatial communication infrastructure and fictional form is quite explicit. Already entwined in a dense network of metaphor and symbol, this interlude adds another figurative layer: the already figurative mirrors take on a layer of simile, the "*as if.*"[54] This cross-referencing, or reentry of figuration into figuration, finds its reflection in the corridor these mirrors form. The interminable corridor, or transit space infinitely replicated on two axes (its lateral openness and recursive interior reflection) is also a figuration of the novel's mediality. That the reflection posited by the overfamiliar trope of the mirror is also rendered in the materiality of pulp ("the steady wink of opaque pages"), which in turn renders a vision of communicating interiors ("face to face"),[55] indicates not an exceptional instance of novelistic communication, but rather a messy display of how it works. It reflexively doubles the medial materiality of paper (which is always metaphorical) in the material metaphor of the corridor, locking them both in referential relays with each other.

The communicative materiality of novels, space, and transit, made exhaustively visible in *Call It Sleep,* relies on specific and repeatable forms at the same time that it portrays them as endlessly portable into one another. It is important that the architectural figure of the corridor in this instance becomes the connective tissue gathering current, interiority, movement, and self-reflection. The corridor, and its ability to encompass other spaces and forms of communication, becomes the trope that figures, as Luhmann might put it, "the transformation of identity into communication."[56] In *Call It Sleep,* the corridor forms a third term between the transit system and the individual involved in its process, asking us perhaps to show the same critical attention to third rails as we do to third terms.

The electrical current that catalyzes David Shearl's theorization of novelistic communication also reaffirms the connection posited between information transport and transit infrastructure. And it is not alone in doing so. One of the more powerful third rails in early twentieth-century American fiction is the nearly eponymous electricity conductor of Dos Passos's *Manhattan Transfer.* The novel's title, as several critics have pointed out, describes the station where railroad travel heading into Manhattan switches to electric power, joining up with the city's underground transit system.[57] "They had to change at Manhattan Transfer," the phrase announcing the novel's title as both place and state change, connects taking up the third rail and participating in fiction. It also demands an account of underground travel and the transfers within it in a novel so invested, on the surface at least, with what happens on the surface.

Dos Passos, who had once planned to be an architect himself, found room in most of his novels for an architect figure. In the *U.S.A.* trilogy, Frank Lloyd Wright gets top billing as "The Architect," and it seems somewhat strange that in the skyscraper world of *Manhattan Transfer* the architect character is not only incidental (appearing only three times, making him more rare than most of the novel's cast of incidentals), but that he spends his time with the city's transit systems of subway, street, and streetcar, and with its buildings only in an elevator.[58] Phil Sandbourne, the architect in question, operates as a connective character in the text, moving briefly in and out of the orbit of several characters to whom the novel grants substantive attention. He is interested in matters of high and low, and sees the subway as part of a vertical system. As they ride underground, Phil tells his wealthy friend George Baldwin that "it does you plutocrats good now and then to see how the other half travels," and hopes that a journey on the subway will induce Baldwin, an attorney, to work on the Tammany Hall powers to "give us wage-slaves a little transportation."[59] Earlier in the novel, before a downward-moving elevator ride, he says, "what do I care if all the architects in New York get bumped off as long as they don't raise the price of commutation."[60] The matter of traveling above or below ground for Sandbourne operates under the easy logic of vertical class structures. The spatial metaphorics of underground travel do more than reinforce this verticality: they take it to extremes. When Baldwin finds himself pressed against the belowground masses he tells Sandbourne, "I'll be seeing the inside of an undertaking parlor if I don't get out of this subway soon."[61] If the pun on underground and undertaker seems strangely informal here, it indicates a casual uneasiness attending movement below ground. The shifting between underground, underclass, and undertake makes the vectors of high and low, over and under, or surface and depth idioms for the text's social and spatial dynamics.

That there seem too many metaphoric resonances for verticality in Phil Sandbourne's relation to the subway becomes further complicated by the movement of the subway and the directionality of its tunnel system. Appropriately enough, the architect's three appearances are each accompanied by speculation about future building possibilities: these include a full-service high-rise building of which J. G. Ballard would have been proud, new towers constructed of steel and glass, and, perhaps more strangely, "a series of endless moving platforms under Fifth Avenue."[62] Sandbourne's vision of "moving platforms" probably refers to a project developed in 1923 by the "Continuous Transit Corporation," which similarly proposed a system of moving platforms as an alternative to subway travel, and which was designed to go between Times Square and Grand Central Station, or under Fifth Avenue.[63] Continuous Transit, according to this plan, meant that instead of boarding a stopped subway car that would then move to the next stop, passengers would instead step on to a series of continuously moving platforms, each subsequent platform moving faster than the previous, until they were traveling at speed, and able to disembark by moving in the reverse direction to subsequently slower platforms until once again on steady ground.

By dreaming of "continuously moving platforms," Sandbourne invokes a transit system that is all platform, no train, all movement, no rest. This is a system of seemingly pure horizontality and unbounded temporality (the platforms are "endless" at the same time that they are "continuous"). According to the patent application for one of many such systems proposed in the early decades of the twentieth century, "System of Transportation" (1922), these platforms engage a communicative sense of "transfer": not only do they facilitate the "conveyance of either passengers or freight," but they "communicate" with non-moving parts of the system.[64] Communication once again operates in the broadest sense, as involving people, things, and information. The idea behind these modes of transit, and their appearance in *Manhattan Transfer,* constitutes something of a paradox, for after all, the one thing a "platform" is not expected to do is "move." Something of the ridiculous also attaches to Sandbourne's fantasy. Another patent, this time filed in 1904 under the title "Moving Platform," describes the platform system for a "circle race," a device set into and kept in motion for nothing other than motion's sake, for "amusement."[65] Motion for motion's sake, in the language of *Manhattan Transfer* and these proposals, is a kind of communication for communication's sake. The novel's quasi-utopian vision of the subway, instanced in the model of moving platform, deals not with origins and destinations—or if so, they are as incidental as the characters describing them—instead, it seems to answer Brian Massumi's call "to build for recursive duration," or "'see time in space'—continuing modulation: don't mediate, modulate."[66]

If the subway comes to resemble a fairground amusement in *Manhattan Transfer,* its thrills are predictably not uncomplicated. After Sandbourne announces his plan for moving platforms, his friend retorts, "Did you cook that up when you were in hospital, Phil?"[67] The answer is yes, for Sandbourne's earlier appearance in the novel involved his nearly fatal collision with street traffic, and does something to explain his desire to go below ground even if it doesn't account for the substitution of platform for subway: "A pouncing iron rumble crashes down on him from behind. Fifth Avenue spins in red blue purple spirals."[68] While this may seem like anything but continuous transit, in *Manhattan Transfer* continuity and blockage, or unobstructed movement and bloody crash, start to look a lot alike.

Endless movement and sudden obstruction make the often-transparent transit systems above and below ground visible. This visibility

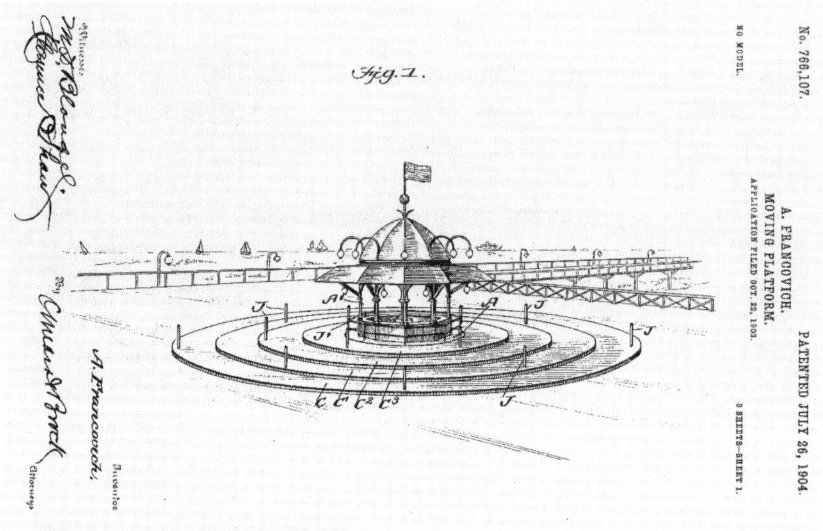

Figure 14. From the Patent Application for "Moving Platform." A. Francovich, Moving Platform. U.S. Patent 766,107, filed Oct. 22, 1903, issued July 26, 1904.

also calls attention to the affinities underlying the competition staged between these modes of transit. Just as a road too full of taxis, streetcars, and pedestrians leads to a dangerous entangling of each of these moving bodies, the modes of transportation below ground start to proliferate rather than offer respite from street noise. This is structurally fitting with the narrative complexity of *Manhattan Transfer,* which anticipates the *U.S.A.* trilogy's moves between multiple media by incorporating newspaper reports, popular songs, and radio broadcasts into its proliferating narrative modes (poetic interludes, free indirect discourse, etc.). Not only do infrastructural and media systems here replicate themselves within each other through this staged competition, but they also observe themselves as communications media by doing so. This can be thought of as a problem of the media themselves: for Friedrich Kittler, for example, "in a discourse network that requires an 'awareness of the abysses which divide one order of sense experience from the other,' transposition necessarily takes the place of translation."[69] But this is also a problem of the relationship of the built world to the media: for Beatriz Colomina, who reads modern architecture "as" mass media, it is precisely by engaging with the media that "modern architecture becomes 'modern.'"[70] And for Reinhold Martin, the "organizational complex" of space makes architecture "one among many media."[71] If the "always-on" continuity of the moving platform sounds a little like a radio broadcast, according to these terms it probably should. And if those radio broadcasts compete with narrative interiority, newspaper reports, and the figurative process, the prospect of their continued flow appears less enticing.

What this means for the novels I have been discussing is that the systems of discourse that represent infrastructural materiality start to take on the properties of the physical worlds they describe. In Dos Passos's *U.S.A.* trilogy, the staged competition between transit systems announces the association between the three novels—in the prologue to the trilogy, "people have packed into subways, climbed into streetcars and buses; in the stations they've scampered into suburban trains; they've filtered into lodgings and tenements, gone up in elevators into apartmenthouses." The filtration mechanisms of urban movement all work in the same way, and the "young man," operating as a synecdoche of the national multitude, "must catch the last subway, the streetcar, the bus."[72] Participating in each of these systems simultaneously is to encounter and be embedded in their corridoricity.

But the subway ride in which Phil Sandbourne announces his idea about moving platforms opens another layer of referentiality that informs the relationship between mass media and mass transit in *Manhattan Transfer.* Phil and George Baldwin approach the station's stationary platform as part of a metaphoric collectivity: "In a tangled clot of men and women, arms, legs, hats aslant on perspiring necks, they were pushed out on the platform."[73] Both atomized and radically conjoined, their envelopment within the "tangled clot," precisely at the moment that train and platform meet, refers to the disembarkation that opens the novel: "*Gates fold upwards, feet step out across the crack, men and women press through the manuresmelling wooden tunnel of the ferryhouse, crushed and jostling like apples fed down a chute into a press.*"[74] As the ferry passengers, like the subway passengers, are pushed out onto the platform, "men and women press" through the ferry's disembarkation passage as "apples fed down a chute into a press." Accounts of this opening often focus on the birth metaphor of passengers delivered through the ferry's canal-like tunnel, emphasized by the immediate turn in the opening of the novel's narrative proper to the birth of one of its major characters, Ellen Thatcher, who "squirmed in the cottonwool feebly like a knot of earthworms."[75] However, the novel's concern with communications systems requires another look at the multiple valences of this opening. The repetition of "press" in this description of mass movement implies that to enter the movements of crowd and city is also to enter into the circulation of media forms. In a novel hardly unaware of its status as a medium in a complex media ecology, the "press" of the opening interlude finds its echo in a later chapter, in which words "press" against the body. Moreover, in an interlude preceding one of Phil Sandbourne's rare appearances, "*print squirms among the shopworn officeworn sagging faces, sore fingertips, aching insteps, strongarm men cram into subway expresses.*"[76] Newsprint "squirms" like the "knot of earthworms," which is like the "tangled clot" of body parts pushed onto the platform, and they, in turn, are like the passengers disembarking the mass transit system of the ferry as synecdochic "feet," who are once again tied to the "press." This is exhausting, but it is also symptomatic of the novel's entanglement of communications systems. When print and subway travel exist simultaneously and so explicitly as the situation of the text, they nearly burn themselves up in the process of self-reflection. Or, as Baldwin observes to Sandbourne before they part and Sandbourne leaves the novel, "how complicatedly things interact."[77]

In Wolfgang Schivelbusch's account of cultural transformation enacted by railroad development in the nineteenth century, the relationship between train car and platform is also a question of corridors, for a key difference he cites between the class-divided coaches of Europe and their more fluid American counterparts lies in the introduction of the corridor to the architecture of the carriage itself. Corridors within trains move the communal space of platform into the train: in these terms, the space inside the train carriage starts to resemble a moving platform.[78]

There is nothing straightforward about the logic of resemblance as it operates in *Manhattan Transfer.* Networks of associations proliferate in a nonlinear horizontality, putting the underground and overground transit networks of the city in strange relation to the above/below verticality that separates both street and subway, but also horizontal urban movement and vertical movement up escalators and elevators, and into the urban interior of the skyscraper. This becomes also a problem of language and of narrative in the novel, which plays with its own perceived linearity and horizontal proliferation. The "endless moving platform" of *Manhattan Transfer,* much like the "endless corridor" of *Call It Sleep,* calls up the categories of resonance and association as ways of understanding figurality, communication, and space. The moving platform resonates with much of the novel's overt thematics and preoccupations about urban geography, creating a vertical line through its overtones, and happening simultaneously. This image also works via association, moving horizontally to reach out to other figurative moments in the novel's timeline. Figural play is often a favorite pastime of the novel, but *Manhattan Transfer* calls attention to these moments almost deliriously. Spaces and states of communicative sociality are so explicitly thematized that the novel becomes the story of their mutual constitution—such comforting structures as bildungsroman, though they appear now and then, prove themselves red herrings before long.

The strange contradictions attending visions of "endless moving platforms" mark moments where the very image of uninterrupted flow causes pause, and reveal underground transit as a vehicle for the novel to name itself as a communications system. As with *Call It Sleep*'s "endless corridor," the moving platform thematizes communication as a process that, once set in motion, works to keep that motion going.[79] This is the novel's familiar world of communication and sociality. As the third rail makes visible the mediality of these texts, or their own self-description as communicative objects, connectivity as such operates as something to which the narratives both are drawn and from which they recoil.

I have been discussing the novel's mediality by way of its communication systems, and more precisely, by looking at how communication is figured in the making-visible of infrastructure. As it surfaces in these texts, infrastructure in its most everyday forms operates as an index of modern communication processes, and its visibility provides an occasion for the novel to contemplate and continue its own communication. Infrastructure materially encodes connectivity as a basic presupposition of modern sociality. Whether clogged, crumbling, or a target of investment, when infrastructure becomes visible it indicates that something in the relation between things and persons is at stake. It also indicates that something in the social forms it produces, irritates, and describes is irreducible to its materiality.

Infrastructure becomes the particular flavor of modernity in which these texts situate themselves, and the turn to infrastructural systems rather than traditional, technical media (such as print, typewriters, telegraphy, or film) to indicate their own mediality and give it shape becomes a routine medial gesture for these novels, even as the consequences for that gesture are anything but routine. These moments point to the insistent figuring of communication in the conduit structures of infrastructure during a time currently recognized as dominated by a "wireless imagination."[80] They suggest why after all, in an age of wireless transmission—the novels I have discussed in this chapter were published between 1925 and 1940—the "channel" reasserts itself so forcefully as a figure for communication, and why is it so often blocked. The resulting change takes place in how we think of novels themselves and modern American novels in particular, which become networks that we can look at as we do the pipelines of modern infrastructure.

3 THE FLU AND THE MEDIA, OR CONTAGION 1918

There's something the matter with me, Oh Gee,
Something the matter with me.

—"The Influenza Blues"

IN 1918 INFRASTRUCTURAL SYSTEMS across the United States began to shut down. They did so to avoid a common threat: the transmission of an influenza virus that was quickly reaching global pandemic status. Although this shutdown included the expected suspension of public transit and other systems involving the bodily proximity of individuals, it also extended to the postal and telephone systems and to other mass-media outlets involved in communication without bodily co-presence and without, it would seem, an immediate danger of contagion.

On the one hand, this otherwise counterintuitive inclusion of message carriers with body carriers as infrastructure happens by subjecting both to suspension in an effort to prevent the spread of a viral menace (counterintuitive, that is, before the poets of contemporary electronic communications condemn the complex relations between the virus and communications infrastructure to unexamined metaphor). This inclusion, or mutual indication of modes of being infrastructural, should by now be familiar enough: as we have seen with the formalization of communication through blocked and too-open infrastructure in novels like *Native Son, Manhattan Transfer,* and *Call It Sleep,* the explicit gathering of physical and informational infrastructure by the protocols of containment throughout the epidemic also becomes a self-description of communication. What starts to look like an unsurprising similarity of virus and message transmission is registered by a constellation of novels that take up the epidemic in its wake, and seems built in to the structure of the epidemic itself. These influenza novels, in addition to engaging the formal dynamics of communication that I have been describing in relation to social and infrastructural blockage, take the somewhat strange status of communication in the time of influenza seriously by testing out its forms on themselves. Moreover, what emerges in novels that take up the problem of representing a historical phenomenon that itself put pressure on the status of available forms of communication is a sense that this pressure also applies to the historical work these novels can do and the forms of communication with which they engage self-reflexively as novels.

In this chapter I will discuss how, in part because of these reflexive dynamics of communication that it instantiates, the 1918 influenza takes on the properties of media in novels that describe it. Texts like Willa Cather's 1922 novel *One of Ours* or Katherine Anne Porter's later work *Pale Horse, Pale Rider* (1939) not only thematize the flu and the media together, drawing attention to their mutual relation, but formalize them as contagious processes. In addition, they encode contagion in space, not only as a problem of relation, proximity, and perspective, but also as a quality of the architectures that house, produce, and reflect these relations. By presenting the historical fact of the flu in this way, in which it both describes the media situation of the fictional world and its historical referents *and* operates formally as media, these novels provide a self-referential account of the structures and limitations of historical communication in the specific case of the flu, and raise broader questions about the kinds of pressures a formal media history places on historical narratives and their disciplinary expectations.

I will be outlining the processes by which influenza functions as media in the fiction following the epidemic, but a context for that transformation during the time of the epidemic itself involves a version of the reverse: the transformation of some technical media into the flu. One prominent example is the telephone, which became a visible carrier of influenza in 1918. Using the telephone also meant catching the flu, transmitting the flu, and preventing the pandemic's containment. It also meant reframing each of these actions—catching, transmitting, or containing contagion—as forms of communication. While readily available theories of hygiene cautioned against sharing telephone receivers with other potential carriers,[1] more was at stake than the possibility of catching something left behind by the telephone's previous user. In several cities, local officials and the telephone companies themselves urged people to avoid using the telephone whenever possible during the height of the influenza outbreaks.[2] This was in part because so many telephone operators were out with the flu, but also because the epidemic highlighted what Friedrich Kittler has described as a change in the "aesthetics of reception" in the discourse network of 1900 that shifted the focus away from a "myth of two souls or consciousnesses" participating in communication to something else.[3] Taking stock of the forms of reception available to telephone users during an outbreak of influenza requires an account of communication that similarly dispenses with a model of transmission between two interiors. Although all that the action of transmission implies—sending, receiving, or that there is some particulate matter of germ or information that can be sent or received—points to a logical link between the communication of diseases or words between persons, the ways that the technical media become contagious in the epidemic defy the logic of transmission. Instead, receivers in this system are constituted as such not by what they receive, but by their capacity to do so. What you might have caught if you used the telephone in 1918 was a very modern, uncomfortable sense of your own permeable sociability. That, and the flu.

Controversies surrounding telephone use provide one instance of how the influenza made structures of modern sociality visible where they should perhaps have been unexpected: in the communication technologies that dispense with bodily proximity. However, considering that cities all over the United States allowed their inhabitants to enter public spaces only if their mouths were covered with blank white sheets (usually taking the form of gauze masks), encoding the process of contagion in mediated forms of communication is not altogether strange. In a published volume of her letters, a student at the University of California, Berkeley, summarized her experience of contagious sociality during the epidemic as a subtle shift of everydayness, in which mask-wearing becomes both symbolic of and essential for the continued functioning of institutions:

> Don't worry about me catching the influenza. The kids call it the *Floo* or the *Flooey*. It seems to have gone all over the country. We've been expecting to have them close the University, or at least make all the non-military students stop. But instead of that we are going to have to wear a sort of mask made of gauze that goes on over your nose & mouth—craziest looking things. They bro't some into the office this morning, & we all three put them on. Dean Hart dictated thro' his. It certainly looked funny. Even President Wheeler wears one.[4]

Here, as before, it is not simply the case that communication travels through the masks as the transmission of particles or even germs, or that the masks could somehow prevent communication from happening. The masks themselves, it seems, have something to say. These overlapping communications, in addition, show a phenomenon at work in the epidemic that anticipates what Thacker and Galloway locate in the contemporary material culture surrounding public health crises and bioterrorism: "With such systems, we see the layering of different networks on top of each other. Communication is deployed to combat contagion. Distribution of patient records, travel advisories, distribution and delivery of vaccines, identification of the disease-causing agent, selected quarantine: *an information network is used to combat a biological network.*"[5]

A culture of contagion emerges around multiple modalities of communication during the influenza epidemic and in its aftermath, signaling that the representational significance of both infectious disease and communications media shifts as a result of their intensified proximity to each other. In Figure 15, some of the implications of rendering technologies of nonpresence contagious under these alternate laws of proximity start to become clear. In this image, the typist gazes at the sheet of paper, but she does so in a double sense: her mask engages her in a reflective relationship with the paper on which she types, and it shifts the loop of looking to an exchange between the two sheets, locked in reference to each other. It is as if she types on her own screen. It is also as if the mask implies that there is something contagious about the paper on which she types, or the writing machine itself. The face she presents to the technical media is plainly, and almost horrifyingly, a reflection of the face presented to her by the technical media. Of course, this typist is also bound up in a long history of female operators transforming both the machines and discourse networks with which they interact,[6] which renders the potential uncanniness of her mask, operating as a wearable symbol of the relationships between body and apparatus, somewhat routine. But these are, in addition, some of the routine relations made visible by the influenza. They are also the contagious relations of people and paper to which the novels I will describe enjoy a privileged access via their deployment of the influenza. The flu, for these texts, marks out the contours of media relationality, and the adoption of the properties of contagion by communications technologies throughout the epidemic represents a condition that makes the relationship between the flu and the media, as it emerges in the novels that describe the epidemic, a possibility.

I have been describing a situation in which the contagious attributes of media systems were peculiarly literalized or concretized during the 1918 influenza epidemic as members of the class of technical media. Devices such as telephones and typewriters, but in addition newspapers and other communications media, became influenza carriers because they were seen to be contagious in a way that could not

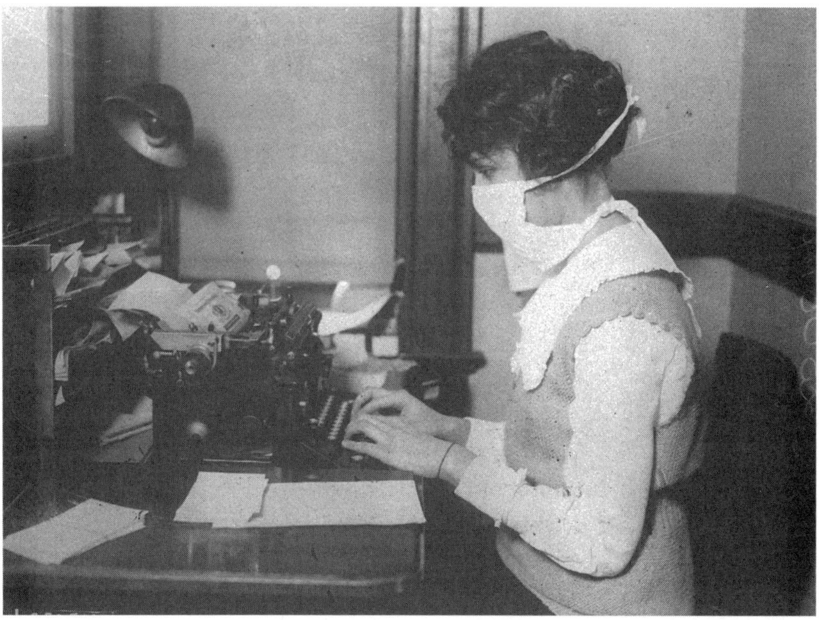

Figure 15. Typist at work during the influenza epidemic. "Typist wearing mask, New York City, October 16, 1918," from the collection "The Deadly Virus: The Influenza Epidemic of 1918," record number 165-WW-269E-16. Courtesy of the National Archives and Records Administration.

be contained by the metaphoric register. That is, they became media in a double sense—the overt linking of viral and message transport (see Figures 16, 17, and 18) that accompanied the rendering-contagious of these media is but one aspect of a larger process at work, one that would be taken up, tested, and transformed by the observational techniques of novels describing the state of contagion in 1918. When the flu and the media begin to indicate each other in the fiction that describes them, they do so as processes, not things: contagion becomes the form through which the flu and the media are thematized together and renamed. It also describes their relationship.

Cultures of Congestion

When novels like *Manhattan Transfer* or the *U.S.A.* trilogy provide an account of the relationship between bodies and the infrastructure connecting them, they also texture their accounts with a cluster of figures that do similar work. Although it may be unsurprising to find figurative associations of organic and infrastructural systems in any modern novel

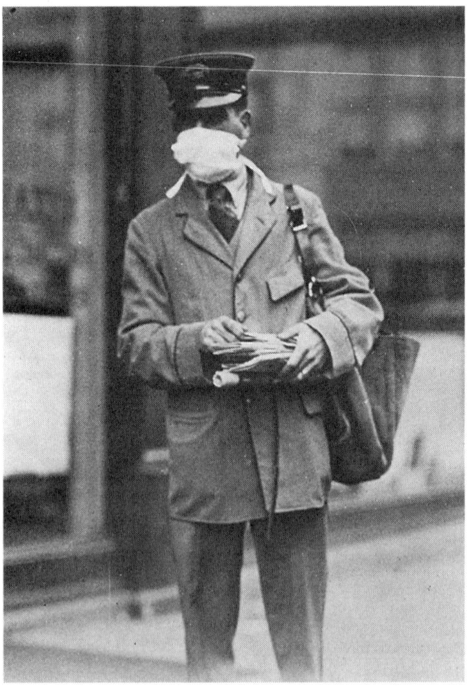

Figure 16. Message transport. "Lettercarrier in New York wearing mask for protection against influenza, New York City, October 16, 1918," from the collection "The Deadly Virus: The Influenza Epidemic of 1918," record numbers 165-WW-269B-15, 165-WW-269B-11. Courtesy of the National Archives and Records Administration.

Figure 17. Message transport. “Street car conductor in Seattle not allowing passengers aboard without a mask, 1918,” from the collection “The Deadly Virus: The Influenza Epidemic of 1918,” record numbers 165-WW-269B-15, 165-WW-269B-11. Courtesy of the National Archives and Records Administration.

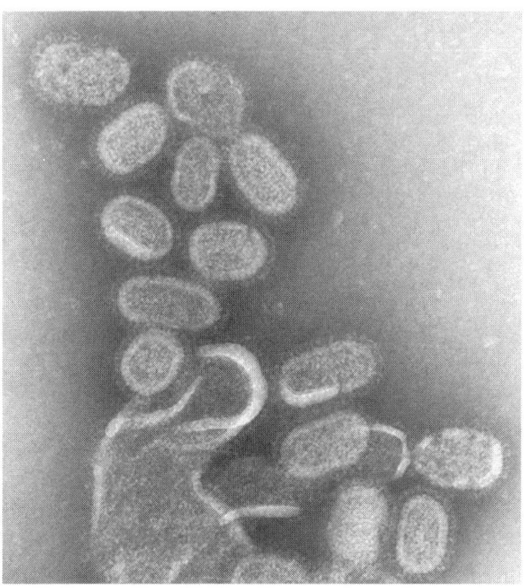

Figure 18. Recreated 1918 Influenza Virons. Courtesy of the Centers for Disease Control. Photo by Cynthia Goldsmith.

concerned with, say, the connective "arteries" traveled in daily life, the influenza epidemic renders these images and associations much more fraught. In *U.S.A.,* for example, the otherwise familiar urban metaphor of congestion seems much less so. As part of the text's spatial idiom, congestion in *U.S.A.* takes place as the piling of paper and commingling of bodies in multiple forms of passageway. But there is another side to this congestion, one that overtly entails bodily systems in its processes. Dos Passos employs the perhaps expected organic systems of the body in his discussions of city streets, sewers, and architectural interiors—respiratory, limbic, and digestive, to name a few—and these figurations start to double back on themselves within the spaces they describe. Take, for example, the "Camera Eye" narrator's trip to the Capitol: "and whispering behind the door of the visitors' gallery and the dead air and a voice rattling under the glass skylights and desks slammed and the long corridors full of the dead air and our legs would get very tired and I thought of the starlings on the grass and the long streets full of dead air and my legs were tired."[7] In this short exercise in repetition with a difference, the gallery, the corridors, and the streets fill with the same "dead air" in a passage that refuses to pause for breath. In the preceding chapter I discussed the doubling of ventilation systems in Dos Passos's *Manhattan Transfer,* and here in *U.S.A.* the rattles and whispers of voices refer also to the respiration of street and hall, and they similarly break down. For architect Rem Koolhaas, this is very much the goal and condition of the grid, the street and the hall, and when he describes a "Culture of Congestion" as being "the real enterprise of Manhattan's architects," he points to the ways in which spatial forms make themselves known as breathing systems through their illnesses.[8]

Discourses surrounding infrastructure rarely stray from the paradoxical logics of disease. As Priscilla Wald points out in her study of outbreak narratives and disease emergence, "contagion in general was a fact of, as well as a metaphor for, life in the crowded conditions of urban spaces."[9] Wald's attention to the figurative allure of contagion is not unfamiliar to the range of work that investigates what happens to fiction when its characters get sick. When René Girard, for example, announces in his literary history of contagion that "the medical plague has become a metaphor for the social plague; it belongs to what we call literature," he also points to its reflexive properties.[10] The proposed "literariness" of plagues lies in their capacity to instance the strange materiality of metaphor, and to demonstrate how the form of a trope or theme itself can be seen as immanent to the thing formalized or thematized. In these terms, the appearance of the 1918 influenza as a topic of fiction provides an occasion to observe its mediality, or the process of its thematization as process, in a local, material context. And what's more, this double movement of figuration attached to the flu is also operative as the modern form of sociality made visible by the outbreak. Luhmann deals in this aspect of contagion when he describes, somewhat uncharacteristically, the functions of social systems by way of figurations of illness. But when he claims that "the communication of contradiction, controversy, and conflict seems to function as a kind of *immune system* of the social system," immunity works not as metaphor generally understood, but function itself—a property and description of the continued functioning of communicative sociality.[11]

What this means for the communicative dynamics I have been discussing in infrastructure as it appears in the work of Dos Passos and others is that descriptions of blocked and free-flowing modalities of connection take the metaphoric cluster of contagion very seriously and encode its form in spatial representations such as architectural structures, position, and point of view. Contagion becomes more than fact, and more than metaphor—it is the condition of the media in these texts. *Manhattan Transfer*'s Jimmy Herf dramatizes this when he thinks, "As I sit here . . . print itches like a rash inside me. I sit here pockmarked with print."[12] Herf's imagined print virus, however, does more than pathologize the relations between human and print characters: it exposes their formal logic. Communications systems in the novel both compete with and refer to one another, and they are catching: "From the outer offices came the sound of typewriters and voice. From outside came the long continuous tapping of riveters at work on a new building."[13] Narrative sympathy between space and media short-circuits their separate categorizations.

Contagion is, more specifically, "the communication of disease from body to body by contact direct or mediate."[14] After the nineteenth-century popularization of the germ theory of disease, this would imply a clear model of transmission, with a focus on the thing being "communicated." But as a concept contagion also circulated widely in the early twentieth century as the Chicago School's formalization of "social contagion," a more process- than message-based movement.[15] When, at the end of *U.S.A.*, "people [keep] away from each other as if to avoid some contagion," what they are trying to avoid is infection by both disease and sociality itself, and in the novels, avoidance of either is not an option.[16] The disease in question, the "Spanish Influenza," reconfigures social relation and describes models of transmission with which the narrative grapples. As a topic, the influenza never strays far from its etymological roots in "influence," as if the most contagious qualities of the virus must reside in its will to reproduce itself rather than the information (albeit genetic) being duplicated. Congestion and contagion point to the two sides of communication I have been discussing in reference to infrastructure—blockage and connectivity—and offer them a peculiar embodiment.

It is perhaps to be expected that the influenza epidemic appears among the extensive coverage *U.S.A.* provides of the war years. After all, more than fifty million people died worldwide from the virus and its complications, far more than in the war itself.[17] And the trilogy is hardly alone in the canon of major modernist novels in providing such coverage of influenza related to the war: one need think only of Clarissa Dalloway's doubling of Septimus Warren Smith's shell shock with her own wartime illness, the flu, in Virginia Woolf's *Mrs. Dalloway* to find treatments of the topic.[18] The flu floats through several of *U.S.A.*'s narrative perspectives, but like Clarissa Dalloway's flu, points to something of a different order than the faithful representation of personal or collective suffering. In a Newsreel section, "persistent talk of peace is an unsettling factor and the epidemic of influenza has deterred country buyers from visiting the larger centers," and in a Camera Eye depiction of an influenza ward, "the barrelvaulted room all smells fever and whitewash."[19] *U.S.A.*'s multiple carriers of the flu point out not only the persistence of the virus as a social and historical marker, but that something else might be at work as well.

At work in the trilogy's most extended treatment of the outbreak is a curious circuit of communication technologies and processes. When Mary French gets off a train to meet her father, a doctor who has "wired" her to let her know that he "got wind" that Mary's mother had been infected by influenza, he warns her to avoid the many lives of the "tricky" contagion: "It's the relapses that kill in this business."[20] The relapse, or the flu's reflexive turn, operates as a case study in novelistic communication. The flu, then, becomes a way for the novel to describe itself as a communication network operating among materially overlapping communication networks. Mary's father emphasizes this fact when he requires Mary to wear a gauze mask over her mouth to work in his office, though which she must answer another technology of communicative presence and absence, the telephone. Through the flu, the *U.S.A.* novels foreground communication and thematize it.[21] Another character, Charley Anderson, witnesses this firsthand while on a train: "Charley held out his hand for the telegram, and standing in the swaying aisle read the strips of letters pasted on the paper: DOWN WITH FLU WIRE ME ADDRESS SEE YOU NEXT WEEK JOE."[22] The train, the aisle, the telegram's strips of letters, the paper, and ultimately the flu all begin to indicate each other in this short passage, and it seems appropriate that Charley feels ill and disoriented when he steps off the train shortly after reading his message.

Manhattan Transfer also stages the "situation" of the war and the flu through mediation. It is important to note that, in a novel temporally organized by the war, its buildup, and its aftermath, the only "war death" it portrays results from the epidemic of influenza. The novel reveals this death when James Merivale returns to his family after the war and the fact of his return contradicts his father's inability to survive the war's duration. Merivale prepares himself to acknowledge this fact with a brief meditation on self-reflection: "On the landing was a mirror. Captain James Merivale stopped to look at Captain James Merivale."[23] Much like *U.S.A.,* the novel's tripartite structure holds the war in its rough center, but unlike the trilogy that center is largely absent. *Manhattan Transfer* presents the war through the mass media and secondhand accounts or memories, and Mr. Merivale's death appears similarly obliquely. When his mother and sister bring up James's new status as "head of the family," their description of his father's ailment avoids naming it directly. "That was something you missed," Mrs. Merivale says, "thousands of people died of it in New York alone."[24] To account for the personal experience of the flu here is to refer (however understated) to body counts in something closer to the vernacular of war reporting.

In the remainder of this chapter, I will take up the ways in which modes of accounting for contagion begin to take on the properties of what they describe. Historians of the 1918–19 influenza epidemic express frustration at what they perceive as the failure of the "forgotten pandemic" to persist in cultural memory, and often turn to a set of novels written in its immediate aftermath to bear that representational burden. However, the best known of these novels, such as Willa

Cather's *One of Ours* and the most celebrated flu narrative, Katherine Anne Porter's *Pale Horse, Pale Rider,* make the topic of the flu very much a vehicle for dealing with contagion as a formalization of the media. To be "one of ours" in these texts means to partake of contagious sociality and its media effects, and to put pressure on the structures of coherence that might define both individuals or the collectivities that claim them. What emerges is a doubling of contagion, as both topic and form, which puts novelistic treatments of influenza in close conversation with fictional pathologizations of media relation as such. The flu novels of the twenties and thirties that I will describe expose an aspect of media culture that circulates in the fiction of these decades as contagion. The concluding discussion of this chapter, therefore, will focus on a novel populated by afflicted persons and publics who do not literally catch the influenza virus, but whose mediations suggest that they share much in common with those who do: Nathaniel West's novel of media sympathies, *Miss Lonelyhearts.*

Influenza Blues

The news media have been remembering the 1918 influenza epidemic, but not only for its perceived parallels with potential mutations of avian flu or other forms of contagious disease. When, in 2005, United States government scientists planned and executed a resurrection of the live flu virus and published its genetic sequence, the resulting furor dealt in the language of both biopower and mechanical reproduction. Amid debates about security levels and biological terrorism, it was with some bemusement that the *New York Times* reflected that "thanks to advances in DNA technology, scientists can now reconstruct new copies of old viruses."[25] To make a new copy of an old virus is also to make a copy of a copying machine, which provokes the fear that such a machine will evade control and copy entire populations to death, and also that its reproduction under the auspices of state control and protection invokes that more precisely Foucauldian notion of a population. But perhaps a description of the reaction to compulsive copying in theses terms misses the point. In his account of the control society, Deleuze himself departs from rather than dwells on these formulations: "There is no need to invoke the extraordinary pharmaceutical productions, the molecular engineering, the genetic manipulations although these are slated to enter the new process. There is no need to ask which is the toughest regime, for it is within each of them that liberating and enslaving forces confront one another."[26] Historians of the flu, however, argue that there is a need to invoke the narrative forms of recording and repeating, and to unpack what they perceive as deficiencies of reporting and memory particular to the 1918 influenza. The laboratory, it seems, does a better job (or perhaps too good a job) of remembering the virus than does the library.

Two of the better-known historians of the 1918 flu, Richard Collier and Alfred W. Crosby, discuss the "puzzling impermanence" of the "forgotten pandemic" in popular and historical memory.[27] What characterizes most discussions of the virus and its effects is heavily dramatized astonishment that something experienced on such a massive scale could also succumb to mass forgetting. When Pete Davies describes "1918's forgotten tragedy," he dwells on details such as bodies "stacked like logs in corridors to the mortuary" to emphasize the nature of past horrors to be considered in our present epidemiological episteme—one in which, according to Crosby, "we are all, so to speak, sitting in the waiting room of an enormous clinic, elbow to elbow with the sick of the world."[28] The statistical and the anecdotal extremes of these histories, which describe the paradoxes of representing mass and individual suffering through competing evidentiary models of universals and particulars, take up the work of mourning that is found missing in other forms of recorded experience of the flu. The influenza blues suffered in histories of the epidemic form a protest of a different order to that expressed by the popular song "The Influenza Blues," which jokes that "If the blues don't kill me the influenza must."[29] The song calls into question the logic of the war and the very idea of taking the flu seriously. For the discussions of the epidemic that I am describing, the only thing worse than mocking the gravity of the illness would be to refuse to acknowledge it.

Critiques of historical reporting on the epidemic extend to media reporting in the epidemic's present. Not only have we failed to represent the flu in its aftermath, the criticism runs, but this is related to the failure of the media to report on it while it was happening. Accounts of the experience and spread of the flu in the United States focus on a lack of coverage in the popular press, which is attributed largely to the national desire to avoid appearing weak in front of a watching wartime enemy. In her examination of the media's role in articulating concepts of disease, Debra Blakely notes that the most recurrent theme in studies of reporting on influenza has been "the reluctance of journalists to report much, if anything, about the severity of the 1918 flu."[30] Moreover, the political dynamics of the wartime press dominate discussions of the flu's nickname, the Spanish Influenza. According to Alfred Jay Bollet, "Suffering in Spain was especially severe, and early reports of the devastation in that country received worldwide publicity, because Spain was not involved in the war and there was no censorship. Because Spain was the first country to have its suffering so widely reported, the disease became generally known as the 'Spanish Influenza.'"[31] But if the news media and other forms of historical record failed to attach to the flu its deserved prominence, and if these omissions can potentially be unpacked in history as a symptom of the media themselves, what of the other potential archives? Is there nowhere to turn for an accurate and sympathetic portrayal of mass suffering with individual consequences? From what old copy does a study of the influenza turn to make new copies?

I am talking, of course, of novels, to which histories of the flu turn to bear the disease's representational burden. For Crosby, this was the particular responsibility of the American modernists, many of whom experienced the flu firsthand: "It is especially puzzling that among those Americans who let the pandemic slip their minds were many members of that group of supposedly hypersensitive young people who were to create some of the greatest masterpieces of American literature, i.e., 'the lost generation' for so many of whom World War I, the other great killer of the era, was the central experience of their lives. (By the way, Gertrude Stein, author of that pitying title, drove an ambulance in France during the pandemic.)"[32] Because authors such as Fitzgerald, Faulkner, and Hemingway were each directly affected by influenza outbreaks (in each case in relation to their involvement with the war), Crosby expects the flu to hold a prominent place in their works of fiction. But this is not a simple case of placing the demand of a kind of biographical realism on the novel. The literary illness narrative is required to be a transmission engine for sympathy, to mediate between the statistical and the anecdotal to represent experience in a way that history cannot. In an article dealing with the memorialization of disease in American culture, addressed to literary scholars, historian of medicine Margaret Humphreys argues for the primacy of the literary as the form best suited to transmit "the emotive power of contagion, epidemics, and the personal experience of enduring them." Works of literature, she claims, "often convey the emotion and fear that surround disease better than many historians can."[33]

This may be true. But what it looks like in fiction offering the direct treatment of the experience of suffering resulting from the flu demanded by these accounts suggests that to "convey the emotion and fear that surround disease" better than the historians might be a mixed blessing. Crosby turns to Thomas Wolfe and Katherine Anne Porter as the "great exceptions" to the literary policy of ignoring the epidemic, and points to their biographical engagement with the flu as the force behind their fiction: "They had no choice but to grant the pandemic due recognition because it struck too close to their hearts to be forgotten."[34] I will be complicating the stakes of Porter's treatment of the flu in more detail shortly. But *Look Homeward, Angel,* presented by Crosby as a "barely fictionalized" witnessing of one of the "chief traumas" of Wolfe's life, offers a version of what "due recognition" of the flu might comprise. Toward the end of the novel, the protagonist suffers from his brother's attack of influenza far more than the unconscious patient does: "Within Eugene, as he paced restlessly up and down the hall or prowled through the house a-search for some entrance he had never found, a bright and stricken thing kept twisting about like a trapped bird. This bright thing, the core of him, his Stranger, kept twisting its head about, unable to look at horror, until at length it gazed steadfastly, as if under a dreadful hypnosis, into the eyes of death and darkness."[35] The narrative transmission of the flu as experience in this instance still operates via a strange attachment to pity as another form of such transmission. Eugene's "bright thing" or "Stranger" is no angel of history. Rather, this near-parodic expression of inward turn made via sympathetic encounter demonstrates that perhaps even the most affectively charged (or in this instance, perhaps the most banal) fictional records of the 1918 influenza also refuse to generalize the particular afflictions to which they refer.

Instead, it makes more sense to conceptualize affinities between literary and viral forms more as Artaud does in his discussion of theater and the plague in *The Theater and Its Double,* which radically links viral and literary forms. For Artaud, the relationship between theater and plague hinges on degrees of relation itself, and more specifically the double relation. He demands that "first of all we must recognize that the theater, like the plague, is a delirium and is communicative."[36] The likeness of theater to plague includes both symptom and operation, redefining illness and genre as constituted by both. This likeness also deals in contagion: "For if the theater is like the plague, it is not only because it affects important collectivities and upsets them in an identical way. In the theater as in the plague there is something both victorious and vengeful: we are aware that the spontaneous conflagration which the plague lights wherever it passes is nothing else than an immense liquidation."[37] Artaud's simile encompasses both terms in their effects. And while his analysis attends to the historical specificities of space, illness, and genre, he shows that what is most productive in a discussion of literary form and viral event is precisely the literariness of that relationship. In addition, the analysis of likeness as both liquidation and gathering of collectivities highlights another dimension of the distinction crisis brought out by flu narratives, and the medial interests of their historical situation. If it is through the epidemic that the uncanny contagion of modern sociality—and its attendant dismantling of coherent persons and collectivities—makes itself known and dramatizes modes of contact and transmission, one result will be that characterizations of that sociality take on symptoms of their own.[38] In the literary environments of the plague of 1918, the double relation is most specifically that between the novel and the flu, and the form of that double relation is explicitly medial.

A commonplace of the influenza as it appears as a topic in historical and fictional narratives is its proclivity for recursion. Most treatments of the flu take into account the basic paradox that the infrastructural systems of modernity both prevent and transmit the virus, or make its management and production possible: the flu is a social disease all the way down.[39] Nor are they unaware of the literal and metaphorical overlap at work in the deployment of phrases such as "media of dissemination" to describe urban and global transit networks in relation to the epidemic.[40] But more pressure can be placed on what it means to think about the dynamics of media and flu in the novel. One account of the place of Katherine Anne Porter's *Pale Horse, Pale Rider* among the forms of flu narrative circulating in the epidemic's aftermath highlights a type of media work done by the text, which is described is "one of the twentieth century's masterpieces of short fiction, but it is something in addition to that for the historian. It is the most accurate depiction of American society in the fall of 1918 in literature. It synthesizes what is otherwise only obtainable by reading hundreds of pages of newspapers."[41] Although their operations may be of a different order, it is the relationships of novels and newspapers exposed by the flu that I would like to take up now in relation to Willa Cather's treatment of the flu and the media in *One of Ours* and then in Porter's text. By examining how the novels thematize the flu and the media together, I will show that the formal doubling of their contagious operations both illuminates and challenges the place of the 1918 influenza outbreak in literary history.

Germ Warfare and Plague Theater

Willa Cather's 1922 novel *One of Ours,* excoriated by Hemingway for its representation of the First World War, has a far more subtle engagement with the figuration of history than its detractors—presumably more authoritative for their access to experience—have room for in restricted definitions of realistic expression. Cather's text is full of half-complete narratives attached to its protagonist, Claude Wheeler, and several of its characters. These narratives, including Claude's movement from farm to university, his marriage, and his life as a soldier, all end abruptly: he returns to the farm, his marriage falters (resulting in the half-complete narrative that his wife, Enid, initiates for herself when she departs), and he dies at the front. Amid these frustrated trajectories, however, sits a set piece staged aboard a troop carrier crossing the Atlantic whose passengers begin to pass the 1918 virus among themselves. The double containment of ship and story in this interlude also encodes the novel's persistent concern with overlapping transmissions, including news broadcasts, sympathetic feelings (or at times, sentiment), and narratives themselves.

A version of influenza blues appears in *One of Ours:* the narrator, setting up the final series of troop and trench movements that will result in the protagonist's "heroic" death, remarks that "the German army still held the north and east of France, and no one could say how much vitality was left in that sprawling body."[42] But this narrator, speaking with overt knowledge of the war's outcome, also knows of many factors already at work on that particular body. One bodily affliction that would be known to the observer but not the observed actors would be the reported outbreak of influenza among German troops as the war was drawing to a close. And in *One of Ours,* influenza can never be isolated from its associative proclivities. The popular song "The Influenza Blues" involves the flu and vitality on their metaphoric as well as more literal registers:

> America knows it's true, So true,
> The Allies know it well too.
> The Flu it come, From the Hun, Gee Whiz, What shall we do,
> The Kaiser said we'll give the Yanks the Flu,
> But poor old Fritzie Bill he got it too.[43]

What the song's Allies and America know is also what the narrator of *One of Ours* knows, that something about the influenza makes the relationship between individual and political bodies resonate in the context of the war. They also know that flu, like metaphoric transfer, likes to share. In a novel perhaps best known for its complex characterizations of intimacy, it is befitting that influenza and its attendant modalities of contagion circulate prominently as figures attached to descriptions of social or collective formations.

Within *One of Ours,* however, figuration appears as the mass media. For example, after a long ocean transport from New York to the French ports, a company of soldiers experiences an object lesson in the subtle seductions of mass-mediated metaphor as they view the untorn fields of "flowery France" through the window of a train taking them to an inland training camp. When they recognize the red flowers adorning the countryside as poppies, a figurative dissonance emerges: "They had supposed that poppies grew only on battle fields, or in the brains of war correspondents."[44] The soldiers' distrust of figurative war reporting does not prevent them from adopting their associative power; the soldiers are still surprised to encounter poppies that have not grown from and embodied the blood of dead soldiers. This is a simple move that reads something like self-recognition in reverse, but it is also a pervasive one in the novel.

A somewhat unkind portrait of an elderly household laborer with dubious literacy, Mahailey, demonstrates that what it means to make a figure is very much at stake. Mahailey participates in Claude Wheeler's preparation for war and decision to enlist by sharing and discussing newspaper reports with Claude and his mother. In one such gathering around the papers, Mahailey contributes clippings of newspaper cartoons "illustrating German brutality," and we are told that "to her they were all photographs,—she knew no other way of making a picture."[45] Mistaking illustration for photograph requires moving between representational categories. But the novel is more interested in the mistake itself than in the boundaries of these categories. Moreover, photographs themselves do not escape the pitfalls of interpretation for Mahailey. Her vigilant attachment to media representations of the war most often means reading photographs: "Pictures of soldiers in gas masks puzzled her; gas was something she hadn't learned about in the Civil War, so she worked it out for herself that these masks were worn by the army cooks, to protect their eyes when they were cutting up onions."[46] Reading photographs for Mahailey, much like reading newspaper reports for others in the novel, involves participating in processes of fiction and figuration that count on the category mistake.

Another possible mistaken interpretation of the gas mask would be its at-home equivalent, the gauze mask that was legally required attire in many American cities, protection from a different threat. The equation of war technology and civilian technology, however, or gas mask and flu mask, is not entirely inappropriate in the context of a novel that stages an outbreak of influenza on an Atlantic transport ship, in which the flu marks the transition between home and battlefront.[47]

Figure 19. Law enforcement officers in masks. Courtesy of the National Archives and Records Administration.

The influenza in *One of Ours* gives a structure to the problems that might attend too-easy transition, and marks these problems as endemic to the novel form as well. When the outbreak hits, the troop ship announces itself as a moving synecdoche of a social system. Although this synecdoche is commonplace, being onboard an encapsulation of the social appears less welcome when people begin to fall ill. When Claude takes his cabin-mate to the ship hospital, the doctor turns several isolated bouts of illness into a collective affliction, reported as his proclamation that "they might as well face the facts; a scourge of influenza had broken out on board, of a particularly bloody and malignant type.*" That does not, however, stop the individuals on board from trying to protect their permeable borders, for "everybody was a little frightened. Some of the officers shut themselves up in the smoking-room, and drank whiskey and soda and played poker all day, as if they could keep contagion out."[48] Contagion operates here as both *contagium,* imagined as the moving germ, but also as the condition of being susceptible to receiving transmissions. It is fitting as well that these officers operate "as if" such defenses were possible, building in something like a shared fiction. The acknowledgment of the epidemic, moreover, calls precise attention to the relationship of the fictional account to a historical real. The asterisk following the influenza's announcement directs attention to the novel's only textual departure from the narrative, and provides the following information as a footnote: "*The actual outbreak of influenza on transports carrying United States troops is here anticipated by several months." That is, remember that the influenza outbreak described here is a work of fiction.

But why, of all of the novel's historical referents, is it the influenza epidemic in particular that must be identified as fiction? Why draw attention to the loosening of historical moorings that must be performed in order to include the epidemic within the novel's timeline? The flu, it seems, offers a particular payoff, and for better or for worse one central to the fictional project of *One of Ours.* The influenza outbreak, narrated as a set piece containing the duration of the transatlantic voyage, participates in a longer tradition of contagion narratives foregrounding the similarity of viral logic to narrative logic.[49] The flu allows the novel to draw attention to itself as a medium, and a fictional one at that. Influenza, breaking out on an ocean voyage, thematizes the international transit networks for moving bodies, goods, and news as bound up in the process of novel making. It also points to the uncertain topographies of communication, access, and intimacy that will be at stake once the ship reaches the shore. The architecture of the ship itself thematizes communication further via the outbreak, for not only are passageways between enclosed spaces implicated in the contagious spread of the virus, but also information about the epidemic must always be communicated in the ship's corridors. The ship's physician often steps into the corridor to provide information regarding a patient to Claude, but not to the patient himself. Corridors in *One of Ours* become the flu's emblematic circulation space: they transmit information in a way that refers to their own status as passages ("From the end of the corridor Claude had heard the frightful sounds that came from his throat, sounds like violent vomiting, or the choking rattle of a man in strangulation"), but they also do more than that. The ship's corridors come to stand in for contagion itself: "The corridors of the vessel had the smell of death about them. Doctor Tureman said it was always so in an epidemic; patients died who, had they been isolated cases, would have recovered."[50] What emerges is not a simple example of the social construction of disease, to which novels contribute, but a case where the flu operates in the novel as the construction of the social.[51] It is no accident that in *One of Ours* "natural death" by contagion, and the sociality it implies, is a more frightening specter than military violence.

Instead of compensating for a failure of the media to report on the flu while it was happening, Cather's novel prefers to report on the contagion of the media. And although the influenza epidemic may not have dominated the national press, or may have even been suppressed as a threat to security or morale, it found a home in reports of the media on the media. As Richard Koszarski has pointed out in his analysis of flu reporting in the trade journal *Moving Picture World,* there was no shortage of discussion of the impact of the flu on the developing motion picture industry, as long as the industry was discussing itself.[52] Reporting on the flu and movies in these accounts focuses on what everyone already knew about the theater and the plague: that the first thing to close in the face of contagion is the theater, or as the case may be, the movie house. Many articles debate the use of masks and staggered seating in the movie theaters, and when *Moving Picture World*'s "Rubbernecking in Filmland" columnist declares, "Filmland is full of gloom and germs. Everyone you meet has a different cure for the Flue, . . . and in spite of this, everyone you meet has either just gotten over an attack of the Flue, or is just getting down with it,"[53] the irony is not limited to the circulation of ineffective cures. The flu does not simply shut the movie theaters—it reveals that gathering in front of screens is also part of gathering behind them, or that the protection offered by a facial screen in the form of a gauze mask also receives and displays projections.

Reflexively playful flu reporting by the movies on the movies starts to suggest that more dangerous than germs themselves are their ubiquitous communication media. Movie theaters as spaces may trade in contagious proximity, but the contagion is not confined to their physical structures of confinement. Instead, the flu provides an opportunity to make contagion from contagion, or at least recognize that it was there all along. And even in the *Moving Picture World* reports, the movies do not have a monopoly on this maneuver: "We have arrived at the humorous stage of the epidemic," the columnist observes. "The poets have busted loose."[54]

It might be said, then, that Katherine Anne Porter's *Pale Horse, Pale Rider,* approaches the flu with the same circularity of this particular brand of humor. For although the novel receives considerable praise for its sympathetic rendering of the pain of both influenza and war, its treatment of media objects and effects suggests that medial forms of communicative sociality are far more powerful than sympathetic affinities. It, too, deals with the relationship of the theater and the plague and novelizes it: by enclosing its audience in front of a stage rather than a movie screen, the novel dramatizes the medial differences between each genre and form even as it cannibalizes them. The novel's protagonist, Miranda, has been "degraded publicly" to a "routine female job" at the local newspaper, writing theater reviews, after suppressing a story that would shame another woman. Her sympathetic act is met like for like, as she must inhabit a space in which "people were crowding into the aisle," a theater space in which she recognizes the symptoms of such crowding as the symptoms of the flu.[55] After Miranda's illness prevents her both from attending the theater and from occupying her desk at the newspaper office (for she is struck by influenza shortly after her theater trip), she learns that the conditions of crowding have been reversed. "It's as bad as anything can be," she is told. "All the theaters and nearly all the shops and restaurants are closed, and the streets have been full of funerals all day and ambulances all night."[56] The emptying of theaters and other conspicuously public spaces corresponds with the filling of the transport channels between those spaces.

Despite its interest in aisles and theater closings, *Pale Horse, Pale Rider* is not a story of the theater and the plague. Miranda, after all, attends the theater as a reporter, and it is the shift between spatial and medial contagion that the novel's treatment of the influenza tracks. This operates within the structure of the newspaper office as well as the newspaper itself, made perfectly clear in Miranda's friend Mary Townsend's nominal movement between the self and the social: "Her column was called Ye Towne Gossyp, so of course everybody called her Towney. Miranda and Towney had a great deal in common, and liked each other."[57] By taking on the society pages, Towney takes on the town itself, and by standing in for the society whose gossip she captures, she seems to demonstrate a penchant for being "in common." Towney and Miranda don't just like each other, but are like each other, and it is into this structure of slippage that Miranda falls when she catches the flu. Towney emphasizes this when she offers a newsworthy theory of contagion. After lampooning reports that influenza germs have been transported via transatlantic sea travel, she finds an alternate version in another town's gossip:

> "They think the germs were sprayed over the city—it started in Boston, you know—and somebody reported seeing a strange, thick, greasy-looking cloud float up out of Boston Harbor and spread slowly all over that end of town. I think it was an old woman who saw it."
>
> "Should have been," said Chuck.
>
> "I read it in a New York newspaper," said Towney; "so it's bound to be true."
>
> Chuck and Miranda laughed so loudly at this that Bill stood up and glared at them. "Towney still reads the newspapers," explained Chuck.[58]

Flu gossip does not need the germ theory of disease, for the generalized miasma implied by Towney's description of a "greasy-looking cloud" preempts the particulate. But this is reported gossip, and that gossip is in turn newspaper reporting. Moreover, to believe in the newspapers is patently ridiculous even if you happen to work for one, perhaps especially so. The flu works as a giant game of telephone, and the message is continually corrupted by the circuits through which it travels.

Whether regarding the flu or the war, the newspaper's role as information provider works as an often-terrible joke. After Adam mentions to Miranda that "men are dying like flies out there"—dying, that is, not in battle but because of "this funny new disease"—he teases her with "Oh, there won't be any more wars, don't you read the newspapers?"[59] Later, when they discuss his life expectancy as a member of a sapping party, this structure persists: "'Just nine minutes,' said Adam; 'I read that in your own newspaper not a week ago.'"[60] The circular motion of the media creates what it describes in these scenes. The newspapers make things real despite the joke, and what's funny about the new disease is that it is subject to the same media logic as the war itself, and both tend toward the same result anyway. It is not that, as several readers of the novel suggest, the flu and the suffering associated with the epidemic symbolize "the pointlessness and horror" of the war.[61] Rather, the uncomfortable similarity of the two makes itself known through the media, and remains locked in tension. The mass media perform a leveling operation on both topics, and in doing so refer back to the social operation of the flu itself, which also regards its separate topics (or persons) with indifference to their individuality.[62] Distinctions between persons look as vulnerable as distinctions between news items.

Architectural technologies of distinction, the walls and corridors marking out such comforting boundaries as inside and outside, take on the properties of sameness in this world of endlessly reflecting contagion and media structures, a world shot through with corridoricity. In the hospitals of *Pale Horse, Pale Rider*, walls, corridors, and persons all reflect one another as blank pages. While Miranda occupies the hospital corridor she participates in this blankness: "The white walls rose sheer as cliffs, a dozen frosted moods followed each other in perfect self-possession down a white lane and dropped one by one into a snowy abyss."[63] Differentiation of self from space appears more difficult when spatial markers of differentiation reflect one another and their affiliated occupants. Although Miranda achieves transfer from the corridor to one of the hospital's so-called private spaces, the situation hardly changes, for "the sheets were folded back, disclosing two speechless men in white, standing, and another speechless man in white, lying." The curtain wall separating patients is revealed to be nothing other than a blank white sheet, which refers to the corridors and to the doctors, whose white drapery in turn refers to the anonymous patient, who then refers back to Miranda. Speechless blankness becomes the novel's preferred description of communication: spaces and persons transfer into each other rather than conducting information. This too describes the novel's early self-identification as a medium, for when the eponymous pale rider regards Miranda "without meaning" in the novel's opening dream sequence, his "blank still stare" evokes not just death but the blank pages from which the narrative must constitute itself.[64]

From which, that is, and through which, for the pages maintain their affinity-producing blankness even as they perform specific mediating functions. That this logic attaches to the influenza in *Pale Horse, Pale Rider* becomes quite apparent in the monitoring of the illness's effects on Miranda's body. Upon her admission to the hospital and its corridors, Miranda's vital signs are read by an intern, one "still quite fresh and dapper in his white coat, though his carnation was withering at the edges," who was "listening to her breathing through a stethoscope, whistling thinly."[65] The strange communication channel of the stethoscope, providing the illusion of access between two interiors, transmits one of two pieces of information. Either Miranda's breathing sounds normal, and she therefore breathes and is like everyone else, or her breathing reveals the symptoms of viral damage due to influenza, which during a pandemic also means she breathes and is like everyone else. Mutual self-regard mediated via the stethoscope: if its paradoxical nature of this regarding wasn't clear enough, the novel offers another image of what it looks like: "Stars gleamed through the window, and Dr. Hildesheim seemed to be gazing at them with no particular expression, his stethoscope dangling around his neck."[66] The doctor's blank stare, reflected back in the gaze of the stars, locates exchange in the disused mediating apparatus hanging from his neck. That apparatus is not required except in reference to itself.

Everybody knows group affiliation can be a very lonely thing, and this holds true for the experience of influenza in Porter's novel. The experience Miranda shares with everyone else somehow avoids being a shared experience. And when her encounters with Adam move from the hallway to the sickroom, or from kind of public to kind of private space, intimacy is precisely what dissolves: "Her eyes followed him about the room, as he did things for her with an absent-minded face." Intimacy dissolves, that is, only to return as contagion, for Adam most likely dies because he has caught influenza from her. The influenza reveals what, for Luhmann, would be the paradox of individuality in a social system comprising communications: "The individual who participates in communication is, in one way or another, simultaneously individualized and de-individualized, that is, standardized or fictionalized."[67] Towney, finally, reminds Miranda that her bout with the flu was also a face-to-face encounter with the communicative topographies of personhood when she tells the newly recovering patient, "You won't recognize yourself in a week."[68] Miranda's illness provides her with a version of self-recognition in the form of both identification (even if as blankness) and alienation, and it should perhaps come as no surprise that the novel presents the recognition of her fictionalization as delirium. Nor should it come as any surprise that the prescription she receives for continuing her recovery, "read your letters, my dear," involves reinscribing that process.

The spatial logic of contagion, then, in *Pale Horse, Pale Rider,* follows only in part the transmission models that would fear permeable architecture. The favorite rhyme of many historical accounts of the epidemic—"I had a little bird / And its name was Enza. / I opened the window / And in-flew Enza"—seems less apropos than the "mutual organization" and "reciprocal topography" invoked in Roger Caillois's description of mimicry.[69] Contagion, like communication, looks less like transmission of discrete packets to discrete individuals and more like a general condition of reciprocality. Miranda reveals her status as a contagious individual to the newspaper office and to the occupants of her building by discussing it on the communal telephone in the corridor. By doing so, she involves communication space with communication technology, and demonstrates her own involvement with a structure of contagion dependent not only on bodily co-presence. Somehow what's catching about her condition is not limited to the proximity of her body to the telephone receiver or to the occupants of other rooms attached to the same corridor. What's catching is in part what has already been caught, and the influenza helps *Pale Horse, Pale Rider* provide it with texture and visibility.

Catch Me If You Can

If the treatments of influenza I have been discussing engage in part what historians claim has been missing from the modern memory of the Great War, they do so with a view to the structures of sociality materialized by the virus. Through the flu, these novels thematize themselves as part of a contagious system of media relations. These novels in effect write themselves through the flu, but the flu then begins to write itself out of the picture. The most contagious aspects of the influenza in the novels I have been describing can be found in the dangerous structures of sociality, sympathy, and publicity invoked in representations of the virus, and its ties to the media and the materialities of communication. This contagion-as-process, or self-thematization of the novel as medium, can take another turn, and apply its reflexive drive to a description of the media themselves as the illness. This is the case for Nathanael West's 1933 *Miss Lonelyhearts,* which diagnoses its own novelness as a reflexive pathology of its media relations. When the novel's Miss Lonelyhearts wonders, "Was he sick? In a great cold wave, the readers of his column crashed over the music,"[70] he highlights these dynamics at work. *Miss Lonelyhearts* also points to the transfer of the flu from media event to media theory that characterizes the flu novels of Cather and Porter, unpacking a concept of mediality that makes contagion explicitly formal.

Miss Lonelyhearts the character coincides with Miss Lonelyhearts the category, and play between the two describes *Miss Lonelyhearts* the novel. Or, as the novel's opening puts it: "The Miss Lonelyhearts of The New York *Post-Dispatch* (Are-you-in-trouble?—Do-you-need-advice?—Write-to-Miss-Lonelyhearts-and-she-will-help-you) sat at his desk and stared at a piece of white cardboard."[71] What it means to be any of these copies of Miss Lonelyhearts depends on occupying a position or address. It also means always being a copy associated with a medium. Miss Lonelyhearts is "the" Miss Lonelyhearts "of" but one paper, but this Miss Lonelyhearts, perhaps like all who occupy that address, dreams of syndication.[72] The Lonelyhearts exchange service enacts a mutual constitution of selves via the newspapers, for reader and writer both operate as individual positions and as categories simultaneously in this formulation. This mutual constitution of defined and distributed selves, their communicability, appears quite at home among epidemiological descriptions of community. But "the materialization of interdependence" often associated with the flu here requires only the mere materiality of reading for its self-awareness.[73]

Plenty of readers and writers get sick in *Miss Lonelyhearts.* Often Miss Lonelyhearts exhibits symptoms of illness after he encounters his readers face-to-face: "Soon after Mrs. Doyle left, Miss Lonelyhearts became physically sick and was unable to leave his room."[74] But even physical symptoms call up a metaphysics of illness tied to Miss Lonelyhearts's odd literalization of an identity crisis, for during the illness described above he turns the language of disease into a meditation on entropy. "The physical world has a tropism for disorder," he thinks. "Keys yearn to mix with change. Mandolins strive to get out of tune. Every order has within it the germ of destruction." Some readers and writers (for Miss Lonelyhearts's readers often constitute themselves as such by writing letters) also get the flu. "Broad Shoulders" writes to Miss Lonelyhearts complaining of romantic and financial trouble tied in part to hospital bills incurred in the wake of her daughter's bout with influenza and her own pneumonia. The context for her description of the flu and illness, however, is the relationship of the physical body to its figurations. "Broad Shoulders" takes pains at the end of her letter to point out that her shoulders, in fact, are not broad ("that is the way I feel about life and me I mean"), and in the context of publicly printed letters, how bodies and persons feel are often at odds with each other. Miss Lonelyhearts ultimately places physical illness in direct service of figurative ills, so that diseases of mind and body become part of the same process. He reflects on this after his fiancée administers to both: "He knew that she believed he did not want to get well, yet he followed her instructions because he realized that his present sickness was unimportant. It was merely a trick by his body to relieve one more profound."[75] Placeholders for physical symptom and figurative ambiguity have trouble holding their places. That is, they double the acts of figuration they describe, and diagnose themselves in the process.

To become ill in *Miss Lonelyhearts* is to play, quite literally, the newspaper game. The editor of the *New York Post-Dispatch,* Shrike, ensures that Miss Lonelyhearts realizes this when he demands that the columnist attend his party. Shrike needs Miss Lonelyhearts at the party because he has invented a game—"Everyman his own Miss Lonelyhearts"—that he claims requires Miss Lonelyhearts to be played. "We will proceed systematically," Shrike says when they arrive in the crowded room of the party with a pile of letters sent to Miss Lonelyhearts that Shrike has stolen from the newspaper office. "First, each of you will do his best to answer one of these letters, then, from your answers, Miss Lonelyhearts will diagnose your moral ills."[76] This game works as more than an exercise in reflexive irony in the novel, for it labels the process of being Miss Lonelyhearts as something that simultaneously diagnoses and is diagnosed. Being Miss Lonelyhearts means receiving, reading, and responding to letters, but those responses function as objects of diagnosis. Stepping into the communication circuit necessarily involves attaining the position of Miss Lonelyhearts and Everyman, and reveals that they just might be the same thing. Diagnostics works here not as the revealing of inward condition from outward symptom, but rather as the reverse: it makes visible the exteriority of the available forms of inwardness in the communication circuit.

Like *Pale Horse, Pale Rider*'s Miranda, Miss Lonelyhearts constantly confronts blank pages: after all, he too claims a journalistic vocation. As in Porter's novel, that blankness also begins to formalize contagion as a media effect via multiple materialities of communication. The page transfers easily to the body's exterior when Miss Lonelyhearts communicates in person rather than in the paper, and is perhaps best exemplified by his editor's deadpan performance: "Although his gestures were elaborate, his face was blank. He practiced a trick used much by moving-picture comedians—the dead pan. No matter how fantastic or excited his speech, he never changed his expression."[77] This short passage engages multiple forms of mimicry, in which Shrike models his face on those projected on movie screens, and those screens in turn reference the blank pages he must fill with a version of expression. It also shows how far a medial engagement can go: in Justus Nieland's reading of the scene, Shrike's face "epitomizes the nature of human nature in West's novel—a human physis so besieged that it has mimetically incorporated the alienated image sphere of mass culture for its very existence."[78] But expression, for Miss Lonelyhearts, is too literary: "At college, and perhaps for a year afterwards, they had believed in literature, had believed in Beauty and in personal expression as an absolute end."[79] Literariness in *Miss Lonelyhearts* describes an absurd belief in both expression and the personal, and in rejecting both, the novel turns instead to a literary world comprising endlessly reflecting media. Through the protocols of these media forms, including an insistent transferability, the persons populating the novel observe themselves. Their observations aggressively engage them in the reproductive compulsion of the media with which they interact.

In his discussion of the negentropic processes of communication, Vilém Flusser gleefully describes the improbable structures developed to store and transmit information as a kind of "dead waste," always condemned to appear only in observation and always perversely oriented toward the solitude and death they work to conceal.[80] Communication media, for Flusser, provide the material means for the self-deception of the social. In *Miss Lonelyhearts,* the observation of these storage and transmission devices often includes a similar double movement: although individuals manage to enter into communicative relation via the media, they observe their relations as violent and dangerous. Readers deploy the newspaper literally as a weapon against the body's other communication organs ("she rolled a newspaper into a club and struck her husband on the mouth with it"), and newspapers also figuratively violate body boundaries. The novel anticipates the reflexive violence of Cronenberg's *Videodrome* by nearly a half century, for "it was as if a gigantic, living Miss Lonelyhearts letter in the shape of a paperweight had been placed on his brain."[81] The self-deceived sociality of *Miss Lonelyhearts,* oddly literalized as communication enacted in violent contact between persons and media, seems aware of its own perversity. This means that transmission serves as a distinctly inadequate description of how communication and its contagious operations work. This is true for a range of modalities of message transport, including postal and transit systems, and the viral version of both.

Tiny self-replicating information packets, the recreated 1918 influenza virons shown earlier work a lot like the letters and persons engaged in masked communication: they seek their own continuation. The transmission of information takes a back seat to the recursive process, and what's catching is the propensity to perpetuate contagious transfer. The repetitive nature of the letters sent and received in *Miss Lonelyhearts* emphasizes the process rather than the message: "And on most days he received more than thirty letters, all of them alike, stamped from the dough of suffering with a heart-shaped cookie knife."[82] These letters, sent to a newspaper columnist whose identity overtly constitutes a position within a category and to a newspaper that calls itself simultaneously "post" and "dispatch," demand the continuation of letter writing. When Miss Lonelyhearts attempts to parse the clamoring multitudes appearing in letterform on his desk and massed on the street, he finds that "no repeated group of words would fit their rhythm and no scale could give them meaning."[83]

Faced with such legibility, Miss Lonelyhearts chooses to pursue empathy instead of interpretive relation. For him, empathy represents an opportunity to achieve unmediated connection, but he fails to realize that empathy also perfectly describes the forms of mediation with which he and his correspondents have been engaged. Several of West's readers turn to this manner of relation as an arbiter of his novels' degrees of success—for example, Tom Cerasulo recently described *Miss*

Lonelyhearts as a more powerful work than several of West's others, including *The Dream Life of Balso Snell,* because "West's savage black humor is present, but so is a new note of empathy, and the result is that we care about the characters in a way we don't in *Balso.*"[84] What empathy itself looks like as a topic in *Miss Lonelyhearts,* however, points to something else at work. Empathy in the novel describes a desire for intersubjective relation that transcends the personal: instead of seeking out vicariously the experience of a distinct other, and occupying that person's place, empathy reveals that what has been sought is identification with another who is just like everyone else. Empathy becomes a pathological identification with a self who, also, is just like everyone else. Empathy is how the persons populating *Miss Lonelyhearts* identify themselves with the social, and recognize their boundedness to the media systems through which the social gathers. In Nieland's account of affect and humor in the novel, he refers to the embedded critique of Miss Lonelyhearts's "project of sympathetic publicity," and locates in the novel's "deadpan affectivity" and West's specific engagements with "modernist anti-sentimentality" a redefinition of the social also implied by the intersections of persons and media forms in the text.[85] This redefinition highlights the aspect of publicness that I have been arguing shifts in the age of contagious mediality, for "with horror," Miss Lonelyhearts faces "an alternative, atypical public without qualities—an inhuman community."[86]

The uncertain relations between insides and outsides of explicitly communicative persons and their alternative publics in the novel become more visible as medial relations. Testing out these boundaries also means testing out the communication media that facilitate movement between them. In *Miss Lonelyhearts,* this appears most clearly when the advice columnist attempts face-to-face interaction with his subscribers. In one such encounter, Miss Lonelyhearts meets the deformed husband of one of his readers in the back room of a speakeasy. Peter Doyle "looked like one of those composite photographs used by screen magazines," and as they sit together, "the strain of wordless communication began to excite them both."[87] Miss Lonelyhearts cannot understand any of the words Doyle attempts to employ as speech, but that kind of interaction matters little among persons inscribed by their media roles, for Doyle then hands Miss Lonelyhearts a Miss Lonelyhearts letter. The letter looks like all of the other letters written to the advice columnist, with the exception of Doyle's final request:

"Please write me an answer not in the paper because my wife reads your stuff."[88] But Miss Lonelyhearts prefers to dispense with writing, and instead grasps Doyle's hand, after theirs had met accidentally under the table, and they sit "silently, hand in hand."[89]

The closest it seems Miss Lonelyhearts can come to putting himself in Mr. Doyle's place is by making contact as direct as possible. This also represents a squaring of Miss Lonelyhearts's earlier attempts at empathetic transference with Mrs. Doyle. She, like her husband, signs her letter to Miss Lonelyhearts with her name, but her letter requests rather than replaces face-to-face communication. "I am not very good at writing," she says in her letter, "so I wonder if I could have a talk with you."[90] The letter seeks as its answer a telephone call, which he makes in the hall and arranges to meet her in person. They eventually rendezvous in his room, and it is as soon as she leaves that he becomes "physically sick" and "unable to leave." Miss Lonelyhearts's interactions with Peter and Fay Doyle demonstrate just how much the methods of message transport are at stake in the communication circuit, and also just how little they convey. *Miss Lonelyhearts* provides a case study in what kinds of recipients populate an epistolary novel whose letters arrive at a news desk. He may become ill after establishing bodily contact in an attempt to achieve some kind of meaningful empathy after his role as columnist addressing a faceless public leaves him feeling alienated, but his "physical" sickness offers an overt manifestation of his mediated condition. That condition is a case of sociality characterized by dedifferentiation, only not the kind Miss Lonelyhearts seeks empathetically.

When his editor presents a series of diagnoses for Miss Lonelyhearts's general malaise, he ends with a double-voiced letter addressed to "Christ Dentist," or "Miss Lonelyhearts of Miss Lonelyhearts," and signs the letter with a reversal of the Lonelyhearts role: "Thanking you very much for a quick reply, I remain yours truly, A Regular Subscriber."[91] When a Miss Lonelyhearts writes a letter to Miss Lonelyhearts, or to a version of his category, he does so as a "regular subscriber." Regular and subscriber here access their multiple associations, for regularity functions in both newspaper time and as a marker of likeness, and subscribers to faith and newspapers become two versions of the same kind of person. Being Miss Lonelyhearts and being a regular subscriber to Miss Lonelyhearts come together in an endless looping that exposes the structure of communicative, medial sociality in the novel. The only tools available for self-making, like the selves, are shared.

The letter writers of *Miss Lonelyhearts* enjoy a similarly paradoxical status to that assigned by Georg Simmel to strangers—they synthesize modes of attachment and detachment in their movements as bodies and messages. The novel's ruthless combination of persons in media and in space, moreover, points to what Simmel describes as an "indication that spatial relations not only are determining conditions of relationships among men, but are also symbolic of those relationships."[92] It matters, then, that Doyle works as a meter reader for the municipal gas company—a wanderer of the hallways and stairwells of buildings, he is simultaneously a stranger to the residents and intimately connected to their infrastructure—and that he, too, is a regular subscriber. Just how much this matters the novel makes perfectly clear in its final scene, when Miss Lonelyhearts rushes from his sickroom into the hallway to meet Doyle, with his arms spread: "Doyle was carrying something wrapped in a newspaper. When he saw Miss Lonelyhearts, he put his hand inside the package and stopped. He shouted some kind of a warning, but Miss Lonelyhearts continued his charge. He did not understand the cripple's shout and heard it as a cry for help from Desperate, Harold S., Catholic-mother, Broken-hearted, Broad-shoulders, Sick-of-it-all, Disillusioned-with-tubercular-husband. He was running to succor them with love."[93] Doyle's newspaper, of course, contains a gun. It also contains the Miss Lonelyhearts column, and if the columnist fails to understand that his readers are not always comfortable with the interchangeability they call up by writing letters to the public media, he can always be replaced himself with another Miss Lonelyhearts.

If the anxiety of influenza persists outside of novels that take up its specificity, it is in their contagious medial relations. In the next chapter, I will be taking up hallway encounters, such as the fatal collision of Miss Lonelyhearts and Doyle, via the twentieth century's two major theorists of the corridors of power: C. P. Snow, who coined the phrase in his novels, and Carl Schmitt, whose concept of *Korridorbildung* got there first. Through their work, I will examine the logic of institutional space as it works with the contagious forms I have been describing.

4 CORRIDORS OF POWER

The hallways smell different.

—Barbara Starr, *CNN* (November 28, 2006), reporting on the expected resignation of U.S. Secretary of Defense Donald Rumsfeld

THE MODERN FORM OF BUREAUCRACY, as described by one of its most prominent theorists, Max Weber, has its own spatial contagions. "It does not matter for the character of bureaucracy," he says, "whether its authority is called 'private' or 'public.'"[1] The mimetic compulsions of structure appear throughout his categorical project of describing bureaucratic rationality; and bureaucracy, like the flu, works with something other than a banal opposition of public and private when it addresses distinctions between persons, spaces, or institutions. The spatial sensibilities that I have been describing as activated by the influenza epidemic in its literary and historical afterlives—the contagious transfer between spatial and social formations and all that this makes visible—are familiar associates in Weber's accounts of bureaucratic rationality. Weber, who himself was a late victim of the influenza pandemic,[2] calls bureaucracy a "type of organization," and takes seriously the etymological background of this organizational system as "rule from the desk." The desk becomes a position in space, and matters for the formalization of communication channels that makes the bureaucratization of modern society possible. For Claude Lefort, for example, Weber's bureaucracy presupposes a kind of spatial formalism that describes the relations between those who move within it, "a determinate spatial context of bureaucratic activities."[3]

But what kinds of contextual work does space perform for the persons, papers, and administrative structures that together form the modern institution? Bureaucratic architectures are organizational forms that describe both built structures and informational command chains—as contexts for the activities within organizations, they are something other than constraints or determinations. The architectural forms that inform institutional activities also *are* those activities, which exhibit the properties of the structures that house them. If a spatial determinism underlies the functioning of organizational life, it is because organization produces its own context. And as the context and action of institutions, the spatial forms encoded in architecture are in a unique position to comment on what seems most formal about how institutions work. In this sense architecture may be context, but it is also text—it reveals, structures, figures and formalizes relationships.

This chapter will take up the spatial figurations and configurations that surface in the work of two observers of modern institutionality who might be seen to enjoy quite disparate fates within the institution of the academy: C. P. Snow and Carl Schmitt. These writers represent the self-reflexive turn of the corridor trajectory I have been describing. The anxieties about medial materiality and its effects on the persons who inhabit the media environments of modernity so violently registered in the clogged channels and spatial substitutions of novels in the decades leading up to the Second World War reach a different kind of apotheosis in the institutional discourse of the immediate postwar period. The self-described heyday of the corridor reorients to what Reinhold Martin calls "the organizational complex," a system within which "architecture acts as a conduit for organizational patterns passing through the networks of communication that constitute the system's infrastructure."[4] This systemization of space, entrenched by the 1960s, Martin says, produces "new kinds of architectures, and with them a new 'self,' none of which could be said to possess the traditional properties that divided inside from outside in any meaningful sense."[5] These are the emergent selves foregrounded in and foreshadowed by the spatial forms of the resolutely material, exteriorizing, wayward novels of American modernism.

Both Snow and Schmitt look directly to architecture for clues about the formal structure of modern power and institutional culture. Their writings are both local and internationalist in orientation—each describes the dynamics of power and institutionality in the administered environments of Britain and Germany, respectively, but it is their legacy, particularly in the critical theory invoked in many debates in Americanist literary criticism, that draws attention here. The discussions of modern institutional life that inform literary accounts often take for granted a set of terms for thinking about subjects and space firmly established first in the writings of Snow and Schmitt, both of whom turn explicitly to the corridor in their analyses of modern institutions and the structured relations within them. The waiting rooms and corridors of the built world they describe take on and direct social configurations. These emerge as distinctions, between disciplines and spaces; the positions from which distinctions are observed and how positionality affects observation; and the dialectical process of spatial formation. It is, I will argue, no accident that the formalizations I will discuss appear in novels, lectures, and dramas, for when space performs its work of revealing in these accounts, it often lives a double life as trope, cliché, or idiom. Like the figures of language they inhabit, these spaces are often transparent, and can be observed only from within.

Figure 20. Craig Kalpakjian, *Corridor,* 1997. Copyright Craig Kalpakjian.

Dashing Metaphors, Cultural Maps

In his 1962 Richmond Lecture, "Two Cultures? The Significance of C. P. Snow," F. R. Leavis expressed his outrage at the adoption of C. P. Snow's 1959 Rede Lecture, "The Two Cultures and the Scientific Revolution," as required secondary school reading. Although this use of the lecture forms just one outrage among a dazzling catalogue of offenses, the appearance of doctrine, Leavis claims, required and initiated his sharp response. Of particular concern for Leavis is Snow's technique, for "if his lecture has any value for use in school—or universities—it is as a document for the study of cliché."[6] Snow's lecture describes a disciplinary schism that feels at the very least outmoded in the culture of contemporary humanist scholarship, yet his often-derided description of the two cultures maintains an odd persistence. Its tenacity doubles back on the clichés so abhorred by Leavis, providing a perhaps appropriate legacy for a document so initially concerned with forms of doubling.

In what follows, I will return to Snow's lecture to get behind the cliché, ask how it works, and provide an account of what figurations of disciplinary space can offer to descriptions of disciplinary structure. In Snow's own interdisciplinary work, as well as the debates in its orbit, the figure of the corridor not only offers a particular form for the modes of distinction so important to understanding disciplinary culture, but it also makes visible their workings. The corridors of Snow's novels reveal a tropology of space and form that feeds back into the two cultures argument, and suggests that any continuation of the discussion Snow began about the modes of communication between the disciplines demands a consideration of the architectures of that communication in all of their literal and metaphorical complexities. This requires taking seriously both figurative and built spaces, as well as the relation of figuration to building, in order to track conceptualizations of disciplinarity.

Early in C. P. Snow's lecture "The Two Cultures and the Scientific Revolution" he presents his project of describing the relationship between literary and scientific culture as one that turns on a question of figuration. By choosing "two cultures," he says, he was "searching for something a little more than a dashing metaphor, a good deal less than a cultural map."[7] But what is it about twoness, or culture, that together they are almost, but not quite metaphor, and almost, but not quite map?

And why would metaphor and map be the two poles demarcating a rhetorical strategy? The answer in part comes from Snow's approaches to engaging with both of the cultures he wants to distinguish between in naming the nature of the distinctions between them. The concept of culture, for Snow, is behavioral, drawn from anthropology and recognizable now as something like a habitus. But the doubling of culture he describes is dialectical, although this dialectic comes with a warning. Two "is a very dangerous number," Snow says, "that is why the dialectic is a very dangerous process."[8] His critique of the two cultures is not, as is often misunderstood, that there are two. Neither is it that disciplines operate through distinctions from each other. Rather, what emerges is a concern with how these distinctions work, and what kinds of communication they do or do not enable. Specialization and autonomy become Snow's bugbears only when they mean that the disciplinary culture refuses to acknowledge the dialectical nature of the distinctions through which it has formed itself—distinctions marking its relation, even negative relation, to other disciplines. More dangerous than the dialectic itself is the world of make-believe that denies its existence.

The examples to which Snow directs his analysis—primarily his utterly lambasted critique of the "anti-social" and "misguided" tendencies of literary modernism and intellectual movements, as well as his more engaging extended call for reform of the British educational system—survive in both parody and policy. Yet what remains interesting about the problems he describes is that they are formal ones. When Leavis argues that Snow "doesn't know what he means, and he doesn't know he doesn't know,"[9] he both highlights and dismisses the contradictions in Snow's argument so crucial to its tenacity. The basic dilemma that arises with Snow's two cultures becomes how to approach specialization critically when disciplines describe, and therefore produce themselves, on their own terms. The two cultures lecture critiques what Snow sees as a mutually constitutive rigidity of social and disciplinary formations, but the alternative to rigidity is not the abolition of specialization, but rather a refining of the processes by which disciplines observe themselves. Snow ties the process of specialization to what he sees as a particularly English "tendency to let our social forms crystallise."[10] A crystallized form, in this account, no longer continues to work.

Snow charts a relation between the crystallization of social forms and disciplinary forms that, perhaps despite his intentions, points to something like what Niklas Luhmann would later refer to as "The Modernity of Science." Luhmann claims that the formal operations of the social system, the ways that it differentiates itself from other systems, connect directly to the distinctions informing a constructivist "self-understanding of science." The basic differential structure of society—that is, its communications—finds its precise echo in the organization of the disciplines. These communicative systems must differentiate themselves and continue to trouble and be troubled by that distinction in order to keep operating. For Luhmann, "modern society's form of differentiation makes possible, or even enforces, the autonomy of separate functional areas; this is accomplished by the differentiation of certain operationally closed, autopoetic systems. Functional differentiation thus imposes on systems an obligation to reflect on their own singularity and irreplaceability, but an obligation that must take into account that there are other functional systems of this kind in society."[11] Both Luhmann and Snow deploy differentiation to explain to the interdependent workings of both social and institutional systems.[12]

The "communication" Snow demands between the two cultures can thus be seen as operating in systems-theoretical terms: disciplinary autonomy for Snow must dialectically involve its outside, or in other words be something like a *functional* autonomy. I am not suggesting that Snow's essay should be read as Luhmann *avant la lettre;* after all, what for Snow is a dangerous dialectic is for Luhmann a productive paradox. It could also be that the nature of Snow's "dangerous" dialectic is what Leavis would call one of his "panoptic pseudo-cogencies."[13] But whether Snow knows, doesn't know, or doesn't know that he doesn't know (as we will see later, he appears to inhabit a state of consistent surprise at the persistence of his phrases), the distinction he describes—the "two cultures" distinction itself—is continually observed as the cliché and idiom for the kind of disciplinary "self-understanding" to which Luhmann refers.

In fact, Snow's attention to the distinctions structuring the operation of modern institutions makes him an unlikely exception to Luhmann's primary assertion in "The Modernity of Science" that for the scientific disciplines, their "modernity seems to go without saying."[14] Luhmann's formalism refuses the reduction of the relationship between science and technology to a rigid opposition of pure and applied science, with the latter in a position of dependence. For Snow, the categories of pure and applied science operate, like the disciplines themselves, via a distinctly modern dialectic, one he sees as historically conditioned by the overt mutual dependence of theoretical and practical science in the development of nuclear technologies throughout the twentieth century. The project of describing the overlap of pure and applied science informs his theory of the two cultures: in his expanded edition of the lecture, "A Second Look," Snow looks twice at forms of two by reflecting on the parallels between the cultural divide he described and its kindred forms, the internal division of the modern sciences and the economic division of the modern world.[15] Characteristic of all of these divides is their dialectical nature, but Snow draws explicit attention to the internal distinction within the sciences: "This complex dialectic between pure and applied science is one of the deepest problems in scientific history."[16] That is, the complex dialectic forms a problem not in the structure of the discipline itself, but in how the discipline observes itself and its distinctions.

Snow describes a modernity that operates via distinctions, and the texture of Snow's dialectic is shaped by the constant reincorporation of the distinctions separating disciplines back into the disciplines themselves. This he simplifies by example: the distinctions producing the disciplines of science and art through dialectical involvement with each other reappear in form within science as the dialectic between pure and applied. These distinctions are bound to the systems of observation and self-observation (such as the history of science) that constitute the functional autonomy of the disciplines. The two cultures lecture, of course, must also be included as a self-observation of each "culture," as Snow would have it, from the inside. Although his critics held that he had claim to authority neither as a scientist nor a literary intellectual, Snow's experiments with both points of view *as* points of view—in the lecture as well as in his large body of fiction—demonstrate that his reporting on disciplinary and institutional cultures takes into account the positions from which the cultures are observed and what it might mean to occupy those positions.

Corridors and Power

As a 1964 *Time* article announcing Snow's appointment to the British Technology Ministry, "Two Cultures in the Corridors," observed, the technocrat's fascination with the dialectics constituting relations between science and art or pure and applied sciences may have had something to do with his own, at times simultaneous occupation of points of view within these disciplines: "Life imitates art. Thus did Snow, 59, sometime physicist, Cambridge don, civil servant, business executive and portrayer-in-fiction of Britain's rulers, begin a new career."[17] Snow, who was reported to have been included on Hitler's blacklist as a double entry, "Dr. C. Snow" and "C. P. Snow, writer," knew something about observing multiple systems from within.[18] While the two cultures lecture provides one look the self-observation of the disciplines, Snow's fiction, in turn, observes that observing in action.

The *Time* article also makes clear the association of the two cultures with a particular space in Snow's work. I have been discussing the 1959 Rede Lecture, but Snow first outlined the argument for his two cultures thesis in a 1956 article in the *New Statesman.* That same year, he published *Homecoming,* a novel in the popular *Strangers and Brothers* series he released over several decades. This 1956 novel chronicled the rise of the technocrats within the pre- and postwar development of nuclear technology. The novel that takes place immediately before *Homecoming* in the series, *The New Men,* moreover, prefigures the bureaucratic power struggles surrounding the use and advance of nuclear technology by dramatizing the "complex dialectic" between theoretical and applied science in government nuclear labs toward the end of the war.[19] In an interview published after the two cultures lecture, Snow said that he would like his novels to be read with the lecture "as a kind of explicit gloss or social commentary at the side."[20] It was in *Homecoming* that Snow would coin a more powerful idiomatic legacy even than the two cultures, the simple phrase with which we are all a bit overly familiar, "the corridors of power." The phrase appears in the novel at a crisis point in the relationship between Snow's semi-autobiographical narrator, the civil servant Lewis Eliot, and his future wife. As they prepare to part, Margaret alludes to her interest in a doctor who is unencumbered by the professional demands responsible for the breakdown of her relationship with Eliot: "The official world, the corridors of power, the dilemmas of conscience and egotism—she disliked them all. . . . So, with a touch of insistence, she mentioned this new acquaintance's work in his hospital."[21] The novel reveals that the joke is on her, however, when after she reunites with Eliot they find themselves negotiating access through corridors of this doctor's hospital.[22] The corridors of power traverse more than one institution.

A reviewer of *Homecoming* noted the phrase, and Snow repurposed it for his next novel, now titled *Corridors of Power,* in 1964. In his preface to this later work, he noted with some irony the sudden everydayness of his words: "The phrase has kept swimming in print before my eyes about twice a week and four times on Sundays, and has, in fact, turned into a cliché. But I cannot help using it myself, without too much inconvenience. I console myself with the reflection that, if a man hasn't the right to his own cliché, who has?"[23] Snow, it seems, has the right to more than one cliché. Moreover, his simultaneous development of both ideas in separate genres suggests that there may be something behind the placement in the popular press of the two cultures idea *in* the corridors. But what kind of "explicit gloss" or "social commentary" do the corridors of power, as both idiom and novel, provide on the two cultures? And what kinds of observation and distinction-making do spatial forms, and specifically these corridors, make visible?

"The corridors of power," in its idiomatic use, activates a spatial metonymic sensibility common to well-worn representations of political power. One can think of the basic substitution of "lobbyist" for those who linger in the corridors previously mentioned (as well as in the waiting-room termini of bureaucratic stagnation) as a nontrivial instance of institutional space standing in for positions of personhood. All of Snow's novels in the *Strangers and Brothers* series deal with the shared forms of institutions, whether the institution in question be the academy, government, or the family. Appropriately enough, *Corridors of Power* engages all three. Throughout the novel, the narrator takes pains to ensure that these homologies do not go unnoticed: "Rose spent the afternoon with our own Minister, talking about a scheme for redistributing the work between the two departments. I had seen the same in a smaller world twenty years before, when I was living in a college."[24] Architecture becomes a key indicator of the shared functions of institutions across the *Strangers and Brothers* series. In his second look at the two cultures in the expanded edition of the lecture, Snow mentions that his novels track the structures of high-level decision making: "I have written, both in novels and essays, more about politics, in particular 'closed' politics (that is, the way decisions are really taken in power-groups, as contrasted with the way they are supposed to be taken)."[25] This also is the situation of the *Corridors of Power,* with its proliferating descriptions of "channels of 'closed' politics—the corridors, the committees."[26] Snow draws attention to the word "closed" in both of these passages, making "the way decisions are really taken" an over-explicit function of the corridors and doors that line them.

Accordingly, Snow's corridors put pressure on what counts as a "channel"—they do not work as mere conduits connecting the private spaces where decisions are taken. Rather, they become the literal and figurative locations of power. The corridors organizing movement in Snow's fiction, like those in the novels I have been discussing thus far, become destinations. They have been destinations all along, in the hospitals, universities, laboratory complexes, and government offices housing the action of the eight *Strangers and Brothers* novels published before *Corridors of Power,* but the novel that takes back the cliché works, at times too hard, to reveal them. Two of the major narrative climaxes happen in the corridors—one involving a secondary, or "corridor" door to Lewis Eliot's private office, and another in a labyrinthine maze connecting several departments, offices, and occupants. Both take place, also appropriately enough, in a chapter titled "Quarrel in the Corridor," in which the novel's dénouement is revealed when its corridors block rather than facilitate movement.

Of course, blocking movement is also a standard function of the corridor, which becomes clear in the novel as it dramatizes the corridor's role in arranging access to people and spaces. When Eliot's civil service superior, Hector Rose, arrives uncharacteristically at his office door (Rose prefers written communication to be sent the short distance between their offices), he also chooses an uncharacteristic route: "A knock sounded on my door, not the door leading to my assistants, through which visitors should come, but the corridor door, usually inviolable. Hector Rose came in, perhaps for the second time since we had been colleagues, paying me a visit unannounced."[27] What Eliot refers to as the "corridor door" is not the corridor-like space through which people move and encounter one another; instead, it is the corridor-like space demarcating boundaries and establishing institutional categories of public and private. When Rose enters through Eliot's corridor door, he demonstrates just how inseparable both points of access appear in relation to the corridors. He also demonstrates that these spatial forms of relationality are precisely what is stake in the most fraught of institutional power struggles.

Corridors of Power dramatizes a conflation of persons and spaces, marking this conflation as a basic indicator of the smooth flowing of modern institutional life. That the organizational condition of the corridor also conflates likeness and distinction is taken for granted. What for earlier observers of so-called individuals occupying positions within institutions had aroused suspicion becomes in Snow a basic presupposition. Take Henry James's early twentieth-century text *The American Scene,* in which the likeness of corridors to the spaces from which they seem intended to be distinguished frames the process of distinction as a crisis for the experience and constitution of modern architecture. In the section "The Multiplied Apertures," in the chapter on New York "social notes," James observes that the problem with spatial differentiation is also tied to structures of institutionality: "This diffused vagueness of separation between apartments, between hall and room, between one room and another, between the one you are in and the one you are not in, between place of passage and place of privacy, is a provocation to despair which the public institution shares impartially with the luxurious 'home.'"[28] The "despair" James describes registers the early experience of what sociologist Ulrich Beck formulates as the institutionalization of the private. Not only do the private spaces of the home refer structurally to public institutional space in the shared form of "passage" or corridor, but the displaced differentiation between public and private, "between hall and room," also inflects the position of individual interiority in the interior. According to Beck, this situation is characteristic of the emerging forms of reflexive modernity James already seems to inhabit: "[individual situations] *span the separated areas of the private sphere and the various areas of the public sphere.* They are no longer merely private situations, but also always institutional. They have the contradictory double face of *institutionally dependent individual situations.*"[29] Rather than as a provocation to despair, the "double face" of institutional situation and institutionalized domesticity and privacy, the institutionality operationalized by the corridor appears comfortably in Snow's fiction, as well as in the proliferating body of midcentury corporate novels, as the self-organization of the organization man.

The corridors of *Corridors of Power* formalize institutional communication as a double-sided and spatial process, one in which the facilitation and prevention of access to its outside (paradoxically, the insides of private offices and their occupants constitute the outside of the corridor) work as two versions of the same movement. As the narrative of "Quarrel in the Corridor" moves out of Eliot's office and into these corridors, however, the corridors themselves begin to disappear:

> I went out, through my private office, into the corridor, past the doors of my own department, round three sides of the Treasury quadrangle, on my way to Osbaldiston. I didn't notice, as I had done times enough, the bizarre architecture, the 19th Century waste of space, the gigantic unfilled hole in the centre of the building, like a Henry Moore sculpture pretending to be functional. I didn't even notice the high jaundiced walls, the dark stretch of corridor up to the next bend, the compartments where the messengers sat on stools reading the racing editions, the labels on the doors just visible. . . . It was just dark, domesticated, familiar: a topological journey: the doors passing me by like the stations seen from an underground train.[30]

When the corridor becomes most visible as the place where institutional distinctions are drawn and battles fought, it also turns into specifically what Eliot does not or cannot see. Moreover, the bizarreness of the corridor, or what on reflection Eliot calls a pretend functionality, disappears into a blur of movement that transforms Eliot into a passive spectator on a subway train. It is no accident that corridor and tunnel, or office door and underground station, indicate each other here—they form, after all, no dashing metaphor. But their straightforward affinities, brought out at the expense of the vector space through which Eliot travels, reveal at the same time an instability in Eliot's position as the observer of these institutional architectures and the spaces and subjects they shape.

Eliot's observational position in *Corridors of Power* can be located only by triangulating the interiors he inhabits with their exteriors and observers, which means that interiority and exteriority start to look, similarly, like points of view. This also means that, viewed in the context of Snow's fiction, the call for thirdness in Leavis's critique of Snow's distinction making perhaps misses the point. "It is in the study of literature, the literature of one's own language in the first place," claims Leavis, "that one comes to recognize the nature and priority of the third realm (as, unphilosophically, no doubt, I call it, talking with my pupils), the realm of that which is neither merely private and personal nor public in the sense that it can be brought into the laboratory and pointed to."[31] It is true that Snow makes no claims for the priority of the literary in revealing situations uncharacterizable as "merely private" or "public." But even his most basic dramas of the technocracy call into question the relevance of those categories in the first place, discounting rather than trying to transcend them. Or, as Eliot's friend-enemy tells him at the end of the eponymous quarrel in the corridor,

"You've felt yourself entitled to your private view. Not so private, if I may say so. So have I. I've made no secret of it."[32] There can be no making-public of the private in this world—all any of its players can do is bring into the open what was already in the open, and then relativize its publicness.

The spaces of Snow's fiction are novelistic in the sense that they provide a tropology of communication and distinction. The connections they establish between space, sociality, and the institution, and their formalization of those connections, make them appropriate to the structure of cliché. If corridors stand in as the carriers of messages and the messages themselves—even persons operate as corridors in this system—it is because they instance the *coincidence* of space, trope, and even cliché itself. They also provide commentary on distinctions and decisions in the context of institutional power, a commentary that operates by form and figure. Although the running gag in the novel is that Hector Rose will summon Eliot from three doors down by delivering a message and then congratulate him for his "athletic feat" of traversing the corridor to see him, corridors are serious business.[33] Their overdetermination only highlights the fact that they offer an architecture for distinction making in the novel even as they seem to turn it inside out. The organization and functionality of corridors in *Corridors of Power* reencodes the complexities of differentiation that float through the pages of the two cultures lecture. But it also does more than that: the space of the corridor in *Corridors of Power* demands that distinction, even at its most clichéd, be taken seriously as form.

Divided Space, Corridor Formation

There is also another context for the play between corridors and culture that I have been describing. Although Snow can claim credit for the cliché, he was not the first to outline a theory of the corridors of power. Just a few years earlier, in his 1954 work *Gespräch über die Macht und den Zugang zum Machthaber* (*A Conversation about Power and Access to the Dictator*), Carl Schmitt described a process of *Korridorbildung* as the concrete realization of a formal power dialectic.[34] Much as in Snow's idiom, for Schmitt *Korridorbildung* describes both the form and location of struggles for the highest power. In this work, Schmitt is interested in the process of *Korridorbildung* as the mode by which power consolidates through the creation of spaces that both prevent and permit access to the person who holds the highest position of power. The catch is that this process too is dialectical—although the formation of corridors concentrates power in a single person, it also requires sequestration from those over whom this person holds power. The more power is consolidated, the more isolated that person becomes.

Schmitt is also interested in the corridors themselves, for they reveal the nature of struggles for power. He attends to what he calls the "occupation of the anterooms and control of the corridors" as modes of power struggle, and claims that in these spaces, "the inner dialectic of human power takes place."[35] Moreover, there is something peculiar about the access he describes. He refers to both "access to the ear" and also "a corridor to the soul" of the occupant of the highest power position.[36] Power is a position, but a managed one. Its outer spaces and access points, and those who control them, are constantly dialectically involved in constituting the power (and power-holder), and this process is both attached to the minutiae of daily life and ongoing.

Corridors that provide access to rooms and souls alike look like metaphors, but refer also to the built structures of the institutions Schmitt describes. This tension is characteristic of the role of spatial forms in much of Schmitt's thought: the distinctions that produce spaces, whether they be borders or walls, reveal the inherent formalisms of the political. Schmitt's formalism treats marked space as the concrete realization, or disclosure in the world, of the abstract ordering and distinction-making processes at stake in the formation and maintenance of individual and collective power positions. Schmitt's discussion of the corridor, then, has consequences for his better-known descriptions of modern power: Fredric Jameson, for example, refers to Schmitt's friend–enemy distinction as "a genuinely original form of spatial thought, a 'concept' that cannot be thought independently of spatial relations."[37] Corridors are "spatial articulation[s]"[38]—built structures and abstract formalizations of power. Their perceived triviality or secondariness (Schmitt pairs corridors with other spaces prefaced by "anti," "hinter," "um," and "unter," all prefixes of subordinated relationality) only fold them further into dialectical complexity.[39]

Although the dialectic revealed by the corridor produces powerful exteriors, it too is subject to itself: it is an "inner" dialectic. The process of *Korridorbildung,* as a process, involves distinction making and a familiar nod to the structure of the decision. But separation always connects in this architecture of distinctions. Schmitt's most direct turn to architecture in *Gespräch über die Macht und den Zugang zum Machthaber* puts pressure on how form can be deployed in relation to built structures as well as their conceptual frameworks. Form does not operate as an empty container; rather, it encodes and discloses distinctions.[40] For Schmitt the dialectic, like the corridor, is what it does.

It makes sense, then, that the form of the text itself follows this model. Not only do tropes and locales reconfigure each other throughout the work, but their very relation also works as the mode of expression. Schmitt's discussion of *Korridorbildung* appears as a book-length dialogue, or play complete with intermission, providing another turn on the formalism of the process of corridor formation. The text opens with a cast of players: C. S., a Schmitt-like character, J., an interviewer of "a younger vintage," and a possible third, an optional voice for the Intermezzo section's description of historical examples of "the struggle for the corridor."[41] Immediately the "conversation" announced as the text deploys the dialogue as an introduction to its formal concerns. As we have seen with the corridors of Snow, what looks like a spatial articulation contains many layers of dimensionality that reorient the distinctions between the built world and its figurations when they come to account for institutional processes. What looks initially like a question of the relationship between literal and figurative space emerges as a reconfigured description of form itself.

The other side of Schmitt's spatial formalism involves the repositioning of the holder and subject of power, for the corridor reveals the importance of indirection to maintaining both of these positions. Power relationships, spatially encoded, become points of view. Job descriptions such as dictator or secretary work instead as spatial positions, and are ruled by the relations, divisions, and access structures produced by the spaces they inhabit, yet which they in turn produce. This is a power always displaced, always observed at a remove. The organization of power brought into view by the corridor, and the process of *Korridorbildung* as the encoding of that organization in architecture, demands a shift from thinking about individuals and what might be thought of as subjects to formal positions. The "orders and orientations" that Schmitt sees unified by juridical life cannot be seen without concretized divisions in space, and neither can those who inhabit them.[42] The consequences for this spatial ordering on Schmittian sovereignty, then, are not insignificant: the decisions through which the sovereign is disclosed have architectural preconditions. Or, as the C. S. of *Gespräch über die Macht und den Zugang zum Machthaber* puts it, "there is no human power without these antechambers and without these corridors."[43]

Schmitt claims to have prepared this 1954 discussion of power in a conversation that took place while he inhabited the institutional space of the prison in 1947. In his 1950 work *The* Nomos *of the Earth,* he anticipates much of this argument when he writes that "from its compulsion to self-affirmation, daily and hourly power seeks to secure, to justify, and to consolidate its position anew. This creates a dialectic, whereby the ruler, in order to maintain this position, is compelled to organize new security systems around himself and to create new anterooms, corridors, and accesses to power. The inescapable dialectic consists in the fact that, through such security measures, he distances and isolates himself from the world he rules."[44] Although he does not name the process of *Korridorbildung* here, this should by now sound familiar. For Schmitt, something as abstract as law not only refers to, but absolutely depends on the guarantee of a "fundamental *nomos,*" which he says is explicitly a "spatial structure, the unity of order and orientation."[45] Spatial structures in *The* Nomos *of the Earth* provide concrete access to abstraction: they make divisions and distributions visible. This late instantiation of Schmitt's concrete-order thinking attached to the corridor both particularizes the distinctions produced and revealed by the space itself, and generalizes them. And despite the mutual goodwill of arcades and corridors, this is not a Benjaminian account of architecture received in a state of distraction; rather, the architectural form makes insistent demands on attention.[46]

But the attention architecture demands in this account does not involve a gaze that takes in an exterior. For Schmitt, it is only after "the solid ground of the earth is delineated by fences, enclosures, boundaries, walls, houses, and other constructs" that "the orders and orientations of human social life become apparent."[47] What corridors and other built structures of distinction provide is an opportunity for self-reflection, for it is through them that the social can acknowledge and account for itself. This kind of self-reflection, then, as a "unity of order and orientation," is also one that sees the ordering, or "divisions and distributions" of itself only through its orientations, or concretely structured points of view. My claim that Schmitt's concretization of perspective and orientation should not be unfamiliar to readers of novels (even the likes of Snow's) does not partake of critiques that attack the "aestheticizing formalism" of his attention to structures of decision.[48] Instead, what seems most literary about the *nomos* is its deictic formalism: although the shifter logic of "here" and "there" renders perspective contingent, it also concretizes it in space. The social sees itself where and when it places itself, and turns its perspective around to that point. It must reorient to recognize its orientations.

What emerge as "the orders and orientations of human social life" are also the spatial preconditions of sovereignty and the political. The spatiality of these concepts underlies many of the contemporary debates circulating around Schmitt's legacy. When Peter Hallward, for example, argues against the "salvage" of Schmitt's theories of the *nomos* as visionary, he takes issue not with Schmitt's insistence on taking stock of emerging spatial orders and orientations, but with the fact that Schmitt adjudicates the new *nomos* to be not spatially demarcated *enough:* "But *Nomos* is not a prophetic book. It anticipates a disordered, rootless, and centerless world, a world of a 'spaceless' and thereby ungovernable universalism. . . . Outside of the world imagined by Deleuze or Negri, however, along with certain tendencies of postcolonial and postmodern theory, this picture bears little relation to any contemporary reality."[49] Any account of Schmitt's concepts and formal articulations of power structures must first consider their visible forms in architecture. The sovereign requires corridors, and corridors in turn reveal the form of that sovereignty, for in this world decision-making is always encoded in architecture, and it can always be seen.

This reliably modern ocularity can be counted on to change what it sees as it sees it. Schmitt's utterly familiar spaces appear unfamiliar because of their constant becoming-visible and the insistent presentness of the process of self-recognition, a presentness that accompanies the temporalities of precondition and inevitability that I have been discussing. Schmitt describes not just corridors and antechambers, but *Korridorbildung,* the emergence and recognition of these spaces, as a constantly evolving process. It is in this motion that the institution emerges as a working system of positions and access that can include persons, spaces, and information. When in *Gespräch über die Macht und den Zugang zum Machthaber* C. S. describes footsteps in the corridors and those who produce them, he insists that the corridors of state power prove instructive far beyond the institution in which they are housed, for although these corridors reveal the nature of struggles for the highest power, "all the same, a motley and mixed company has converged in these antechambers of power throughout the course of world history."[50] A cross-section of social positions forms in and forms the corridors, and this attribute of *Korridorbildung* travels across institutions. After C. S. juxtaposes the Augustas, Rasputins, Richelieus, and Messalinas—as well as the more general managers, kings, and cleaners whose convergence makes *Korridorbildung* possible—his interlocutor points out that the same dynamic characterizes the corridors of institutions such as hospitals, where it is the nurses who "rule the world" in a manner recognizable among the institutional wanderings of Snow's Lewis Eliot.[51] Within these corridors, power held by the nurses, secretaries, and butlers indicates anything but topsy-turveydom. The true struggle, after all, is for the occupation of antechambers and control of corridors.

The sociality and institutionality of space emerges when it is seen, and in this version of seeing, when it is also read. Schmitt's account of the other spaces of modern institutional life shares its interest in the legibility of architectural forms with, and perhaps surprisingly echoes, the work of Siegfried Kracauer, whose essay "On Employment Agencies: The Construction of a Space" explicitly takes up the parsing of institutional space as text and who asks, like Schmitt, what spatial structures reveal about social relationships. Kracauer claims that "spatial images are the dreams of society." But these dreams, of course, are subject to interpretation, for "wherever the hieroglyphics of any spatial image are deciphered, there the basis of social reality presents itself."[52] The spaces of the institution (in this case, the employment agency) reveal how much these organizations express and encode the basic forms of modern sociality. In these spaces "the concepts governing [the institution] ooze through all pores."[53] That is, the institutional space is rendered permeable as a readable object, even as that readability becomes complicit with the forces restricting the movements of the occupants of the waiting room. So when the collective spaces of the unemployed become a "collection of texts" complete with a "preface" (the door plate announcing the contents of the building), they also operate as agents of confinement.

In the back rooms of the modern institution, Kracauer observes the constant disclosure of social forms by spatial ones, but finds the results of this disclosure gloomy when experienced by the interiors deciphering the spaces. These interiors, the unemployed, "occupy themselves with waiting" while they occupy the waiting room. When occupation of space and self collide, the space reveals more than the social relationships at stake, but that these relationships also constitute the occupied self. And although the discussion of waiting rooms appears to focus on the terminus or enclosed space, it turns out that "this space is actually not a room but, at most, a passageway."[54] The waiting room is a corridor, or "an arcade, through which the unemployed should once more attain a gainfully employed existence." In addition to its specific institutional function, the waiting room refers to the category of spaces the likes of which are so important to Schmitt. The waiting room is also antechamber, corridor, and lobby. Its mode is displacement and indirection, and it exists only in relation to other spaces, by coming before, after, under, or between them. These are the relations it discloses between the interiors otherwise known as the unemployed or the bureaucrat. "Unfortunately," Kracauer says, "the arcade is heavily congested."[55] He begins this analysis of employment agencies by remarking that "each social stratum has a space that is associated with it," but if the corridors of Schmitt and Snow reveal anything, it is that stratifications of space *or* the social are rarely one-sided.[56]

Inhabited Selves

The negotiations of form and space that I have been tracing reposition the interiors and exteriors of persons and buildings. This happens as selves and spaces come to account for one another—what persons populate the corridor spaces of modern institutional life are occupied like the spaces they inhabit and by those spaces. The situation between corridors and cultures as it is described by these observers of modern institutionality looks much like that presented in John Stezaker's *Amnesia* (see Figure 21)—it is not just that architectural forms of access stand in for other recognizable portals of communication and expression. Instead, the corridor to the soul begins with the rough equivalent of window and door for eye and mouth, and looks back at the observer, blocking and reincorporating the observation as part of the same operation. Spatial structures reveal the forms of modern power and personhood at stake for the disciplines and the dictator, the scientist and the bureaucrat, and the inner walls of the house, the hospital, or Parliament. They also reveal that both architecture and personhood are bound to each other in loops of self-observation.

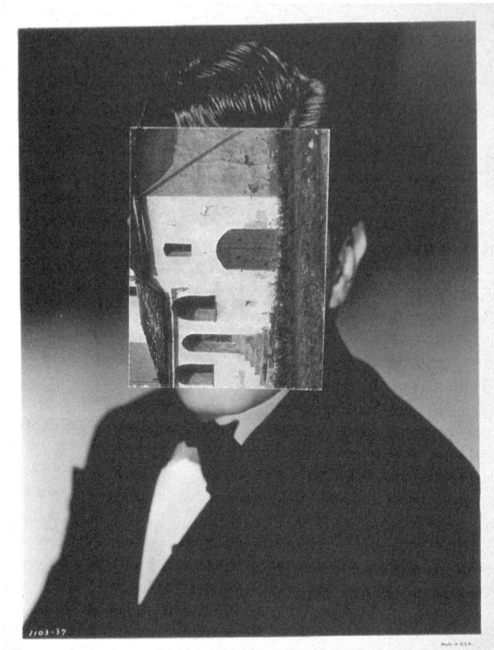

Figure 21. John Stezaker, *Amnesia*, 2006. Courtesy of Richard Telles Fine Art.

The kinds of figuration that emerge in the works of Snow and Schmitt—and, as I have discussed in the previous chapters, in novels interested in something like *Korridorbildung* as a model of narrative interiority—are masks (see Figure 22). As an insistently built and material metaphor, the corridor paradoxically disappears into a vanishing point and yet, in the position of the observer, gazes back at the same time. In Stezaker's portraits, the cinematic image and the headshot betray the impossibility of this form of mediation: what Kracauer calls "picture postcard greetings from the happy upper world" become letters from nowhere, placed on top of the likenesses that would otherwise form the addresses, or reading interiors constituted by the sending of the postcard.[57] The likenesses between spaces and between spaces and persons renders spaces and persons alike nearly unrecognizable other than as forms. What becomes strange is that something distinctly social, or something like meaning persists as formal organization rather than in opposition to it.

These images, produced by a conceptual artist interested in "the periphery of image culture, the sideways, the byways of image culture," are also picture-postcard greetings from the nowhere described by Snow and Schmitt, a self-referring maze of corridors that is, in fact, everywhere.[58] And the rendering of the relation of persons and spaces as formal does not become an occasion for mourning—it instead coolly indicates that this also describes the structure of relations among persons as well (see Figure 23).

What I have been outlining here is a provisional layout of the spatial forms, which are also medial forms, that insistently surface in an archeology of contemporary debates about disciplinarity. Embedded within the now-clichéd idioms of institutionality is a topology of corridors and antechambers that offer a compellingly awkward perspective through which to view the distinctions and connections that participate in the formal self-observation and reproduction of the disciplines. They are neither dashing metaphors nor cultural maps, and yet they provide a basis for taking both metaphor and map seriously as figurations that make a difference for how architecture works within this observational world, and what it can reveal.

The previous chapters took up these forms of distinction and observation as they were already at work in the proliferating interiors of

Figure 22. John Stezaker, *Mask xxv,* 2006. Courtesy of The Approach.

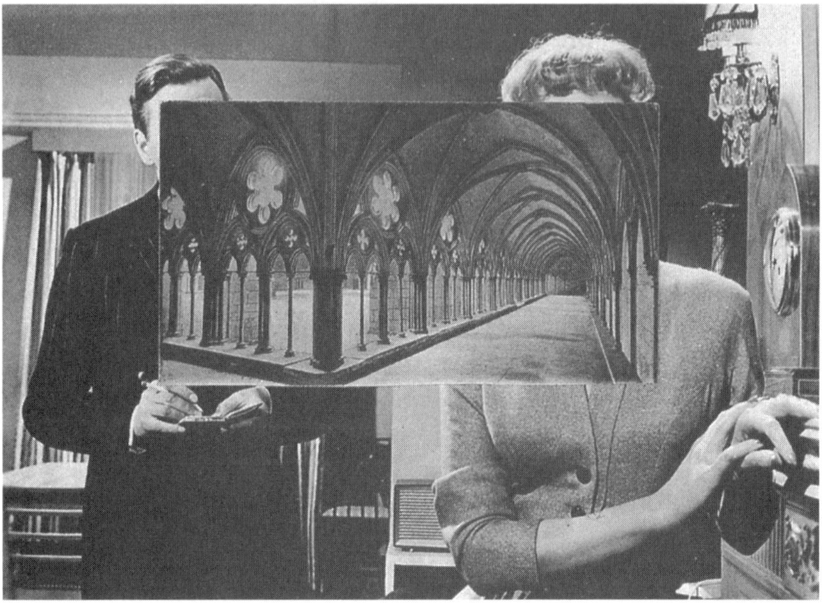

Figure 23. John Stezaker, *Untitled,* 2005. Courtesy of The Approach.

novels likewise concerned with observing themselves through their spaces. What emerged in the decades leading up to and through World War II was a world of corridoricity, somewhere between the likenesses of *Winesburg* and the distinctions of Snow and Schmitt. These instances of the American corridor idiom locate processes of identification in both technical apparatus and architecture—revealing a formal relationship among space, media, and personhood inseparable from the institutional dynamics localized and concretized by the works I have been discussing. This is a relationship encoded in the long history of the corridor as a location, and in its primary substitution of place for person in the corridors of power.

EPILOGUE

Open Plan

AN ARCHITECT OF COMMUNICATION in the modern novel loves walls, partitions, and channels that organize vectors of movement and transfer. These structures of division—inside from outside, private from social space—indicate and make possible that from which they are divided. Corridors also connect.

Thus, when Virginia Woolf draws the form of *To the Lighthouse* she imagines a structure analogous to both house and closed system. Ann Banfield suggests that this spatial diagram points to a constitutive multiplicity of form encoded by the corridor: "'break' and 'bridge,'" as well as the rendering of time as "in-between."[1] This is a conspicuous assertion of the conduit in a moment of modernity now known for its wireless imagination, and as I hope to have shown, it is not alone. These channels, moreover, operate on the level of self-description that Woolf's diagram makes most literal: novels are not only material artifacts of

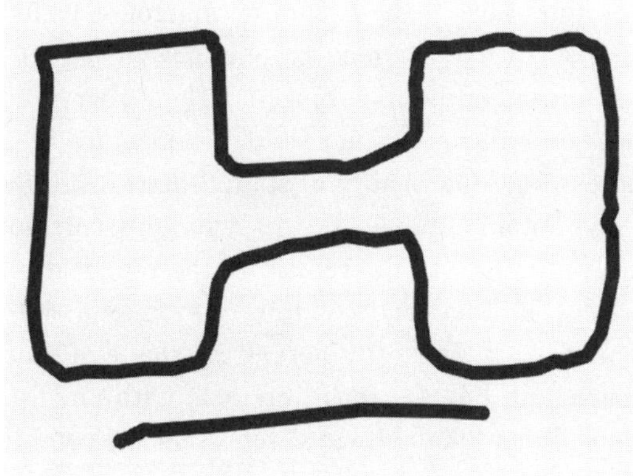

Figure 24. "Two blocks separated by a corridor." Adapted from Virginia Woolf's notes for *To the Lighthouse*. Cited in Ann Banfield, "Time Passes."

communication, but also produce that communicativeness discursively through reference to other materialities.

The insistent location of novelistic communication in places of passage constitutes the crucial reflexive gesture of the wayward texts of American modernism. It can also be described as their corridoricity. The novels for which I have been providing an account enact their own medial operations in and as corridors.

Michel Serres includes this form in the fable-world of *The Parasite* as the character of Poros, who appears at the end of Serres's observations on the noisiness of modern communication. He asks: "But who is Poros, who comes out of the black box? Alas! he is the passage itself, the path. Poros is the name of the passage."[2] A certain horror, or vertigo, attends this rendering of self-reference as an embodied labyrinth, but also a kind of glee. Serres concludes that "the only information that comes out of the black box is that there is a channel through which information passes. The only message that comes out of the path is that there is a path by which messages pass. A thread comes out of the box. The only thing that passes in the channel is the name of the channel."[3] What amounts to the corridoricity of passage in these novels, or the naming of channels as channels, is also part of the task of a reflexive modernity: the self-thematization of communication as communication becomes also the making visible of modernity to itself in its localized and specific forms.

Later in the twentieth century, after the self-theorizations of the corridor I have been discussing, the unchecked proliferation of corridors takes on a more overt aspect of horror. When the speaker of Regina Barreca's 1986 poem "Nighttime Fires" looks into her father's eyes, she gets her metaphors for accessing interiority all wrong: "I could see his quiet face in the / rearview mirror, eyes like hallways filled with smoke."[4] First, she mediates her gaze using a tool usually assigned to self-regard (although appropriately a "rearview" mirror), and she sees opaque hallways rather than windows to the soul. By doing so, she accesses a long history of spatial figures standing in for the interiors they contain or reflect, be they windows, corridors, or mirrors. She also calls attention to the refusal of these figurations to operate as transparent, uninterested conduits. At stake in shaping the spatial representation of interiority here is the shape of that interiority in the first place, and how its form interacts with and is encoded in its mediations. Eyes "like hallways" represent the conduit to itself, a process of vertigo-inducing observation in which the architectural form can only reflect itself into infinity.

Barreca's hallway eyes instance their uncomfortable reflexivity as a problem specific to the medium: the simile renders the overtly literary project of making interiority available both literary and literal, and demonstrates how unsteady the relationship between the two may be. This in turn may be a somewhat routine slippage characteristic of a form of literary self-reflection that structurally examines itself through structures, but it also puts some pressure on a tendency in accounts of literature's operations as a medium to take sides.

The corridors I have been describing in Barreca and others point to the limitations of approaches to media in literary study that either make assumptions about the transparency of language as a medium for representing interiority or about the material force of the technical media making the production and dissemination of literary language possible. Both formally abstract and materially specific, these corridors demand inclusion in a conceptualization of media precisely when they encode literary reflexivity in the process of rendering modern interiority concrete. It is not simply that machines for writing and other technical media provide no account of the self-production of the literary when they appear within its content or produce its material instantiations, but that they do not tell the whole story. Rather, they operate as one version of a media process that takes on other guises, and it is through the interaction of these forms that the shape of modern interiority, and the role of literary texts in producing it, comes into view.

This is a problem that can turn to look back at itself in its novelistic afterlives. In recent fiction, the dynamics of medial interiority play out as a resurfacing of an old problem, that of figuring the relationship of mind to machine. For example, the third story or semi-novella of Michael Cunningham's 2005 novel of variations, *Specimen Days,* places something understood as a historical problem of machine cognition in an updated home: the filtered perspective of Simon, a part-clone, part-android inhabitant of the near future who suffers from a poetry complex. Simon recognizes himself as "a dream his skeleton was having,"[5] and tests the relationship of consciousness to that which houses it through predictable experiences of "beauty," "empathy," and "love." On the one hand, Simon answers questions posed earlier in the novel, such as whether "machines could believe" or "if the machine had loved."[6] But he also provides a palliative for the discomfort provoked by an idea of consciousness that allows it to wander and take residence in persons and machines alike. Through his aesthetic and emotive capacities (side effects of his "fucking poetry chip") and his rendering in the free indirect, Simon reads like a more familiar, or even familiarly modern character.

Whatever version of interiority Simon's character can be said to possess depends also on the form it takes in the novel's tripartite exercise in pattern recognition, for a version of "Simon" appears in each of *Specimen Days'* three novellas. The Simon of the first novella, "In the Machine," has been eaten alive by the factory machine he operates, yet his presence is perceived as a form of consciousness lingering in the metal by his poetry-encumbered brother, who has taken up Simon's vacant post in the factory. Missing from the title of the first novella, of course, is "the ghost"—paradoxically enough, the object of the novel's often peculiar literalizing moves. These moves become part of the project of genre fiction with which *Specimen Days* engages, and the genres of "In the Machine," industrial realism and the ghost story, begin to parody themselves as they compete for authority. Ghosts and machines, however idiomatically familiar, find dissonant voices in the 1911 factory world being described.

In part, what *Specimen Days* registers is the incompatibility of a range of narrative techniques with an idea of consciousness that each attempts to capture. But what's interesting here is not the elusive, and often banal version of consciousness to which the narratives of Cunningham's novel aspire, but that the genres themselves become more compatible through their failure to capture their object. Although the containers of consciousness (factory machines, terrorists, aliens, androids) and the containers of fiction (ghost stories, suspense dramas, sci-fi) are what vary, the relationship to the contained does not. Variations of bodies and stories become visible as reflexive enactments of themselves: containers that contain, housings that house.

Two factories form the key sites of "In the Machine": the Mannahatta Clothing Company, a not very loose allusion to the Triangle Shirtwaist Factory that caught fire and killed 146 garment workers in New York in 1911, a date that is in turn a not very loose allusion to 9/11, which appears as the immediate background to the novel's second section. The second factory, the location of Simon's death, and his brother Lucas's subsequent employment, remains unnamed except as homonym, or "the works." Lucas himself works at the same machine responsible for his brother's demise, in the "cutting-and-stamping room," a room "full of steady, creaturely life."[7] The machine stamps metal and unfortunate humans with the same regard for either, but the product of its stamping remains as opaque as the ultimate product of the works. When Lucas asks, "what are these things I'm making?" he discovers only that "they're housings."[8]

Where ghost and factory story come together, appropriately enough, is on the question of housings. Lucas resolves to observe the workings of the machine closely to discover precisely "what the housings housed," and instead discovers what the machine houses: "Simon was imprisoned in the machine. It made sudden, dreadful sense. He was not in heaven or in the pillow; he was not in the grass or in the locket. His ghost had snagged on the machine's inner workings; the machine held it as a dog might hold a man's coat in its jaws after the man himself had escaped. Simon's flesh had been stamped and expelled, but his invisible part remained, trapped among the gears and teeth."[9] The novel thus begins a process of adding housings to Simon, depicted here as the literalized ghost in the machine, and his transformation into the third novella's futuristic form results in a character recognizable as Simon housed in a mechanized brain, housed in turn in cloned human flesh. The catalyst for Simon's initial release into the machine, the stamping of his flesh as housing, comes full circle as he trades places with the humanoid machine's animated and toothy gears. Satisfied that the house is haunted, Simon's brother inserts his own hand to be stamped, "partner to the iron and the machine."[10]

Cunningham's novel approaches its dilemma of consciousness by way of two processes that also involve an insistent materiality: stamping and housing. The relationship of those populating the novel who could be said to have interiors to the stamping and the housing, however, is confined to passivity: they are housed and stamped in regressive layers. Although structured to provide a future-oriented account of the state of interiority and its fictional homes that emerges out of a fluid relation to the past, *Specimen Days* instead rejects its own premise. It substitutes a general notion of history (Cunningham himself is at pains, in the novel's preface, to discuss the role of historical fidelity to the process of fiction, calling his own effort "semi-accurate" and "true to historic particulars")[11] for any pressure that might be placed on how that narrative mode may itself be an agent of stamping and housing. And yet these actions, largely because of their grammatical fungibility, also point back to the everyday material of novel making (such as stamps or houses). Although *Specimen Days* absorbs its paradoxes of stamping and housing into its discussion of consciousness, they are not unfamiliar players in earlier accounts of factory machines and clothing manufacturers, such as the medial housings and stamping rooms of Dreiser's *An American Tragedy*.

The corridors and corridor-like spaces I have been describing have become in our contemporary medial landscape increasingly spectral, and de-differentiated, eerily replicating themselves into an oblivion of sameness that emerges in postwar American fiction alongside anxieties over ubiquitous media. Consider the following scene, from Thomas Pynchon's *The Crying of Lot 49:*

> When he opened the door of his apartment/office she saw him framed in a long succession or train of doorways, room after room receding in the general direction of Santa Monica, all soaked in rain light. Genghis Cohen had a touch of summer flu. . . .
>
> She glanced down the corridor of Cohen's rooms in the rain and saw, for the very first time, how far it might be possible to get lost in this.[12]

Or, more recently, Mark Z. Danielewski's *House of Leaves* puts this another way: "Resistance to representation, however, is not the only difficulty posed by those replicating chambers and corridors."[13]

Replicating chambers and corridors, room after receding room: from Pynchon's postal labyrinth to the haunted paper houses of contemporary fiction, the novels emerging from a postwar American media culture stage their compulsive reflexivity in corridors. For the revelation of the channel to itself is how the novel enacts its own mediality, as a self-producing communication system articulated through specifically articulated historical forms. When Pynchon's Oedipa Maas or Danielewski's Zampanò look down a corridor to find that it contains within itself merely another corridor, and that this repetition never ends, what they encounter is an overt rendering of the local form of the novel they inhabit in architecture. What they also encounter in these simultaneously odd and banal spaces is a concrete image of a formal process, for through their corridors these novels point to their own operations as media.

The more recent literary corridors to which I refer lay out the evolving networks of modern communication, and like the modern corridors I have been discussing, offer the literary medium a location through which to test its forms. These are examples of the mutual self-reference of fiction, architecture, and media, and very explicit examples at that. Both *The Crying of Lot 49* and *House of Leaves* stage themselves through reflexively produced communications systems—postal conspiracies and deconstructive media networks that make and regulate themselves—and do so in channel spaces that either look or are impossible. These are also examples of what it might look like to inhabit a media culture, and a modernity, whose forms are reflected everywhere in corridic space—a kind of space that exhausts itself in referentiality. When Oedipa Maas comes face to face with her situation in *The Crying of Lot 49,* it is in a category-evading "apartment/office," whose thoroughfares appear as a "train of doorways" or "corridor of Cohen's rooms." To "get lost" in this world is to experience a horizontal vertigo, and to register that discomfort as figural confusion.

House of Leaves encapsulates this dynamic in a brief interaction between a child and her father, a filmmaker who finds his house haunted by its own corridoricity:

> Navidson lifts his daughter onto his lap.
>
> "Okay. What do you want to play?"
>
> "I don't know," she shrugs. "Always."
>
> "What's always?"
>
> But before she can answer, he starts tickling her around the neck and Daisy dissolves into bursts of delight.
>
> Despite the tremendous amount of material generated by Exploration A, no one has ever commented on the game Daisy wants to play with her father, perhaps because everyone assumes it is either a request "to play always" or just a childish neologism.
>
> Then again, "always" slightly mispronounces "hallways."
>
> It also echoes it.[14]

What this interaction and the commentary provided with it show is that the dynamic interplay between communication and space—or communicative space—that I have been describing is always at heart an explicit problem of language and figuration for these novels. The implicit demand to "play hallways," which is the novel's demand as well, also requires that those hallways be misrecognized, mispronounced, and heard as echoes of something else.

The demand to "play hallways," as it is invoked by Pynchon's and Danielewski's novels (published in 1966 and 2000, respectively), resonates as an echo of what I have been exploring in these pages. The cannibalization of space by corridors of infinite regress, or what becomes the nightmarish topography of these texts, forms a possible vector for what is a long history of novels observing their own mediality through reference to physical channels.

The ruthless reassertion of corridoricity in the face of a perceived dematerialization of the channel through the development and increased ubiquity of broadcast signals and wireless communication is not a simple or reactionary clinging to a materiality of communication now deceased. Something of the corridor persists in the move to a Corbusian "freedom" represented by the domestic open-plan architecture that produces a distinctive spatial mode in the postwar period. Do the channels, pores, and vectors of corridic space dissipate along with the walls in an open-plan interior? Is interiority itself, in part the purview of novels, subject to radical redefinition when the wireless imagination is literalized in the architectural "open"? Deleuze describes a "generalized crisis in relation to all the environments of enclosure" emerging in the latter half of the twentieth century that operates as a crisis of interiors and institutions alike.[15] What happens to these enclosures is that they become subject to change, or "deformation," just like the individuals thought to inhabit them. The call to "describe what is already in the process of substitution for the disciplinary sites of enclosure, whose crisis is everywhere proclaimed,"[16] remains a call to describe, or to redescribe a series of social forms that are describing themselves no longer as sites, but systems. The open plan is another name for such a redescription, enacted in architecture.

What the open plan looks like and how it works, however, are never easy to describe. An open-plan domestic interior may be what Marc Augé refers to as a non-place, a paradoxical combination of spatial circulation network, transit mechanism, and destination. This refusal of "place" as traditionally understood depends on accounting for the "spatial overabundance of the present" by using something other than double-entry bookkeeping.[17] Instead, non-places are observed by "totaling all the air, rail and motorway routes, the mobile cabins called 'means of transport' (aircraft, trains and road vehicles), the airports and railway stations, hotel chains, leisure parks, large retail outlets, and finally the complex skein of cable and wireless networks that mobilize extraterrestrial space for the purposes of a communication so peculiar that it often puts the individual in contact only with another image of himself."[18] And if the spatial equivalences of contagious "openness" are the nonlocations of non-places in the open-plan model, its time could be that of a liquid modernity. In Zygmunt Bauman's discussion of such liquidity, "the solids whose turn has come to be thrown into the melting pot and which are in the process of being melted at the present time, the time of fluid modernity, are the bonds which interlock individual choices in collective projects and actions—the patterns of communication and co-ordination between individually conducted life policies on the one hand and political actions of human collectivities on the other."[19] The solidity of walls in a liquid time, along with what it might represent and encode, is also here subject to melting forces.

In this world, the homogeneous spaces of flow start to stand in for corridors. Bauman refers to "the crowds filling the corridors of shopping malls" who "come as close as conceivable to the imagined ideal 'community' that knows no difference."[20] When contemporary novels attempt to inhabit these spaces and the persons filling and moving through them, such as the office spaces and inmates of Joshua Ferris's postbureaucratic 2007 novel *Then We Came to the End,* the first person shifts to a collective "we" with as little regard for the stakes of that shift as the omnivorous spaces have for their distinctions. Take the following account of what non-place looks like from the "collective":

> We had wide hallways. Some contained offices running along both sides, while others had offices on one side and cubicles on the other. Jim Jackers' cubicle was unique in that it was set off in a corner. He had a wonderful view because of that location and we questioned whether he deserved it. To get there you had to walk past the toner stain in the carpet on sixty. He shared that prime space with one other person, a woman named Tanya something who worked on a different partner's team. A retractable wall separated them, made of thick privacy glass, the kind used in shower windows. Behind it, one moved about, it seemed to the other, as if scrubbing and deodorizing, when really they were just filing or inputting.[21]

Not only do the hallways assume the agency of containment here, but they also demarcate the banal pseudo-divisions of open-top cubicle life. Navigating these "walls," retractable or otherwise, requires moving between "me," "you," and "one." This is a move that requires some effort, experiencing the transfer of domesticity to the corporate home with more certainty than the process of self-identification, made subtly alien.

Alien, that is, because it is without alienation. Even as the corridor disappears into its referentiality, the interiors, like those of *Winesburg, Ohio*'s Enoch, *Absalom, Absalom!*'s Quentin, or *An American Tragedy*'s Clyde, disappear with it only to reappear within themselves recursively. And the employees of Ferris's novel are hardly alone: when Howie, the narrator of Nicholson Baker's 1988 novel of minutiae *The Mezzanine* (the real-time setting of which is confined to the narrator's lunchtime mechanical passage from ground to middle floor) announces that the novel springs from "the escalator ride that is the vehicle of this memoir," the looping structures of language, architecture, and persons coincide.[22] What Howie refers to as his "escalatorial happiness," then, is another way of pointing to the kind of sublimations attached to that coincidence. Just before the reference to his transit-shaped happiness, as he catalogues "systems of local transport" such as airport luggage carousels, supermarket conveyor belts, milk-bottling machines, clothing hanger systems at the dry cleaners, rotating watch displays, and the like—their cylindricality becomes the basic agent of reference. And the escalator, he says, "shared qualities with all of these systems, with one difference: it was the only one I could get on and ride."[23] Howie's genuine enjoyment of the escalator (which appears not without its hints of violence throughout the novel) appears on the one hand quite different from the experience of the escalator's contemporary counterpart in communicative non-place, the elevator. But as Lila Mae, the elevator inspector focalizing much of Colson Whitehead's 1999 novel *The Intuitionist* observes, the distinction can also be labeled an interpretive choice: "Taking their cue from the early days of passenger-response criticism, Arbo equipped their newest model with an oversized door to foster the illusion of space, to distract the passenger from what every passenger feels acutely about elevators. That they ride in a box on a rope in a pit. That they are in the void."[24]

The escalators and elevators that loop deliriously through levels of allegory and other figurative grey zones in these texts do so as messengers, as Poros, or channels that insistently name themselves as such. They are the inescapable counterparts of any dream of openness. They also signal a confrontation with a modernity that is reflexive rather than beyond itself. What happens to the corridor in the move to an open-plan aesthetic is not a melting, liquification, or disappearance—instead, it travels and looks back at itself. What it sees is a vector, a network, or a lateral movement, or perhaps what Bruce Nauman visualizes in *Live-Taped Video Corridor*. In Nauman's installation, a television monitor at the end of a passage shows an image of the viewer (who may not in any case any longer be a "subject") as he or she approaches the monitor, but in reverse: the image you confront in the glass of the monitor is one of yourself simultaneously walking away and receding from view, and the closer the approach the more distant the image.

Nauman, of course, presents his corridor "closed-circuit." By doing so, he deploys perhaps another version of a box on a rope in a pit, or makes visible an anxiety about closure that tends to accompany any call for the open. In this I also include the recent interventions of Quentin Meillassoux, whose critique of what he calls "correlational exteriority"

Figure 25. Bruce Nauman, *Live-Taped Video Corridor,* 1970; wallboard, video camera, 2 video monitors, videotape player, videotape; dimensions variable, approximately 144 × 384 × 20 in. (365.8 × 975.4 × 50.8 cm). Solomon R. Guggenheim Museum, New York, Panza Collection, Gift. Courtesy Sperone Westwater, New York / Copyright 2012 Bruce Nauman / Artists Rights Society (ARS), New York.

assumes that the correlational moves of post-Kantian philosophy, particularly when they stem from reflexive structures of observation, are also moves of imprisonment and enclosure. His call for the speculative, the absolute, or the un-totalizable in *After Finitude* is also a lament, that "the space of exteriority is merely the space of what faces us, of what exists only as a correlate of our own existence."[25] What is so "mere" about a self-facing exteriority is precisely its looping, reflexive, and in this account limiting structure. Meillassoux speculates that "it could be that contemporary philosophers have lost the *great outdoors,* the *absolute* outside of pre-critical thinkers: that outside which was not relative to us, and which was given as indifferent to its own givenness to be what it is, existing in itself regardless of whether we are thinking of it or not; that outside which thought could explore with the legitimate feeling of being on foreign territory—of being entirely elsewhere."[26] The "great outdoors" imagined here is after interiority as well.

Rather than moving after finitude, my account of corridors and their postmodern afterlives is comfortable in its closures and lateral motion. It abides in a spatialized sociality such as that formalized by Bruno Latour as a "movement, a displacement, a transformation, a translation, an enrollment."[27] This movement, a movement of reassembly, is constitutively and brazenly reflexive, and has a flexibility that Latour himself locates in the theorizing of narrative (and its self-theorizing in fiction).[28] This is a redescribing, rather than a replacing, of modern interiority from the perspective of the interior itself. That interior is connective, and it has walls, and its closed circuit is also a kind of vanishing point that renders any closure paradoxical.

NOTES

Preface

1. Gerber, Roth, and Silver, "All That I Need Is a Hallway."

2. Ibid.

3. I take the phrase "materialities of communication" from a collection of essays by the same title that moves between two poles of this book's theoretical background, namely the discourse analysis of Friedrich Kittler and the systems theory of Niklas Luhmann. See Gumbrecht and Pfeiffer, eds., *Materialities of Communication.*

4. Colomina, *Privacy and Publicity,* 20.

5. Jarzombek, "Corridor Spaces," 728–70. Deleuze, "Postscript on the Societies of Control," 3–4.

Introduction

1. See Kern, *The Culture of Time and Space.*

2. Benjamin, *The Arcades Project,* 125.

3. Benjamin quotes the *Illustrated Guide to Paris* on "inner boulevards": "These arcades, a recent invention of industrial luxury, are glass-roofed, marble-paneled corridors extending through whole blocks of buildings, whose owners have joined together for such enterprises. Lining both sides of these corridors, which get their light from above, are the most elegant shops, so that the passage is a city, a world in miniature" (ibid., 31).

4. J. Frank, *The Idea of Spatial Form.*

5. Faulkner, *Absalom, Absalom!,* 7.

6. Parrish, *From the Civil War to the Apocalypse,* 52.

7. Kelly, "Telling Questions in *Absalom, Absalom!,*" 123.

8. Hönnighausen, *Faulkner,* 63.

9. Chandler, *Dwelling in the Text,* 271–72. Chandler's divisions make literal those described by Eric Sundquist in *Faulkner.*

10. Faulkner, *Absalom, Absalom!,* 124.

11. Ibid., 67.

12. Ibid., 109. The specific association of "sentience" with the house could also be seen to dehumanize Clytie and other characters subject to its empty echoes, such as Quentin himself, and Rosa's sister Ellen, referred to in these passages as an "empty shell."

13. Brooks, "Incredulous Narration," 264.

14. Ibid., 266.

15. There are many discussions of the loom as an important piece of medial and literary history. See, for example, Alan Liu's discussion of the loom as digital ("Imagining the New Media Encounter"), or Liedeke Plate's location of digital textuality in the figure of Penelope's loom ("Is Contemporary Women's Writing Computational?").

16. Faulkner, *Absalom, Absalom!,* 80.

17. Thus, I share in this study the interest Jennifer Fleissner declares in *Women, Compulsion, Modernity* in looking beyond Americanist criticism either overtly or implicitly committed to what she refers to as "hyperbolic accounts of modernity's meanings for the American individual" (7) as well as the sense that emerges in the conclusion of her book that the more dynamic, obsessive naturalism she describes has a long and undertheorized life in the twentieth century. I also respond in part to Bill Brown's suggestion that the "material unconscious" he locates in Stephen Crane and modernized recreational space continues to develop, so that in "private modernist techniques" one sees how the space he examines "spatializes modern mental life—allowing the subject to inhabit a materialized interiority" (Brown, *The Material Unconscious*, 26). Taken together, these texts show broadly that the scholarship focused on the turn of the twentieth century is too rich a resource for thinking about the persistence of materiality and the strangeness of form not to feature prominently in a more capacious account of novelistic interiority as it travels into late modernity.

18. See Simmel, "The Metropolis and Mental Life"; and Goble, *Beautiful Circuits*.

19. Evans, "Figures, Doors and Passages," 74.

20. Ibid., 75. Evans presents his findings as a glimpse of the history of the corridor rather than its full view. He claims that the first corridor in domestic architecture was designed in 1597 by John Thorpe in England, but that the form remained dormant until the late eighteenth century, when it became a requirement for all domestic interiors.

21. Ibid., 70.

22. Jarzombek, "Corridor Spaces," 766.

23. Ibid., 738, 752, 764–66.

24. Muthesius, *The English House,* 79.

25. Blau, *The Architecture of Red Vienna, 1919–1934,* 200.

26. Ibid., 202.

27. Hayden, *Redesigning the American Dream,* 7.

28. Archer, *Architecture and Suburbia*, 112.

29. Evans, "Figures, Doors and Passages," 79.

30. Ibid., 88.

31. Archer, *Architecture and Suburbia,* xvi.

32. Peters, *Speaking into the Air,* 7–8.

33. Kittler, "The History of Communication Media," 1.

34. In his chapter on communication in *Social Systems,* Luhmann writes: "Processes that can be applied to themselves are reflexive. With communication, this means that one can communicate about communication. One can thematize the communicative process in communication, can inquire about and explain how something was meant, can request communication, can reject communication, can establish communicative connections, and so forth. All this continues to be based on the difference between information and utterance, but in reflexive communication, communication itself is treated as information and made the object of utterances" (153).

35. De Certeau, *The Practice of Everyday Life,* 115. Mark Seltzer takes this connection between fiction and transport a step further, extending it to the marketplace: "News and novels supply a shorter or longer movement between the reader's private space and the world; the market productions of news and novels transport and 'beguile' the reader doubly shuttling between home and marketplace. The novel is thus both for commuters and a commuter itself, representing and enacting an exchange between domesticity and the market-place of the world" ("Reading Foucault," 88).

36. A brief survey of such texts would include: Carsten and Hugh-Jones, *About the House*; Chandler, *Dwelling in the Text*; Elam and Wiegman, *Feminism Beside Itself*; Eriksen, *The Building in the Text*; E. Frank, *Literary Architecture*; Gill, *Happy Rural Seat*; Gleason, *Sites Unseen*; Johnson, *Home, Maison, Casa*; Levy, *Fiction of the Home Place*; Romines, *The Home Plot*; R. Rubenstein, *Home Matters*; Tristram, *Living Space in Fact and Fiction*. See also Bachelard, *The Poetics of Space*.

37. Elmer, "Blinded Me with Science," 244.

38. Clarke and Hansen, eds., *Emergence and Embodiment*; Huhtamo and Parikka, eds., *Media Archaeology*.

39. See, in particular, Winthrop-Young, "Silicon Sociology, or, Two Kings on Hegel's Throne?"

40. Rasch and Wolfe, *Observing Complexity*, 9–10.

41. Clarke and Hansen, *Emergence and Embodiment,* 5

42. Ibid, 6. In David Wellbery's 2009 essay, "The General Enters the Library: A Note on Disciplines and Complexity," he discusses Luhmannian "transdisciplinarity" as one of three types of interdisciplinary forms, and points out that these kinds of theories "can have a considerable impact on research, but perhaps their most interesting feature is that they are, for the most part, short-lived" (989). The point is that the disciplines themselves adapt and change in response to transdisciplinary pressures, and they adapt and change because they are systems. I will discuss some of the ramifications of disciplinary thinking and Luhmann in chapter 4.

43. Clarke and Hansen, *Emergence and Embodiment,* 6.

44. Ernst, "Media Archaeography," 239.

45. For a description of what this theory entails, see the issue of *Grey Room* dedicated to "The New German Media Theory," including the editorial introduction (Horn, "Editor's Introduction").

46. Parikka, *Insect Media,* xiii.

47. Vismann, *Files,* 39.

48. Jarzombek, "Corridor Spaces," 731.

49. Vogl, "Becoming-Media," 16.

50. See Wellbery, introduction, xi.

51. Kittler, "Thinking Colours and/or Machines," 40.

52. Such a move would more likely look something like the reaction of the unnamed narrator of J. G. Ballard's posthumously published short story "The Dying Fall" to what he perceives to be a more generalized obliteration of the traditional humanities: "Elaine had married me on the rebound, to spite an unfaithful lover, but soon decided that her husband, a classics lecturer at a minor university, was minor in all other respects. I was losing my students in a ferment of curriculum changes that would eventually lead to the descheduling of Latin and Greek and their replacement by cultural and media studies. My refusal to sue the university, Elaine decided, was a sign of my innate weakness, a frailty that soon extended to the marriage bed." Ballard's narrator responds to this situation by single-handedly causing the collapse of the Leaning Tower of Pisa, destroying his wife, the tower's occupants, and the symbol of "fossilised time" all at once. But at least he feels bad about it. See Ballard, "The Dying Fall."

53. Vogl, "Becoming-Media," 15.

54. Luhmann, *Social Systems,* 153.

55. Levinson, "What Is New Formalism?," 560.

56. Ibid., 561.

57. Marin, *On Representation,* 5, 7.

58. C. Wolfe, "The Idea of Observation at Key West," 261. Cary Wolfe's reading of Stevens also appears in his more recent *What Is Posthumanism?,* which also includes an important consideration of the reception of Luhmann in the American academy. Wolfe sees "second-order systems theory" as "'the reconstruction of deconstruction,'" and sees many parallels to the reception of both modes of thinking in the United States. According to Wolfe, an understanding of the relationship between the two "hinges on systems theory's extraordinarily rigorous and detailed account of the fundamental dynamics and complexities of meaning that subtend the reproduction and interpenetration of psychic and social systems" (*What Is Posthumanism?,* 8).

59. Thacker and Galloway, *The Exploit,* 5.

60. Ellmann, *The Nets of Modernism,* 2.

61. Ibid., 39.

62. Cohen, *The Networked Wilderness,* 28.

63. Ibid., 146.

64. See McGurl, *The Program Era;* Cicciorico, *Reading Network Fiction.*

65. See Biers, "Syncope Fever." Biers mentions "American *autopoesis*" on page 100.

66. See Seltzer, *Serial Killers* and *True Crime.*

67. Biers, "Syncope Fever," 99.

68. Goble, *Beautiful Circuits,* 159.

69. Ibid., 158.

70. Ibid., 224.

71. For David Roberts, the "doublevoicing" of first-order observation differentiates the novel from other forms of narrative observation, such as biography: "The social autonomy of literature is the outcome of the process of the differentiation, that is fictionalization of the novel in the seventeenth and eighteenth centuries. Its inner literary complement is the externalization of second-order observation in the self-reflection of the novel as form. Through self-reflection—the visible re-entry of form—the novel demonstrates its autonomy in relation to the world" ("Self-Reference in Literature," 41).

72. Foucault, "Of Other Spaces," 24.

73. Siegert, *Relays,* 14.

74. Ibid., 59.

75. Ibid., 17.

76. Kracauer, "On Employment Agencies," 62.

77. Evans, "Figures, Doors and Passages," 78.

78. Gallagher, "The Rise of Fictionality," 360–61.

79. Luhmann, *Observations on Modernity,* 7.

80. Luhmann, *Social Systems,* 456.

81. Martin, *The Organizational Complex,* 7.

82. Hayles, *Writing Machines,* 22.

83. Vogl, "Becoming-Media," 16.

84. Steinbeck, *The Wayward Bus,* 1.

85. Ibid., 117.

86. Ibid., 170.

87. Ibid., 226.

88. Ibid., 240.

89. Ibid., 261.

90. This is one of several translations of Stendhal's aphorism, sometimes translated as "a mirror carried along a high road." Thanks to Jonathan Grossman for first pointing me to this reference.

91. Jarzombek, "Corridor Spaces," 770.

92. Latour, *Aramis,* 24.

93. For more specific discussions of the political engagements of late naturalist, social realist, and proletarian forms see Bell, *Culture, Genre, and Literary Vocation*; Douglas, *Terrible Honesty*; Foley, *Radical Representations*; Geismar, *Writers in Crisis*; Mullen and Smethurst, *Left of the Color Line*; Szalay, *New Deal Modernism.*

94. Fleissner, *Women, Compulsion, Modernity,* 276.

95. Said, *On Late Style.*

96. Adorno, "Late Style in Beethoven," 564.

97. Deleuze, *Kafka,* 73–74.

98. Anderson, *Winesburg, Ohio,* 9.

99. Ibid., 3, 105, 122.

100. The language of "expression" here also refers to generic debates surrounding the placement of *Winesburg Ohio* within a modernist literary canon. Seen at times as a work of "expressionist" literature prefiguring modernist innovation or also as an outmoded naturalist work, Anderson's text highlights a problem characterizing many of the works I take up.

101. The particular story of "hands," so often anthologized as a discrete work, has received recent critical attention in accounts of *Winesburg, Ohio* that focus on its often contradictory positions on sexuality (and, therefore, on what the hands do rather than what they represent). See Whalen, "Dreams of Manhood." See also Haralson, *Henry James and Queer Modernity.*

102. Anderson, *Winesburg, Ohio,* 151.

103. Ibid., 152.

104. Ibid.

105. Luhmann, *Social Systems,* 139. See also Baecker, "The Reality of Motion Pictures"; and Esposito, "The Arts of Contingency."

106. Among the range of systems-theoretical discussions of distinction, the accounts of the medium/form distinction upon which I rely here are interested not only in the drawing of distinctions (taken from George Spencer-Brown's injunction in *Laws of Form*), but in the drawing through *observation.* These ocular metaphorics are apropos to the following discussion of film as well as an analysis of narrative observation. A primary distinction for an analysis of social systems, and particularly for art systems, is the distinction between medium and form (see Luhmann, *Art as a Social System*).

107. Baecker, "The Reality of Motion Pictures," 570.

108. Koolhaas, *Delirious New York,* 125.

109. Luhmann puts this proximity another way when he says, "we arrive at a time in which literature and life in literature can no longer be separated." The "time" to which he refers corresponds with that of *Winesburg,* for he is discussing redescriptions of "self" and "self-realization" by thinkers such as Georg Simmel and William James. See Luhmann, *The Reality of the Mass Media,* 114.

110. Brian Massumi identifies proprioception as the most overtly self-referential of the senses, and the aspect of self-referentiality reconfigures the understanding of space: "Position emerges from movement, from a relation of movement to itself . . . Place arises from a dynamic of interference and accord between sense-dimensions" (*Parables for the Virtual,* 180).

111. For an account of this relationship seen from the perspective of the "spatial turn" in critical theory, see also the analysis of the "socio-spatial dialectic" in Soja, *Postmodern Geographies.*

112. The drive for a kind of "containment culture," in light of these proliferating distinctions, forms here the opposite logic of the corridor. See Nadel, *Containment Culture*.

113. Karatani, *Architecture as Metaphor,* 145.

114. Derrida, *Dissemination,* 95.

1. Becoming Media in *An American Tragedy*

1. See Crane, *Maggie*; Norris, *McTeague*. Here I am only briefly alluding to the body of literature on Norris's text that accounts for the relationship of Trina McTeague to what might be understood as factory labor. For a discussion of how the "worn-out machine" Trina's production of animals signals not only her "inability to reproduce" but also her affiliation with immigrant forms of labor, see Fleissner, who argues that "the machine that competes with [Trina] might be seen not simply as history's product but as history itself, its reproductions far exceeding those of any single household" (*Women, Compulsion, Modernity,* 219).

2. Crane, *Maggie,* 17.

3. Ibid., 25, 45.

4. Dreiser, *An American Tragedy,* 3. Richard Lehan has pointed out that "Clyde's story takes place between walls," which he reads as a general metaphor for the "walls of society," and its constraints. I will be arguing that the formation of walls into corridors, halls, rooms, and passages throughout the text has consequences that complicate this picture of the individual and the social that emerges in earlier accounts of the novel. See Lehan, "Dreiser's *An American Tragedy,*" 189.

5. Dreiser, *An American Tragedy,* 49.

6. Ibid., 185.

7. Ibid., 206.

8. Ibid., 554.

9. See also Mitchell, "'And Then Rose for the First Time'"; Lehan, "Dreiser's *An American Tragedy*."

10. An exception would be the recent volume: Cassuto and Eby, eds., *The Cambridge Companion to Theodore Dreiser*. This collection features one essay devoted specifically to *An American Tragedy* among its twelve, a piece by Leonard Cassuto on gender and crime fiction. The novel appears more frequently in recent criticism that takes up its film adaptations, which I will discuss in more detail later in this chapter.

11. Denby, "The Cost of Desire."

12. Davis, "Life in the Iron-Mills, or the Korl Woman," 260.

13. Banta, *Taylored Lives,* 299.

14. Michaels, "An American Tragedy, or the Promise of American Life," 93.

15. Sergei Eisenstein makes the mediality of the collar's movement between thing and symbol explicit in his unfilmed screenplay for the novel. He marks Clyde's arrival at his uncle's factory thus: "The letter fades out and we see the city of Chicago and, resplendent on one of the buildings, is an electric sign. The sign

outlines a collar, a collar gorgeous, in apotheosis—straight lines of light, like a fiery star, like a halo, shoot out around it, bursting and extinguishing like the opening and shutting of a fist. And ever and anon, beneath it, shows the illuminated signature: *Samuel Griffiths*" ("An American Tragedy").

16. Here I am deliberately echoing Michaels's assessment of collars in *An American Tragedy,* but with a key difference. In Michaels's elegant formulation, "the literature of the Progressive Era is a literature of white-collar promises and tragedies, like the promises and tragedies—the white-collar people and the white collars—produced in the Griffiths Collar and Shirt Company" ("An American Tragedy, or the Promise of American Life," 95). What I would like to point out, however, is the shift that this construction will not allow, a shift registered in *An American Tragedy*'s focus on the collar factory's stamping room rather than the collars themselves.

17. See also U.S. Patent No. 567,866, in which Henri Edouard Couzineau says of the design for his printing press apparatus for garments, "An apparatus according to my invention consists, essentially, in the combination of a fixed table, over which is placed or stretched the fabric or material on which the printing or impressing is to be effected, and of a carriage, as hereinafter described, which is moved over the fabric or material, which carriage supports the cliché or stereotype-plate or other printing or marking device, which may be a thin plate of metal or other flexible material and which is formed in relief with the shapes to be printed or impressed. I will refer to it as the 'cliché.'"

18. Dreiser, *An American Tragedy,* 276.

19. Flusser, *The Shape of Things,* 28.

20. Hayles, *Writing Machines,* 22.

21. Kittler, *Discourse Networks 1800/1900,* 370.

22. "And as she thought of all this, stamping at her desk along with the others, she suddenly discovered that a bundle of collars which she had already stamped as sixteens were not of that size but smaller" (Dreiser, *An American Tragedy,* 307).

23. The newspaper report detailing the search for Clyde makes the link between stamp, identity, and guilt very clear: "The fact that a man's straw hat found nearby contained no lining or other method of identification, has caused Coroner Heit to assert that unless the body of the man is found he will assume that murder has been committed" (ibid., 624).

24. Ibid., 840.

25. Luhmann, *The Reality of the Mass Media,* 114.

26. Dreiser, *An American Tragedy,* 568.

27. Ibid., 592.

28. Vogl, "Becoming-Media," 16.

29. Vismann and Krajewski, "Computer Juridisms," 91.

30. Dreiser, introduction, vii.

31. "Yet, several years since, when it was filmed as *Greed* . . ." (Dreiser, introduction, vii).

32. Erikson, *Zeroville,* 15.

33. For a comprehensive history of the interactions between twentieth-century adaptations of the novel, see Merck, *Hollywood's American Tragedies*.

34. Dreiser, *An American Tragedy*, 27.

35. Ibid., 734.

36. Ibid., 567.

37. Merck, *Hollywood's American Tragedies*, 113.

38. Rancière, "The Saint and the Heiress," 116. Rancière also incorporates a discussion of Stevens's adaptation in his more extended analysis of Godard's *Histoire(s)* in *Film Fables*. See Rancière, *Film Fables*, 183–86.

39. Dreiser, *Art, Music, and Literature 1897–1902*, 112.

40. Rancière, "The Saint and the Heiress," 114.

41. Ibid., 113.

42. Ibid., 118–19.

43. Ibid., 119.

44. Rancière, *The Philosopher and His Poor*, 133.

45. Rancière, *Dis-agreement: Politics and Philosophy*, 90–91.

46. Rancière, *The Names of History*, 3.

47. Ibid. Rancière describes the paradoxical rendering of history as narrative thus: "The difference between history as science and history as narrative was necessarily produced in the heart of narrative, with the latter's words and use of words."

48. Derrida and Stiegler, *Echographies of Television*, 162.

49. Vismann and Krajewski, "Computer Juridisms," 92.

50. Vismann, *Files*, xii.

51. This is also another way of saying that the study of media is a communicative process. For Luhmann, "communication is possible only as a self-referential process," and "processes that can be applied to themselves are reflexive." Media studies, thus conceived, present a specific form of communication communicating about itself. See Luhmann, *Social Systems*, 143, 53.

52. Eisenstein, too, was interested in *An American Tragedy* for the possibilities it afforded to experiment with the changing of registers of meaning. Chris Robé, in his discussion of the role of Eisenstein's *An American Tragedy* work in developing techniques that would eventually appear in his *Qué Viva México!*, points out that Eisenstein was explicitly interested in using the combination of individual shots to express the relationship between separate objects and the concepts that emerge through their juxtaposition. See Robé, "Eisenstein in America," 24.

53. Dreiser, *An American Tragedy*, 6.

54. Merck likens Eisenstein's interest in internal monologue and his experimentations with technique planned for *An American Tragedy* to an objectification of distraction, pointing out that in his reflections on the scenario Eisenstein pointed to his project as one oriented toward the changing places of otherwise incommensurable registers of meaning, such as when he asks "what is the syntax of inner language, as distinct from external? . . . What contradicts what?" (qtd. in Merck, *Hollywood's American Tragedies*, 48).

55. Dreiser, *An American Tragedy,* 529.

56. Ibid., 506.

57. Ibid., 532.

58. Ibid., 532–33.

59. Flusser, *The Shape of Things,* 82.

60. Dreiser, *An American Tragedy,* 533.

61. Ibid., 535, 36, 41.

62. Peters, *Speaking into the Air,* 5.

63. Jarzombek, "From Corridor (Spanish) to Corridor (English)," 7. See also Jarzombek, *Corridor Spaces*. For earlier histories, see Evans, "Figures, Doors and Passages"; Blau, *The Architecture of Red Vienna, 1919–1934*.

64. Dreiser, *An American Tragedy,* 541.

65. Vismann, *Files,* 139.

66. Jarzombek, "From Corridor (Spanish) to Corridor (English)," 10.

67. Dreiser, *An American Tragedy,* 776.

68. Luhmann, *The Reality of the Mass Media,* 115.

69. See Deleuze, "Postscript on the Societies of Control"; Nancy, *Being Singular Plural*; Virno, *A Grammar of the Multitude*.

70. Dreiser, *An American Tragedy,* 559.

71. Ibid., 306.

72. Ibid., 586.

73. Habermas, *The Structural Transformation of the Public Sphere,* 44. Habermas cites changes in architectural style that lead to "the lofty, raftered hall" going "out of fashion."

74. Klimasmith, *At Home in the City,* 5, 31.

75. Rosner, *Modernism and the Architecture of Private Life,* 128, 47.

76. See also Marcus, *Apartment Stories*.

77. Dreiser, *An American Tragedy,* 933.

2. Infrastructural Modernity

1. Ellison, *Invisible Man,* 13.

2. Ibid., 6–7.

3. Ibid., 13.

4. Qtd. in Denes, "Interview: Picture Perfect." For a fascinating backdrop to Wall's image, see Gordon Parks's spread in *Life* magazine (August 25, 1952, pp. 10–11), in which he depicts the same scene with a lone man against a circuit background.

5. See Kittler, *Discourse Networks 1800 / 1900*.

6. I take the phrase "media landscape" from Esposito, "The Arts of Contingency."

7. See Luhmann, *Art as a Social System*.

8. Robbins, "The Smell of Infrastructure."

9. See M. Rubenstein, *Public Works;* and Herring, *Another Country,* 60.

10. Herring, *Another Country,* 154.

11. M. Rubenstein, *Public Works,* 46.

12. Latour, *We Have Never Been Modern,* 117.

13. See Karatani, *Architecture as Metaphor.*

14. Roth, *Call It Sleep,* 17.

15. Esposito, "The Arts of Contingency," 10.

16. Calvino, *Six Memos for the Next Millennium,* 45.

17. Benjamin and Arendt, *Illuminations,* 223.

18. Ibid., 219.

19. Laporte, *History of Shit,* 56. One of Laporte's many texts in this volume is a bathroom that doubles as corridor: "When people emerged from the Koun-tse-fan (a public bathroom in the shape of a hallway 'lined by stalls in the fashion of the boxes in an opera house'), they did not leave a tip in the custodian's bowl. Rather, it was the custodian who distributed a *sapèque* to all comers in exchange for the shit they left behind" (134). The likeness of public bathroom to public hallway becomes part of the reversal of the exchange process.

20. Dos Passos, *Manhattan Transfer,* 335.

21. Ibid., 321.

22. Ibid.

23. "He grabbed the gas jet, the gas jet gave way" (Dos Passos, *Manhattan Transfer,* 214).

24. Ibid., 180.

25. Siegert, *Relays,* 1.

26. Ibid., 2.

27. See Elizabeth Klimasmith's *At Home in the City* for a compelling account of increased "permeability" in urban domestic architecture. What I would like to emphasize here, however, is that this permeability is not necessarily new, but intensified, and part of a broader conception of communications space and process.

28. For example, Jacqueline Stewart reads Wright's treatment of the cinema in *Native Son* as a point of departure for analyzing the relationship between African American moviegoing and larger national movement, comparing spectatorship, the Great Migration, and urbanization. See Stewart, "Negroes Laughing at Themselves?"

29. Wright, *Native Son,* 53, 57. "This is" remains the common language for introduction, with Mary being told, "This is Bigger Thomas," and shortly after this scene introducing Bigger and Jan: "Oh Bigger, this is Jan. And Jan, this is Bigger Thomas." The refrain, however, works differently for the elder Daltons. Henry Dalton introduces his wife to Bigger belatedly ("That was Mrs. Dalton") and, significantly, is the only character to introduce himself ("Well, I'm Mr. Dalton"). See Wright, *Native Son,* 66, 47.

30. Ibid., 57.

31. Ibid., 58.

32. Stewart, "Negroes Laughing at Themselves?," 655.

33. Wright, *Native Son,* 331.

34. Ibid., 332, 12.

35. The term "reentry" describes, in systems-theoretical terms, an operation in which a system-producing distinction is incorporated back into the system, thereby continuing its self-production. I will be discussing this operation later as part of a media logic. See "Medium and Form" in Luhmann, *Art as a Social System*.

36. Wright, *Native Son,* 380.

37. Ibid., 381.

38. Elmer, "Spectacle and Event in Native Son," 783.

39. Goble, *Beautiful Circuits,* 158.

40. Wright, *Native Son,* 215.

41. The furnace in *Native Son* explicitly stages the workings of what Steven Shaviro, in his collection of observations on the contemporary "network society," calls a network: "As it seems to us now, a network is a self-generating, self-organizing, self-sustaining system. It works through multiple feedback loops. These loops allow the system to monitor and modulate its own performance continually and thereby maintain a state of homeostatic equilibrium. At the same time, these feedback loops induce effects of interference, amplification, and resonance. And such effects permit the system to grow, both in size and in complexity. Beyond this, a network is always nested in a hierarchy. From the inside, it seems to be entirely self-contained, but from the outside, it turns out to be part of a still larger network" (*Connected,* 10).

42. Dos Passos, *Manhattan Transfer,* 12.

43. Wright, *Native Son,* 238.

44. Ibid., 231.

45. Ibid., 238.

46. Qtd. in Thompson, *The Soundscape of Modernity,* 131. For a discussion of noise both explicitly audible and information-theoretical, see Schweighauser, *The Noises of American Literature, 1890–1985*.

47. Wright, *Native Son,* 92.

48. Ibid., 248.

49. Luhmann, *The Reality of the Mass Media,* 115.

50. Biers, "Syncope Fever"; Goble, *Beautiful Circuits*.

51. See Peters's *Speaking into the Air* for an extended account of the multiple valences of communication in philosophical and literary history. Peters focuses on the role of mass mediation in transforming the cultural idea of communication in the twentieth century, claiming that "only moderns could be facing each other and be worried about 'communicating' as if they were thousands of miles apart" (2). Peters's emphasis on disruption and breakdown as constitutive of modern communication, however, is something I would like to complicate in these pages.

52. On the historical distinction of "communications systems" as multimedia transit systems of "information, persons, goods" as opposed to "information systems" that are "optimized in terms of the storage, processing and transmission of messages" see Kittler, "The History of Communication Media."

53. Roth, *Call It Sleep,* 426–27.

54. The construction "as if," of course, invokes the conditional, but the sense of simile is preserved in the "as" in this instance.

55. For Peters and others, face-to-face communication in a hypermediated world represents an attempt (though clearly always doomed) at unmediated communication. We could think, then, about the recent critical turn to ethics, so often premised on the Levinasian encounter of the "face to face," as an effect of the media. See Peters, *Speaking into the Air.*

56. Luhmann, *The Reality of the Mass Media,* 114.

57. See, for example, Nazare, "Backtrack to the Future." The mention of "Manhattan transfer" in the novel occurs when the characters are traveling out of the city, however, moving out of the electrical transit infrastructure.

58. Stan Emery is the more developed character in the novel to have a connection to architecture as a career choice. After he kills himself by setting his apartment on fire, uttering, "Kerist I wish I was a skyscraper," his wife informs the crowd watching the fire from the street that Emery planned to ask his father for money to go abroad and study architecture. Although the novel presents this as a doubtful possibility should he have lived, Stan Emery's relationship to the built world throughout the novel marks "architecture" in reference to his character a very different project. It is also useful to observe that Stan's death and the revelation of his plans to study architecture are immediately followed by Phil Sandbourne's final appearance in the novel. See Dos Passos, *Manhattan Transfer,* 214–15.

59. Ibid., 216–17. Note here that George Baldwin begins his vertical ascent of the class ladder in the novel by arguing and winning a suit against the New York Central Railroad.

60. Ibid., 143.

61. Ibid., 216.

62. Ibid., 217.

63. For a description of this project in relation to the development of shopping transit systems, see Chung et al., *Harvard Design School Guide to Shopping.*

64. Sachs, "System of Transportation."

65. Francovich, "Moving Platform."

66. Massumi, *Parables for the Virtual,* 198. Massumi's call is for building to become more Deleuzean, or at least to represent the kind of countermodel to Foucauldian "enclosure" (though anticipated by Foucault) that Deleuze sees in the society of control: "Enclosures are molds, distinct castings, but controls are modulation, like a self-determining cast that will continuously change from one moment to another, or like a sieve that will transmute from point to point" (Deleuze, "Postscript on the Societies of Control," 4).

67. Dos Passos, *Manhattan Transfer,* 217.

68. Ibid., 144.

69. Kittler, *Discourse Networks 1800/1900,* 265.

70. Colomina, *Privacy and Publicity,* 335.

71. Martin, *The Organizational Complex,* 8.

72. Dos Passos, *U.S.A,* 1. Paul Giles sees the spatial moves of the trilogy as a more direct combination of map and culture, with a more literal geography: "The symbiotic equation in the 1930s between U.S. national identity and cultural geography was epitomized by the publication in 1938 of John Dos Passos's *USA*, whose projection of the country as contiguous in space" (*The Global Remapping of American Literature,* 129).

73. Dos Passos, *Manhattan Transfer,* 217.

74. Ibid., 3.

75. See Hughson, "Narration in the Making of *Manhattan Transfer,*" 187.

76. Dos Passos, *Manhattan Transfer,* 142.

77. Ibid., 219.

78. Schivelbusch, *The Railway Journey.*

79. For Luhmann, this is the process of the social, for the setting-into and keeping-in-motion of communication is what makes the formation of social systems both possible and inevitable. See Luhmann, *Social Systems,* 162.

80. See Kahn and Whitehead, *Wireless Imagination.*

3. The Flu and the Media, or Contagion 1918

1. In Dos Passos's *U.S.A.*, for example, one character's physician father requires that she wear a gauze mask to answer the telephone when she contributes to the efforts of his office to combat the epidemic locally.

2. For a collection of accounts dealing with the impact of the flu on particular cities, see Hartesveldt, ed., *The 1918–1919 Pandemic of Influenza*; Paul A. Buelow's chapter dealing with Chicago discusses the advertisements brought out by Chicago telephone companies cautioning against overuse of the phone during the pandemic.

3. Kittler, *Discourse Networks 1800/1900,* 225.

4. Moremen, ed., *Student Life at the University of California, Berkeley during and after World War I,* 147. For another treatment of public reaction to mask ordinances in the San Francisco Bay Area, see Hays, *Epidemics and Pandemics.*

5. Thacker and Galloway, *The Exploit,* 121.

6. For two accounts of the implications for media history of the role of the female operator, see Hayles, *My Mother Was a Computer*, and Kittler, *Discourse Networks 1800/1900.*

7. Dos Passos, *U.S.A,* 90.

8. Koolhaas, *Delirious New York,* 125.

9. Wald, "Contagious," 116.

10. Girard, "The Plague in Literature and Myth," 138.

11. Luhmann, *Essays on Self-Reference,* 14.

12. Dos Passos, *Manhattan Transfer,* 301.

13. Ibid., 283.

14. "Contagion," in *Oxford English Dictionary.*

15. According to Wald, "with its circulation in the sociological literature, 'contagion' gradually evolved from a metaphor to a carefully articulated sociological concept" ("Contagious," 164).

16. Dos Passos, *U.S.A,* 1153.

17. For many years after the war the estimate of flu deaths hovered at around forty million, but more current scholarship puts that figure much higher, from fifty up to one hundred million. I will be discussing a range of histories of the epidemic in the pages that follow.

18. Although critics often read illness in the works of Woolf as a rejection of models of "conventional sympathy," or highly original experience, I would argue that the mediation of Clarissa Dalloway's and Septimus Warren Smith's parallel relationship puts some pressure on this hypothesis. For a detailed account of Woolf's illness writing, see Coates, "Exposing the 'Nerves of Language.'"

19. Dos Passos, *U.S.A,* 479, 507.

20. Ibid., 867.

21. For Luhmann, this reflexivity is the basic operation of communication as such: "Processes that can be applied to themselves are reflexive. With communication, this means that one can communicate about communication. One can thematize the communicative process in communication, can inquire about and explain how something was meant, can request communication, can reject communication, can establish communicative connections, and so forth" (*Social Systems,* 153). In *U.S.A.,* and in the novels I will describe, one version of this is that contagion and influenza are contagious and influential, or communicative.

22. Dos Passos, *U.S.A,* 815.

23. Dos Passos, *Manhattan Transfer,* 232.

24. Ibid., 233.

25. Zimmer, "Old Viruses Resurrected through DNA."

26. Deleuze, "Postscript on the Societies of Control," 1.

27. See Collier, *The Plague of the Spanish Lady*; and Crosby, *Epidemic and Peace, 1918*, and *America's Forgotten Pandemic*. Crosby's 2003 reissue of his widely circulated 1976 volume adopts the phrase from the previous work that was paradoxically best remembered. Both historians lament the perceived relegation of the event to "folk-memory." Collier's history, famed for its "novelistic" attention to anecdote and narrative, is particularly concerned with the generalized ambivalence of reaction to the flu both "in the height of the slaughter" and afterward.

28. Crosby, *America's Forgotten Pandemic,* xiii.

29. "The Influenza Blues" can be read in relation to similar songs that circulate in Dos Passos's novels as well. For John Trombold, songs such as "The Alcoholic Blues" subtly demonstrate an argument for political revolt. See Trombold, "Popular Songs as Revolutionary Culture," 298.

30. Blakely, *Mass Mediated Disease,* 7.

31. Bollet, *Plagues and Poxes,* 104. See also Hartesveldt, ed., *The 1918–1919 Pandemic of Influenza.*

32. Crosby, *Epidemic and Peace, 1918,* 315.

33. Humphreys, "No Safe Place," 846.

34. Crosby, *Epidemic and Peace, 1918,* 317.

35. T. Wolfe, *Look Homeward, Angel,* 446.

36. Artaud, *The Theater and Its Double,* 27.

37. Ibid.

38. Priscilla Wald locates this sociality in space and time: "Contagious and infectious epidemics underscore the contact unrelated people, often strangers, have with each other; they are very much located in the present, emphasizing the rupture with the past and the uncertainty of the future" ("Future Perfect," 685). It is also interesting to note here how the discussion of the theater and the plague echoes the symptomatology provided by Paolo Virno in his *Grammar of the Multitude*: "In liberal thought, the uneasiness provoked by the 'many' is toned down by means of having recourse to the pairing of the terms public-private. The multitude, which is the polar opposite of the people, takes on the slightly ghostly and mortifying features of the so-called *private*." Virno diagnoses a weakness of liberal thought through its use of the term "multitude" to warm up an idea of the many with the hopeful proposition that enough residue of private individualism remains in socio-political life to provide immunity from undifferentiated publicness (*A Grammar of the Multitude,* 23).

39. For a more contemporaneous history of the epidemic that posits such recursion, see Sigerist, *Civilization and Disease*.

40. Immediately following the epidemic's worldwide outbreak, a physician in India composing a treatise on influenza for the Helmutty Tea Company drew explicit attention to global and urban transit as a medial operation of the flu: "In India it was conclusively proved by the health officer in Bombay that the first cases arrived there in ships at the end of May, 1918. At this time of the year Bombay acted as a huge incubator with suitable media for the dissemination of the disease among the over-crowded population" (Sen, *A Treatise on Influenza,* 12).

41. Crosby, *Epidemic and Peace, 1918,* 318.

42. Cather, *One of Ours*, 421.

43. Klark, "The Influenza Blues : . . . Song."

44. Cather, *One of Ours,* 339.

45. Ibid., 215.

46. Ibid., 233.

47. It is often the ship itself that is implicated not only as a culprit for the rapid worldwide spread of influenza, but for frustrating writers' desires to participate in the war. Crosby points out that an outbreak of influenza occurred on the ship carrying John Dos Passos across the Atlantic (and is frustrated that Dos Passos's account of a shipbound epidemic in *Three Soldiers* is of spinal meningitis). He also notes "Spanish influenza frustrated F. Scott Fitzgerald's ambition to get into the war and see something worth writing about. In October 1918, his division was ordered to France, but fear of an outbreak of flu on the high seas delayed its embarkation. When the division finally boarded ship, the war ended and she never cleared port. Fitzgerald, to his sorrow, had missed World War I" (Crosby, *Epidemic and Peace, 1918,* 315).

48. Cather, *One of Ours,* 292.

49. In an article tracing the relationship of epidemiological metaphors to theatrical space in the thinking of Artaud and theater history, Stanton Garner notes a generic interest on the part of the theater to the tropes of disease informed by germ theory: "Both theatre and medicine, after all, are technologies of the body, and in the modern period the two disciplines foregrounded similar issues: the interaction of the human organism with its environment, the relationship of inside and outside, the nature of visibility and somatic disclosure, and the definition of individual and social pathology." For Garner, the dialectical corporealities of metaphoric and literal plague turn on the medium of the theater itself, and its gathering of "actual bodies" in the same space. I would like to argue that the epidemic and the novel are similarly conjoined via the play between event and figure, but that the novel, a medium that does not require physical co-presence, is also implicated as a medium of transmission. See Garner, "Artaud, Germ Theory, and the Theatre of Contagion," 2.

50. Cather, *One of Ours,* 299, 310.

51. Blakely, for example, identifies the relationship between the flu and the media as representational rather than mutually constitutive. She examines the social construction of disease by the mass media as a project of articulation. However, this approach perhaps does not take its constructivism far enough. I propose that a narrative of the social construction of the flu must take into account that the social itself is a construction reflexively bound up in its media operations. See Blakely, *Mass Mediated Disease.*

52. Koszarski, "Flu Season."

53. Qtd. in ibid., 475.

54. Qtd. in ibid., 478.

55. Porter, *Pale Horse, Pale Rider,* 149, 72.

56. Ibid., 184.

57. Ibid., 149.

58. Ibid., 162–63.

59. Ibid., 157.

60. Ibid., 159.

61. For example, Daniel Gordon singles out *Pale Horse, Pale Rider* as an exception to the lack of literature dealing with the 1918 influenza, but he sees a limit to its exceptionality because the flu, for Gordon, ultimately cedes to the war and operates on the level of the merely symbolic: "Indeed, the specter of the war looms larger than that of the epidemic in the story as a whole. In the twentieth century, pain and tragedy have been represented primarily in the context of politics" ("The City and the Plague in the Age of Enlightenment," 69).

62. Gary Ciuba deals with the affinities of news items to one another in *Pale Horse, Pale Rider* as a sign of "the writing of everydayness," but also looks to the ultimate victory of war rhetoric over that of any topical or structural equivalence. See Ciuba, "One Singer Left to Mourn," 58.

63. Porter, *Pale Horse, Pale Rider,* 195.

64. Ibid., 143.
65. Ibid., 193.
66. Ibid., 197.
67. Luhmann, *The Reality of the Mass Media,* 74.
68. Porter, *Pale Horse, Pale Rider,* 207.
69. Caillois, "Mimicry and Legendary Psychasthenia," 23.
70. West, *Novels and Other Writings,* 84.
71. Ibid., 59.
72. Early in the novel, Miss Lonelyhearts turns to a marked passage in his copy of *The Brothers Karamazov* as his own Miss Lonelyhearts advice column. After reading the passage, he reflects for a moment: "It was excellent advice. If he followed it, he would be a big success. His column would be syndicated and the whole world would learn to love" (ibid., 67). Miss Lonelyhearts then decides that by turning to this novel, he simply fools himself.
73. See Wald, "Contagious," 2.
74. West, *Novels and Other Writings,* 93.
75. Ibid., 99.
76. Ibid., 119.
77. Ibid., 64.
78. Nieland, "West's Deadpan," 75.
79. Ibid., 74.
80. See the essays "What Is Communication?" and "On the Theory of Communication" in Flusser, *Writings.*
81. West, *Novels and Other Writings,* 91.
82. Ibid., 59.
83. Ibid., 70.
84. Cerasulo, "*The Dream Life of Balso Snell* and the Vocation of Nathanael West," 71. See also Greenberg, "Nathanael West and the Mystery of Feeling."
85. Nieland, "West's Deadpan," 58.
86. Ibid., 79.
87. West, *Novels and Other Writings,* 110.
88. Ibid., 111.
89. Ibid., 112.
90. Ibid., 86.
91. Ibid., 98.
92. Simmel, "The Stranger," 143.
93. West, *Novels and Other Writings,* 126.

4. Corridors of Power

1. M. Weber, *From Max Weber,* 197.
2. See, for example, Miller, *Max Weber,* 3.
3. Lefort, *The Political Forms of Modern Society,* 104.
4. Martin, *The Organizational Complex,* 4.

5. Ibid., 7.

6. Leavis, *Two Cultures?,* 17.

7. Snow, *The Two Cultures and a Second Look,* 9.

8. Ibid.

9. Leavis, *Two Cultures?,* 10.

10. Snow, *The Two Cultures and a Second Look,* 17.

11. Luhmann, *Theories of Distinction,* 63.

12. The problem of disciplinary communication becomes less acute when the cultures "display, at the least, a family resemblance," as Snow sees happening more in the American than British academy at the time. Their resemblances must be seen to be seen. See Snow, *The Two Cultures and a Second Look,* 70.

13. Leavis, *Two Cultures?,* 12.

14. Luhmann, *Theories of Distinction,* 60.

15. Snow claims in "A Second Look" that an alternate pairing to the two cultures was originally planned as the lecture's title: "Before I wrote the lecture I thought of calling it 'The Rich and the Poor,' and I rather wish that I hadn't changed my mind" (*The Two Cultures and a Second Look,* 79).

16. Ibid., 68.

17. "Two Cultures in the Corridors." For a discussion of Snow's stature within each of his disciplines, and what his figure as "a professional who became a professional amateur" reveals about the nature of the modern professions, see Garber, *Academic Instincts.*

18. See John Halperin's interviews with Snow for an account of his double blacklisting, as well as the cyanide pills he carried as a contingency plan: *C. P. Snow: An Oral Biography.*

19. Snow, *The New Men.*

20. "Interview with C. P. Snow," 107, qtd. in Graves, *The Two Culture Theory in C. P. Snow's Novels,* 67.

21. Snow, *Homecoming,* 147.

22. As the novel ends, the corridors beneath the hospital capture those of the "official world" referred to earlier by Margaret: "Through the underground corridor of the hospital, which smelt of brick dust and disinfectant, Margaret and I were finding our way to Geoffrey's office. Along the passage, whose walls, as bare as those of a tube railway, carried uncovered water-pipes, went mothers with children. At a kind of junction or open space sat a group of women, their children in pushchairs, as though expecting nothing, waiting endlessly, just left there, children not specially ill, their fate now specially tragic, waiting with the resignation that made hospitals seem like forgotten railway stations littered with the poor and unlucky camping out for the weekly train. Nurses, their faces high-coloured and opaque, moved past them with strong, heavy-thighed steps as though they did not exist" (ibid., 393).

23. Snow, *Corridors of Power,* vii.

24. Ibid., 65.

25. Snow, *The Two Cultures and a Second Look,* 97.

26. Snow, *Corridors of Power,* 237.

27. Ibid., 358.

28. James, *The American Scene,* 166. Elizabeth Klimasmith discusses this passage in her account of Henry James's "spatial practice" by drawing attention to what she describes as "vagueness" in architecture as threatening to James's personal identity. Although for my project the relationship between interiority and the organization of interiors is essential, it is viewed from the point of view of the communications system rather than the individual. See Klimasmith, *At Home in the City,* 31.

29. Beck, *Risk Society,* 130.

30. Snow, *Corridors of Power,* 362.

31. Leavis, *Two Cultures?,* 28.

32. Snow, *Corridors of Power,* 364.

33. Ibid., 176.

34. See Seltzer, *True Crime,* 106.

35. "Je mehr die Macht sich an einer bestimmten Stelle, bei einem bestimmten Menschen oder einer Gruppe von Menschen wie in einer Spitze konzentriert, um so mehr verschärft sich das Problem des Korridors und die Frage des Zugangs zur Spitze. Umso heftiger, verbissener und stummer wird dann auch der Kampf unter denjenigen, die den Vorraum besetzt halten und den Korridor kontrollieren. Dieser Kampf im Nebel indirekter Einflüsse ist ebenso unvermeidlich, wie er für alle menschliche Macht wesentlich ist. In ihm vollzieht sich die innere Dialektik der menslichen Macht" (Schmitt, *Gespräch über die Macht und den Zugang zum Machthaber,* 16–17). This text has yet to appear in translation—all in-text translations hereafter are my own, and will be followed by the original text in footnotes. I will cite the published translations of Schmitt's other texts when available.

36. "Vor jedem Raum direkter Macht bildet sich ein Vorraum indirekter Einflüsse und Gewalten, ein Zugang zum Ohr, ein Korridor zur Seele des Machthabers. Es gibt keine menschliche Macht ohne diesen Vorraum und ohne diesen Korridor" (ibid., 15).

37. Jameson, "Notes on the *Nomos,*" 203.

38. I borrow this term from William Rasch, who claims that for Schmitt, "order is always spatially and concretely grounded" (Rasch, "Human Rights as Geopolitics," 128).

39. "Antichambre, Hintertreppe, Umraum, Unterraum: die Sache selbst ist klar und bleibt für die Dialektik der menschlichen Macht desselbe" (Schmitt, *Gespräch über die Macht und den Zugang zum Machthaber,* 16).

40. For an account, informative in this context, of the systems-theoretical understanding of form in relation to contemporary architecture, see C. Wolfe, "Lose the Building."

41. Schmitt, *Gespräch über die Macht und den Zugang zum Machthaber,* 6.

42. See Schmitt, *The* Nomos *of the Earth.*

43. "Es gibt keine menschliche Macht ohne diesen Vorraum und ohne diesen Korridor." Schmitt, *Gespräch über die Macht und den Zugang zum Machthaber,* 15.

44. Schmitt, *The* Nomos *of the Earth,* 337.

45. Ibid., 186.

46. The perspectival shift between Benjamin and Schmitt on the topic of space and architecture, of course, cannot be separated from the controversy attached to their correspondence and theories of violence and the exception. When Sam Weber, for example, discusses the nature of the "decision" that constitutes a Schmittian sovereignty, he looks to the spatial forms that separate the two thinkers: "The question of decision, of its power and status, is always tied [for Schmitt] to a certain determination of space. Whereas in Benjamin, however, this determination is revealed to be the errant stage of an inauthentic and unlocalizable place, for Schmitt decision can be situated in terms of an unequivocal *point*" (S. Weber, "Taking Exception to Decision," 18).

47. Schmitt, *The* Nomos *of the Earth,* 42.

48. For a discussion of this kind of critique, see Pourciau, "Bodily Negation," 1066.

49. Hallward, "Beyond Salvage," 240.

50. "Jedenfalls hat sich in diesem Vorraum der Macht im Laufe der Weltgeschichte eine bunte und gemischte Gesellschaft zusammengefunden" (Schmitt, *Gespräch über die Macht und den Zugang zum Machthaber,* 16).

51. "Oder sogar ein Krankenzimmer, in dem einige Freunde am Bett eines gelähmten Mannes sitzen und die Welt regieren" (ibid).

52. Kracauer, "On Employment Agencies," 60.

53. Ibid., 61.

54. Ibid., 62.

55. Ibid., 59.

56. Ibid.

57. Ibid., 64.

58. Stezaker, "Interview with John Stezaker," 155.

Epilogue

1. Banfield, "Time Passes," 501, 500. Opening image and epilogue also qtd. in Banfield, 500.

2. Serres, *The Parasite,* 240.

3. Ibid.

4. Barreca, "Nightime Fires."

5. Cunningham, *Specimen Days,* 235.

6. Ibid., 18, 20.

7. Ibid., 15.

8. Ibid., 19.

9. Ibid., 47.

10. Ibid., 82.

11. Ibid., ix.

12. Pynchon, *The Crying of Lot 49,* 94–95.

13. Danielewski, *House of Leaves,* 89.

14. Ibid., 73.

15. Deleuze, "Postscript on the Societies of Control," 3–4.

16. Ibid.

17. Augé, *Non-Places,* 34.

18. Ibid., 79.

19. Bauman, *Liquid Modernity,* 6.

20. Ibid., 100.

21. Ferris, *Then We Came to the End,* 58.

22. Baker, *The Mezzanine,* 37.

23. Ibid., 35–36.

24. Whitehead, *The Intuitionist,* 5. Thanks to Sianne Ngai for recommending this text as a possible vector for my argument about infrastructure.

25. Meillassoux, *After Finitude,* 7.

26. Ibid.

27. Latour, *Reassembling the Social,* 64–65.

28. Ibid., 53–54.

BIBLIOGRAPHY

Adorno, Theodor. "Late Style in Beethoven." In *Essays on Music.* Edited by Richard Leppert, 564–68. Translated by Susan H. Gillespie. Berkeley: University of California Press, 2002.

Anderson, Sherwood. *Winesburg, Ohio.* New York: Modern Library, 2002.

Archer, John. *Architecture and Suburbia: From English Villa to American Dream House, 1690–2000.* Minneapolis: University of Minnesota Press, 2005.

Artaud, Antonin. *The Theater and Its Double.* Translated by Mary C. Richard. New York: Grove Press, 1957.

"Artist's Rendering of the Continuous Transit Corporation's Proposal for Moving Platforms." *Scientific American* 130, no. 2 (1924): 88–89.

Augé, Mark. *Non-Places: Introduction to an Anthropology of Supermodernity.* Translated by John Howe. London: Verso, 1995.

Bachelard, Gaston. *The Poetics of Space.* Translated by Maria Jolas. Boston: Beacon Press, 1964.

Baecker, Dirk. "The Reality of Motion Pictures." *MLN* 111, no. 3 (1996): 560–77.

Baker, Nicholson. *The Mezzanine.* New York: Vintage Books, 1990.

Ballard, J. G. "The Dying Fall." *The Guardian,* April 25, 2009.

Banfield, Ann, "Time Passes: Virginia Woolf, Post-Impressionism, and Cambridge Time." *Poetics Today* 24, no. 3 (2003): 471–516.

Banta, Martha. *Taylored Lives: Narrative Productions in the Age of Taylor, Veblen, and Ford.* Chicago: University of Chicago Press, 1995.

Barreca, Regina. "Nightime Fires." *Norton Introduction to Poetry.* Edited by J. Paul Hunter, 787. 7th ed. New York: W. W. Norton, 1999.

Bauman, Zygmunt. *Liquid Modernity.* Cambridge: Polity, 2000.

Beck, Ulrich. *Risk Society: Towards a New Modernity.* London: Sage Publications, 1992.

Bell, Michael Davitt. *Culture, Genre, and Literary Vocation: Selected Essays on American Literature.* Chicago: University of Chicago Press, 2001.

Benjamin, Walter. *The Arcades Project.* Edited by Rolf Tiedemann. Cambridge: Harvard University Press, 1999.

Benjamin, Walter, and Hannah Arendt. *Illuminations.* Translated by Harry Zohn. New York: Schocken Books, 1968.

Biers, Katherine. "Syncope Fever: James Weldon Johnson and the Black Phonographic Voice." *Representations* 96 (Fall 2006): 99–125.

Blakely, Debra E. *Mass Mediated Disease: A Case Study Analysis of Three Flu Pandemics and Public Health Policy.* Lanham, Md.: Lexington Books, 2006.

Blau, Eve. *The Architecture of Red Vienna, 1919–1934.* Cambridge, Mass.: MIT Press, 1999.

Bollet, Alfred Jay. *Plagues and Poxes: The Impact of Human History on Epidemic Disease.* New York: Demos, 2004.

Brooks, Peter. "Incredulous Narration: *Absalom, Absalom!*" *Comparative Literature* 34, no. 3 (1982): 247–68.

Brown, Bill. *The Material Unconscious: Amusement, Stephen Crane, and the Economics of Play.* Cambridge, Mass.: Harvard University Press, 1996.

Caillois, Roger. "Mimicry and Legendary Psychasthenia." *October* 31 (Winter 1984): 16–32.

Calvino, Italo. *Six Memos for the Next Millennium.* Translated by Patrick Creagh. New York: Vintage International, 1988.

Carsten, Janet, and Stephen Hugh-Jones. *About the House: Levi-Strauss and Beyond.* Cambridge: Cambridge University Press, 1995.

Cassuto, Leonard, and Clare Virginia Eby, eds. *The Cambridge Companion to Theodore Dreiser.* Cambridge: Cambridge University Press, 2004.

Cather, Willa. *One of Ours.* New York: Alfred A. Knopf, 1922.

Cerasulo, Tom. "*The Dream Life of Balso Snell* and the Vocation of Nathanael West." *Arizona Quarterly* 62, no. 2 (2006): 59–75.

Chandler, Marilyn R. *Dwelling in the Text: Houses in American Fiction.* Berkeley: University of California Press, 1991.

Chung, Chuihua Judy, Jeffrey Inaba, Rem Koolhaas, and Sze Tsung Leong. *Harvard Design School Guide to Shopping,* Project on the City 2. Cologne: Taschen; Harvard Design School, 2001.

Ciccioric, David. *Reading Network Fiction.* Tuscaloosa: University of Alabama Press, 2007.

Ciuba, Gary M. "One Singer Left to Mourn: Death and Discourse in Porter's *Pale Horse, Pale Rider.*" *South Atlantic Review* 61, no. 1 (1996): 55–76.

Clarke, Bruce, and Mark B. N. Hansen, eds. *Emergence and Embodiment: New Essays in Second-Order Systems Theory.* Durham: Duke University Press, 2009.

Coates, Kimberly Engdahl. "Exposing the 'Nerves of Language': Virginia Woolf, Charles Mauron, and the Affinity between Aesthetics and Illness." *Literature and Medicine* 21, no. 2 (2002): 242–63.

Cohen, Matt. *The Networked Wilderness: Communicating in Early New England.* Minneapolis: University of Minnesota Press, 2010.

Collier, Richard. *The Plague of the Spanish Lady: The Influenza Pandemic of 1918–1919.* London: Macmillan, 1974.

Colomina, Beatriz. *Privacy and Publicity: Modern Architecture as Mass Media.* Cambridge, Mass.: MIT Press, 1994.

"Contagion." In *Oxford English Dictionary*. 2nd ed. Oxford: Oxford University Press, 1989.

Crane, Stephen. *Maggie: A Girl of the Streets and Other Short Fiction.* New York: Bantam Books, 1986.

Crosby, Alfred W. *America's Forgotten Pandemic: The Influenza of 1918.* Cambridge: Cambridge University Press, 2003.

———. *Epidemic and Peace, 1918.* Westport, Conn.: Greenwood Press, 1976.

Cunningham, Michael. *Specimen Days.* New York: Picador, 2005.

Danielewski, Mark Z. *House of Leaves.* London: Anchor, 2000.

Davis, Rebecca Harding. "Life in the Iron-Mills, or the Korl Woman." In *The American Short Story and Its Writer.* Edited by Ann Charters, 256–84. New York: Macmillan, 2000.

de Certeau, Michel. *The Practice of Everyday Life.* Translated by Steven Rendall. Berkeley: University of California Press, 1984.

Deleuze, Gilles. *Kafka: Toward a Minor Literature.* Translated by Dana Polan. Minneapolis: University of Minnesota Press, 1986.

———. "Postscript on the Societies of Control." *October* 59 (1992): 3–7.

Denby, David. "The Cost of Desire: Theodore Dreiser's 'An American Tragedy.'" *New Yorker,* April 21, 2003.

Denes, Melissa. "Interview: Picture Perfect." *The Guardian,* October 15, 2005.

Derrida, Jacques. *Dissemination.* Translated by Barbara Johnson. Chicago: University of Chicago Press, 1983.

Derrida, Jacques, and Bernard Stiegler. *Echographies of Television.* Translated by Jennifer Bajorek. London: Polity Press, 2002.

Dickinson, Emily. *The Poems of Emily Dickinson.* Edited by Ralph W. Franklin. Cambridge, Mass.: Belknap Press, 1998.

Dos Passos, John. *Manhattan Transfer.* 1st Mariner Books ed. Boston: Houghton Mifflin, 2000.

———. *U.S.A.* New York: Library of America, 1996.

Douglas, Ann. *Terrible Honesty: Mongrel Manhattan in the 1920s.* New York: Noonday Press; Farrar, Straus, and Giroux, 1995.

Dreiser, Theodore. *An American Tragedy.* New York: Library of America, 2003.

———. *Art, Music, and Literature, 1897–1902.* Edited by Yoshinobu Hakutani. Chicago: University of Illinois Press, 2001.

———. Introduction to Frank Norris, *McTeague: A Story of San Francisco,* vii–xi. New York: Doubleday, 1928.

Eisenstein, Sergei. "An American Tragedy." http://web.archive.org/web/20060613212337/geocities.com/emruf0/aat.html.

Elam, Diane, and Robyn Wiegman. *Feminism Beside Itself.* New York: Routledge, 1995.

Ellison, Ralph. *Invisible Man.* New York: Vintage Books, 1995.

Ellmann, Maud. *The Nets of Modernism: Henry James, Virginia Woolf, James Joyce, and Sigmund Freud.* Cambridge: Cambridge University Press, 2010.

Elmer, Jonathan. "Blinded Me with Science: Motifs of Observation and Temporality in Lacan and Luhmann." In *Observing Complexity: Systems Theory and Postmodernity.* Edited by William Rasch and Cary Wolfe, 215–46. Minneapolis: University of Minnesota Press, 2000.

———. "Spectacle and Event in Native Son." *American Literature* 70, no. 4 (1998): 767–98.

Eriksen, Roy T. *The Building in the Text: Alberti to Shakespeare and Milton.* University Park: Pennsylvania State University Press, 2000.

Erikson, Steve. *Zeroville.* New York: Europa Editions, 2007.

Ernst, Wolfgang. "Media Archaeography." In *Media Archaeology: Approaches, Applications, and Implications.* Edited by Erkki Huhtamo and Jussi Parikka, 239–55. Berkeley: University of California Press, 2011.

Esposito, Elena. "The Arts of Contingency." *Critical Inquiry* 31, no. 1 (2004): 7–24.

Evans, Robin. "Figures, Doors and Passages." In *Translations from Drawing to Building and Other Essays.* Cambridge, Mass.: MIT Press, 1997.

Faulkner, William. *Absalom, Absalom!* New York: Vintage, 1990.

Ferris, Joshua. *Then We Came to the End.* New York: Little, Brown, and Co., 2007.

Fleissner, Jennifer. *Women, Compulsion, Modernity: The Moment of American Naturalism.* Chicago: University of Chicago Press, 2004.

Flusser, Vilém. *The Shape of Things: A Philosophy of Design.* Translated by Anthony Mathews. London: Reaktion Books, 1999.

———. *Writings.* Edited by Andreas Ströhl. Minneapolis: University of Minnesota Press, 2002.

Foley, Barbara. *Radical Representations: Politics and Form in U.S. Proletarian Fiction, 1929–1941.* Durham: Duke University Press, 1993.

Foucault, Michel. "Of Other Spaces." *diacritics* 16, no. 1 (1986): 22–27.

Francovich, Auguste. "Moving Platform." United States Patent Office, U.S. Patent 766,107, filed Oct. 22, 1903, issued July 26, 1904.

Frank, Ellen Eve. *Literary Architecture: Essays toward a Tradition: Walter Pater, Gerard Manley Hopkins, Marcel Proust, Henry James.* Berkeley: University of California Press, 1979.

Frank, Joseph. *The Idea of Spatial Form.* New Brunswick: Rutgers University Press, 1991.

Gallagher, Catherine. "The Rise of Fictionality." In *The Novel.* Vol. 1, *History, Geography, Culture.* Edited by Franco Moretti, 336–63. Princeton: Princeton University Press, 2006.

Garber, Marjorie. *Academic Instincts.* Princeton: Princeton University Press, 2000.

Garner, Stanton B., Jr. "Artaud, Germ Theory, and the Theatre of Contagion." *Theatre Journal* 58 (2006): 1–14.

Geismar, Maxwell. *Writers in Crisis: The American Novel between Two Wars.* Boston: Houghton Mifflin Company, 1942.

Gerber, Alex, Murray Roth, and Abner Silver. "All That I Need Is a Hallway." New York: M. Witmark and Sons, 1919.

Giles, Paul. *The Global Remapping of American Literature.* Princeton: Princeton University Press, 2011.

Gill, Richard. *Happy Rural Seat: The English Country House and the Literary Imagination.* New Haven: Yale University Press, 1972.

Girard, René. "The Plague in Literature and Myth." In *"To Double Business Bound": Essays on Literature, Mimesis, and Anthropology,* 136–54. Baltimore: Johns Hopkins University Press, 1978.

Gleason, William A. *Sites Unseen: Architecture, Race, and American Literature.* New York: New York University Press, 2011.

Goble, Mark. *Beautiful Circuits: Modernism and the Mediated Life.* New York: Columbia University Press, 2010.

Gordon, Daniel. "The City and the Plague in the Age of Enlightenment." *Yale French Studies,* no. 92 (1997): 67–87.

Graves, Nora Calhoun. *The Two Culture Theory in C. P. Snow's Novels.* Hattiesburg: University and College Press of Mississippi, 1971.

Greenberg, Jonathan. "Nathanael West and the Mystery of Feeling." *Modern Fiction Studies* 52, no. 3 (2006): 588–612.

Gumbrecht, Hans Ulrich, and K. Ludwig Pfeiffer, eds. *Materialities of Communication.* Stanford: Stanford University Press, 1994.

Habermas, Jürgen. *The Structural Transformation of the Public Sphere: An Inquiry into a Category of Bourgeois Society.* Translated by Thomas Burger and Frederick Lawrence. Cambridge, Mass.: MIT Press, 1991.

Hallward, Peter. "Beyond Salvage." *South Atlantic Quarterly* 104, no. 2 (2005): 237–44.

Halperin, John. *C. P. Snow: An Oral Biography.* Brighton: Harvester, 1983.

Haralson, Eric L. *Henry James and Queer Modernity.* Cambridge Studies in American Literature and Culture. Cambridge: Cambridge University Press, 2003.

Hartesveldt, Fred R. van, ed. *The 1918–1919 Pandemic of Influenza: The Urban Impact in the Western World.* Lewiston, N.Y.: Edwin Mellen Press, 1993.

Hayden, Dolores. *Redesigning the American Dream: The Future of Housing, Work, and Family Life.* New York: W. W. Norton, 1984.

Hayles, N. Katherine. *My Mother Was a Computer: Digital Subjects and Literary Texts.* Chicago: University of Chicago Press, 2005.

———. *Writing Machines.* Cambridge, Mass.: MIT Press, 2002.

Hays, J. N. *Epidemics and Pandemics: Their Impacts on Human History.* Santa Barbara, Calif.: ABC Clio, 2005.

Herring, Scott. *Another Country: Queer Anti-Urbanism.* New York: New York University Press, 2010.

Hönnighausen, Lothar. *Faulkner: Masks and Metaphors.* Jackson: University Press of Mississippi, 2006.

Horn, Eva. "Editor's Introduction: 'There Are No Media.'" *Grey Room* 29 (Winter 2008): 1–8.

Hughson, Lois. "Narration in the Making of *Manhattan Transfer.*" *Studies in the Novel* 8, no. 2 (1976): 185–98.

Huhtamo, Erkki, and Jussi Parikka, eds. *Media Archaeology: Approaches, Applications, and Implications.* Berkeley: University of California Press, 2011.

Humphreys, Margaret. "No Safe Place: Disease and Panic in American History." *American Literary History* 14, no. 4 (2002): 845–57.

"Interview with C. P. Snow." *A Review of English Literature* 3 (1962): 107.

James, Henry. *The American Scene.* New York: Scribner, 1907.

Jameson, Fredric. "Notes on the *Nomos.*" *South Atlantic Quarterly* 104, no. 2 (2005): 199–204.

Jarzombek, Mark. "Corridor Spaces." *Critical Inquiry* 36, no. 4 (2010): 728–70.

———. "From Corridor (Spanish) to Corridor (English); or, What's in Your Corridor?" *Thresholds* 32, Access (2006): 6–11.

Johnson, Erica L. *Home, Maison, Casa: The Politics of Location in Works by Jean Rhys, Marguerite Duras, and Erminia Dell'oro.* Madison, N.J.: Fairleigh Dickinson University Press, 2003.

Kahn, Douglas, and Gregory Whitehead. *Wireless Imagination: Sound, Radio, and the Avant-Garde.* Cambridge, Mass.: MIT Press, 1992.

Karatani, Kojin. *Architecture as Metaphor: Language, Number, Money.* Translated by Sabu Kohso. Edited by Michael Speaks. Cambridge, Mass.: MIT Press, 1995.

Kelly, David. "Telling Questions in *Absalom, Absalom!*" *Sydney Studies in English* 19 (1993): 99–132.

Kern, Stephen. *The Culture of Time and Space, 1880–1918.* Cambridge, Mass.: Harvard University Press, 2003.

Kittler, Friedrich. *Discourse Networks 1800/1900.* Translated by Chris Cullens and Michael Metteer. Stanford: Stanford University Press, 1990.

———. "The History of Communication Media." *CTheory.net* (1996): 1–18.

———. "Thinking Colours and/or Machines." *Theory, Culture & Society* 23, nos. 7–8 (2006): 39–50.

Klark, Happy. "The Influenza Blues : . . . Song." McAlester, Okla.: Brown Music Co., 1918.

Klimasmith, Elizabeth. *At Home in the City: Urban Domesticity in American Literature and Culture, 1850–1930.* Durham: University of New Hampshire Press, 2005.

Koolhaas, Rem. *Delirious New York: A Retroactive Manifesto for Manhattan.* New York: Monacelli Press, 1994.

Koszarski, Richard. "Flu Season: *Moving Picture World* Reports on Pandemic Influenza, 1918–19." *Film History* 17, no. 4 (2005): 466–85.

Kracauer, Siegfried. "On Employment Agencies: The Construction of a Space." In *Rethinking Architecture: A Reader in Cultural Theory.* Edited by Niel Leach, 59–64. New York: Routledge, 1997.

Laporte, Dominique-Gilbert. *History of Shit.* Cambridge, Mass.: MIT Press, 2000.

Latour, Bruno. *Aramis: The Love of Technology.* Translated by Catherine Porter. Cambridge, Mass.: Harvard University Press, 1996.

———. *Reassembling the Social: An Introduction to Actor-Network Theory.* Oxford: Oxford University Press, 2005.

———. *We Have Never Been Modern.* Translated by Catherine Porter. Cambridge, Mass.: Harvard University Press, 1993.

Leavis, F. R. *Two Cultures? The Significance of C. P. Snow.* London: Chatto and Windus, 1962.

Lefort, Claude. *The Political Forms of Modern Society: Bureaucracy, Democracy, and Totalitarianism.* Edited by John B. Thompson. Cambridge, Mass.: MIT Press, 1986.

Lehan, Richard. "Dreiser's *An American Tragedy*: A Critical Study." *College English* 25, no. 3 (1963): 187–93.

Levinson, Marjorie. "What Is New Formalism?" *PMLA* 122, no. 2 (2007): 558–69.

Levy, Helen Fiddyment. *Fiction of the Home Place: Jewett, Cather, Glasgow, Porter, Welty, and Naylor.* Jackson: University Press of Mississippi, 1992.

Liu, Alan. "Imagining the New Media Encounter." In *A Companion to Digital Literary Studies.* Edited by Susan Schreibman and Ray Siemens, 3–26. Oxford: Blackwell, 2008.

Luhmann, Niklas. *Art as a Social System.* Stanford: Stanford University Press, 2000.

———. *Essays on Self-Reference.* New York: Columbia University Press, 1990.

———. *Observations on Modernity.* Translated by William Whobrey. Stanford: Stanford University Press, 1998.

———. *The Reality of the Mass Media.* Translated by Kathleen Cross. Stanford: Stanford University Press, 2000.

———. *Social Systems.* Translated by John Bednarz Jr. and Dirk Baecker. Stanford: Stanford University Press, 1995.

———. *Theories of Distinction: Redescribing the Descriptions of Modernity.* Translated by Joseph O'Neil, Elliott Schreiber, Kerstin Gehnke, and William Whobrey. Edited by William Rasch. Stanford: Stanford University Press, 2002.

Marcus, Sharon. *Apartment Stories: City and Home in Nineteenth-Century Paris and London.* Berkeley: University of California Press, 1999.

Marin, Louis. *On Representation.* Translated by Catherine Porter. Stanford: Stanford University Press, 2001.

Martin, Reinhold. *The Organizational Complex: Architecture, Media, and Corporate Space.* Cambridge, Mass.: MIT Press, 2005.

Massumi, Brian. *Parables for the Virtual: Movement, Affect, Sensation.* Durham: Duke University Press, 2002.

McGurl, Mark. *The Program Era: Postwar Fiction and the Rise of Creative Writing.* Cambridge, Mass.: Harvard University Press, 2009.

Meillassoux, Quentin. *After Finitude: An Essay on the Necessity of Contingency.* Translated by Ray Brassier. London: Continuum, 2008.

Merck, Mandy. *Hollywood's American Tragedies: Dreiser, Eisenstein, Sternberg, Stevens.* Oxford: Berg, 2007.

Michaels, Walter Benn. "An American Tragedy, or the Promise of American Life." *Representations* 25 (Winter 1989): 71–98.

———. *The Gold Standard and the Logic of Naturalism.* Berkeley: University of California Press, 1988.

Miller, S. M. *Max Weber.* New York: Thomas Y. Crowell, 1963.

Mills, C. Wright. *White Collar: The American Middle Classes.* Oxford: Oxford University Press, 1951.

Mitchell, Lee Clark. "'And Then Rose for the First Time': Repetition and Doubling in *An American Tragedy.*" *Novel: A Forum on Fiction* 19, no. 1 (1985): 39–56.

Moremen, Grace E., ed. *Student Life at the University of California, Berkeley during and after World War I: The Letters of Agnes Edwards Partin, 1917–1921.* Lewiston, N.Y.: Edwin Mellen Press, 2006.

Mullen, Bill, and James Edward Smethurst. *Left of the Color Line: Race, Radicalism, and Twentieth-Century Literature of the United States.* Chapel Hill: University of North Carolina Press, 2003.

Muthesius, Hermann. *The English House.* Edited by Dennis Sharp. New York: Rizzoli, 1979.

Nadel, Alan. *Containment Culture: American Narratives, Postmodernism, and the Atomic Age.* Durham: Duke University Press, 1995.

Nancy, Jean-Luc. *Being Singular Plural.* Stanford: Stanford University Press, 2000.

Nazare, Joe. "Backtrack to the Future: John E. Stith's/John Dos Passos's *Manhattan Transfer.*" *Extrapolation* 42, no. 1 (2001): 37–52.

Nieland, Justus. "West's Deadpan: Affect, Slapstick, and Publicity in Miss Lonelyhearts." *NOVEL: A Forum on Fiction* 38, no. 1 (2004): 57–83.

Norris, Frank. *McTeague: A Story of San Francisco.* New York: Doubleday, 1928.

Parikka, Jussi. *Insect Media: An Archaeology of Animals and Technology.* Minneapolis: University of Minnesota Press, 2010.

Parrish, Timothy. *From the Civil War to the Apocalypse: Postmodern History and American Fiction.* Amherst: University of Massachusetts Press, 2008.

Peters, John Durham. *Speaking into the Air: A History of the Idea of Communication.* Chicago: University of Chicago Press, 1999.

Plate, Liedeke. "Is Contemporary Women's Writing Computational? Unraveling Twenty-First Century Creativity with Penelope at Her Loom." *Contemporary Women's Writing* 1, nos. 1–2 (2007): 45–53.

Porter, Katherine Anne. *Pale Horse, Pale Rider.* New York: Harcourt Brace, 1939.

Pourciau, Sarah. "Bodily Negation: Carl Schmitt and the Meaning of Meaning." *MLN* 120 (2005): 1066–90.

Pynchon, Thomas. *The Crying of Lot 49.* New York: Harper and Row, 1990.

———. *Gravity's Rainbow.* New York: Penguin, 1995.

Rancière, Jacques. *Dis-agreement: Politics and Philosophy.* Translated by Julie Rose. Minneapolis: University of Minnesota Press, 1999.

———. *Film Fables.* Translated by Emiliano Battista. New York: Berg, 2006.

———. *The Names of History: On the Poetics of Knowledge.* Translated by Hassan Melehy. Minneapolis: University of Minnesota Press, 1994.

———. *The Philosopher and His Poor.* Translated by John Drury, Corinne Oster, and Andrew Parker. Durham: Duke University Press, 2003.

———. "The Saint and the Heiress: A Propos of Godard's *Histoire(s) du Cinéma.*" *Discourse* 24, no. 1 (2002): 113–19.

Rasch, William. "Human Rights as Geopolitics: Carl Schmitt and the Legal Form of American Supremacy." *Cultural Critique* 54 (2003): 120–47.

Rasch, William, and Cary Wolfe, eds. *Observing Complexity.* Minneapolis: University of Minnesota Press, 2000.

Robbins, Bruce. "The Smell of Infrastructure." *boundary 2* 34, no. 1 (2007): 25–33.

Robé, Chris. "Eisenstein in America: *The Qué Viva México!* Debates and the Emergent Popular Front in U.S. Film Theory and Criticism." *The Velvet Light Trap* 54 (Fall 2004): 18–31.

Roberts, David. "Self-Reference in Literature." *Problems of Form.* Edited by Dirk Baecker. 27–45. Stanford: Stanford University Press, 1999.

Romines, Ann. *The Home Plot: Women, Writing and Domestic Ritual.* Amherst: University of Massachusetts Press, 1992.

Rosner, Victoria. *Modernism and the Architecture of Private Life.* New York: Columbia University Press, 2005.

Roth, Henry. *Call It Sleep.* New York: Farrar Straus and Giroux, 1991.

Rubenstein, Michael. *Public Works: Infrastructure, Irish Modernism, and the Postcolonial.* Notre Dame: University of Notre Dame Press, 2010.

Rubenstein, Roberta. *Home Matters: Longing and Belonging, Nostalgia and Mourning in Women's Fiction.* New York: Palgrave, 2001.

Sachs, Philip. "System of Transportation." Edited by United States Patent Office, 1922.

Said, Edward W. *On Late Style: Music and Literature against the Grain.* New York: Pantheon Books, 2006.

Schivelbusch, Wolfgang. *The Railway Journey: The Industrialization of Time and Space in the 19th Century.* Berkeley: University of California Press, 1986.

Schmitt, Carl. *Gespräch über die Macht und den Zugang zum Machthaber.* Frankfurt: Verlag, 1954.

———. *The* Nomos *of the Earth: In the International Law of the Jus Publicum Europaeum.* Translated by G. L. Ulmen. New York: Telos Press, 2006.

Schweighauser, Philipp. *The Noises of American Literature, 1890–1985: Toward a History of Literary Acoustics.* Gainesville: University of Florida Press, 2006.

Seltzer, Mark. *Bodies and Machines.* New York: Routledge, 1992.

———. "Reading Foucault: Cells, Corridors, Novels." *Diacritics* 14, no. 1 (1984): 78–89.

———. *Serial Killers: Death and Life in America's Wound Culture.* New York: Routledge, 1998.

———. *True Crime: Observations on Violence and Modernity.* New York: Routledge, 2006.

Sen, Rajenda Kumar. *A Treatise on Influenza: With Special Reference to the Pandemic of 1918.* Calcutta: Ramnarayan Bhattarcharjee, 1923.

Serres, Michel. *The Parasite.* Translated by Lawrence R. Schehr. Edited by Cary Wolfe. Minneapolis: University of Minnesota Press, 2007.

Shaviro, Steven. *Connected: Or What It Means to Live in the Network Society.* Minneapolis: University of Minnesota Press, 2003.

Siegert, Bernhard. *Relays: Literature as an Epoch of the Postal System.* Translated by Kevin Repp. Stanford: Stanford University Press, 1999.

Sigerist, Henry E. *Civilization and Disease.* Chicago: University of Chicago Press, 1942.

Simmel, Georg. "The Metropolis and Mental Life." In *On Individuality and Social Forms.* Edited by Donald N. Levine, 324–39. Chicago: University of Chicago Press, 1971.

———. "The Stranger." In *On Individuality and Social Forms.* Edited by Donald N. Levine, 143–49. Chicago: University of Chicago Press, 1971.

Snow, C. P. *Corridors of Power.* New York: Charles Scribner's Sons, 1964.

———. *Homecoming.* London: Macmillan, 1956.

———. *The New Men.* New York: Charles Scribner's Sons, 1954.

———. *The Two Cultures and a Second Look: An Expanded Version of the Two Cultures and the Scientific Revolution.* Cambridge: Cambridge University Press, 1964.

Soja, Edward W. *Postmodern Geographies. The Reassertion of Space in Critical Social Theory.* London; New York: Verso, 1989.

Steinbeck, John. *The Wayward Bus.* New York: Penguin, 1995.

Stewart, Jacqueline. "Negroes Laughing at Themselves? Black Spectatorship and the Performance of Urban Modernity." *Critical Inquiry* 29, no. 4 (2003): 650–77.

Stezaker, John. "Interview with John Stezaker." In *The Impossible Document: Photography and Conceptual Art in Britain, 1966–1976.* Edited by John Roberts, 143–62. London: Camerawork, 1997.

Sundquist, Eric. *Faulkner: A House Divided.* Baltimore: Johns Hopkins University Press, 1985.

Szalay, Michael. *New Deal Modernism: American Literature and the Invention of the Welfare State.* Durham: Duke University Press, 2000.

Thacker, Eugene, and Alexander Galloway. *The Exploit: A Theory of Networks.* Minneapolis: University of Minnesota Press, 2007.

Thompson, Emily Ann. *The Soundscape of Modernity: Architectural Acoustics and the Culture of Listening in America, 1900–1933.* Cambridge, Mass.: MIT Press, 2002.

Tristram, Philippa. *Living Space in Fact and Fiction.* London: Routledge, 1989.

Trombold, John. "Popular Songs as Revolutionary Culture in John Dos Passos' *U.S.A.* and Other Early Works." *Journal of Modern Literature* 19, no. 2 (1995): 289–316.

"Two Cultures in the Corridors." *Time,* November 20, 1964.

Virno, Paolo. *A Grammar of the Multitude.* Translated by James Cascaito, Isabella Bertoletti, and Andrea Casson. Los Angeles: Semiotext(e), 2004.

Vismann, Cornelia. *Files: Law and Media Technology.* Translated by Geoffrey Winthrop-Young. Stanford: Stanford University Press, 2008.

Vismann, Cornelia, and Markus Krajewski. "Computer Juridisms." *Grey Room* 29 (Winter 2008): 90–109.

Vogl, Joseph. "Becoming-Media: Galileo's Telescope." *Grey Room* 29 (Winter 2008): 14–25.

Wald, Priscilla. *Contagious: Cultures, Carriers, and the Outbreak Narrative.* Durham: Duke University Press, 2007.

———. "Future Perfect: Grammar, Genes, and Geography." *New Literary History* 31, no. 4 (2000): 681–708.

Weber, Max. *From Max Weber: Essays in Sociology.* Translated and edited by H. H. Gerth and C. Wright Mills. New York: Oxford University Press, 1958.

Weber, Samuel. "Taking Exception to Decision: Walter Benjamin and Carl Schmitt." *diacritics* 22, no. 3/4 (1992): 5–18.

Wellbery, David E. "The General Enters the Library: A Note on Disciplines and Complexity." *Critical Inquiry* 35, no. 4 (2009): 982–94.

———. Introduction to *Discourse Networks 1800/1900,* by Friedrich Kittler, vii–xxxiii. Stanford: Stanford University Press, 1990.

West, Nathanael. *Novels and Other Writings.* New York: Library of America, 1997.

Whalen, Mark. "Dreams of Manhood: Narrative, Gender, and History in Winesburg, Ohio." *Studies in American Fiction* 30, no. 2 (2002): 229–48.

Whitehead, Colson. *The Intuitionist.* New York: Anchor Books, 1999.

Winthrop-Young, Geoffrey. "Silicon Sociology, or, Two Kings on Hegel's Throne? Kittler, Luhmann, and the Posthuman Merger of German Media Theory." *Yale Journal of Criticism* 13, no. 2 (2000): 391–420.

Wolfe, Cary. "The Idea of Observation at Key West, or, Systems Theory, Poetry, and Form beyond Formalism." *New Literary History* 39, no. 2 (2008): 259–76.

———. "Lose the Building: Systems Theory, Architecture, and Diller+Scofidio's *Blur.*" *Postmodern Culture* 16, no. 3 (2006): 1–34.

———. *What Is Posthumanism?* Minnesota: University of Minnesota Press, 2010.

Wolfe, Thomas. *Look Homeward, Angel.* New York: Scribner, 1929.

Wright, Richard. *Native Son.* New York: Perennial Classics, 1998.

Zimmer, Carl. "Old Viruses Resurrected through DNA." *New York Times,* November 7, 2006.

INDEX

Page numbers in italics indicate photographs and other illustrations.

KATE MARSHALL is the Thomas J. and Robert T. Rolfs Assistant Professor of English at the University of Notre Dame.